Another Gold Medal Book by
Sven Hassel:

WHEELS OF TERROR

Comrades of War

by Sven Hassel

Translated from the Danish

by Sverre Lyngstad

A Gold Medal Novel

GOLD MEDAL BOOKS

Fawcett Publications, Inc., Greenwich, Conn.
Member of American Book Publishers Council, Inc.

contents

The slightest pain in your little finger causes you more uneasiness and anxiety than the destruction and death of millions of people.

We were delivered to the main first-aid station. The doctor bawled us out because we were so incredibly filthy and crawling with lice.

He'd never received such pigs before, he told us.

This doctor was very young and had seen very little. Up to then he had only sniffed at medicine in the medical factory in Graz.

Tiny told him off. He called him all sorts of names he should've kept to himself—and not a clean word in the lot.

The doctor flew into a rage. He scrupulously took down everything Tiny had said, as well as his name and detachment. Swearing by his newly acquired military honor, he vowed that Tiny would long remember the punishment he'd get, unless he was lucky enough to die during the transport —which he sincerely hoped he would.

The young doctor displayed vociferous pleasure at Tiny's screaming during the operation, as grenade splinters were extracted from his well-fleshed body.

Three weeks later the doctor was shot, tied to a willow tree. He had operated on a general who'd been bitten by a boar. The general died under the knife. The medical officer had been drunk and was in no condition to perform.

Someone in the Army Corps requested a report, and the medical officer didn't hesitate to place the responsibility on the young doctor. Incompetence and neglect of duty, the court-martial put it.

His screaming as they dragged him off to that willow tree was indecently loud. He couldn't be made to walk, and four men had to carry him.

One of them held the doctor's head in a vise under his arm. Two others held onto his legs. The fourth pinioned his arms to his sides and breast. He could feel the pounding of the young doctor's heart. It raced.

They told him he ought to face it like a man, that a man should be ashamed to cry.

But it's hard to be a man for a person of twenty-three who believes he's a superior being for having become a reserve army surgeon with two stars.

It was an ugly execution, said those who shot him, old

7

*infantrymen from the 94th Regiment. They ought to know,
they had executed many. They were capable guys, the men
of the 94th.*

chapter i

Auxiliary Field Hospital Train 877 East

THE FROST plunged red-hot knives into everything living and
dead and swept the forest with a crackling sound.

The locomotive heading the endless Red Cross train whistled long and plaintively. The white exhaust steam looked
cold against the Russian winter day. The engineers wore fur
caps and padded jackets.

Inside the long string of freight cars with the red cross
marked on top and sides lay hundreds of mangled soldiers.
As the train tore ahead, the snow on the embankment was
sent swirling in the air and pierced through the frosted walls
of the cars.

I was lying in car 48, together with Tiny and the Legionnaire. Tiny was lying on his stomach. An explosive had hit
him in the back, and half his behind had been torn off by a
mortar shell. The little Legionnaire had to hold up a mirror
to him several times a day so he could contemplate the war
damage.

"Don't you think I can wangle a GVH* for the hunk of
meat Ivan has sliced off me?"

The Legionnaire gave a low laugh: "You're as naive as
you're big and brawny. D'you really believe that? *Non, mon
cher*—a person who belongs to a *bataillon disciplinaire* doesn't
get a GVH till his whole head's blown off. You'll get a nice
KV† stamped on your service record, and then you'll be
rushed straight back to the front to get the second half
sliced off."

"I'll give you one in the chops, you wet blanket," Tiny
yelled furiously. He tried to get up, but fell back in the
straw with a scorching curse.

The Legionnaire chuckled and gave Tiny a friendly slap
on the shoulder.

---

* *Garnisonsverwendungsfähig Heimat* (fit only for garrison duty).
† *Kriegsverwendungsfähig* (fully fit for active service).

"Take it easy, you dirty pig, or you'll be chucked out with
the dead heroes next time we unload."

Down by the wall Huber had stopped screaming.

"He's croaked," Tiny said.

"Yes, and he'll have company," the Legionnaire whispered, wiping the sweat from his forehead. He was running
a high fever, and pus and blood had soaked through the
week-old emergency dressing on shoulder and neck.

This was the sixteenth time the Legionnaire was wounded.
The first fourteen were chargeable to the Foreign Legion,
where he had served for twelve years. He considered himself
more of a Frenchman than a German. He even looked like a
Frenchman: he was five feet three inches tall, of slight build,
and had a deep sun tan. A cigarette dangled like a fixture
in the corner of his mouth.

"Water, you damn swine," yelled Huhn, an NCO with a
big open abdominal wound. He threatened, cursed and
begged. Then he started crying. At the other end of the car
someone let out a hoarse, wicked laugh.

"If you're thirsty you can lick the ice off the walls just like
the rest of us."

The sergeant beside me got up halfway, braving the pain
in his abdomen, which had been riddled by a burst of sub-
machine gun fire.

"Comrades, the Führer will provide for us!" He raised his
arm for a stiff Nazi salute like a rookie, then began singing:
" 'Hold high the banner, close tight the ranks. The S. A. is
marching. . . .' "

He skipped some text, as if picking out the words he liked
best: " 'Jewish blood shall flow. Across from us the Socialists
are ranked, our land's disgrace.' " Then he tumbled back in
the straw, exhausted.

Laughter rang mockingly against the hoar-frosted ceiling.

"The hero has grown tired," someone grunted. "Adolf
doesn't give a damn about us. Right now he's most likely
spooning up rabbit-feed and slobbering over his mongrel dog."

"I'll have you court-martialed for this!" the sergeant yelled
hysterically.

"Watch out we don't tear the tongue out of your throat,"
Tiny barked, throwing a mess tin of nauseating cabbage at
the ash-gray face of the sergeant.

Fairly sobbing with rage and pain, the Hitler-happy artillery sergeant yelled: "I'll fix you, you stinking swine, you
skunk!"

"Bah, brag," Tiny sneered, waving the broad battle knife
he always kept hidden in the leg of his boot. "I'll carve

your stupid brain out of your skull and send it to the Nazi goat that mothered you. If I could get up I'd come over and give you the treatment right now."

The train came to an abrupt halt. The jolt made us all moan with pain.

The cold wormed deeper and deeper into the car, numbing our feet and fingers. The hoar-frost faced us with a pitiless grin.

One fellow was amusing himself by drawing animals in it with a bayonet. Nice little animals. A little mouse. A squirrel, and a puppy we named Oscar. All the other animals were erased by the frost, but Oscar was redrawn again and again. We loved Oscar, and talked with him. The artist, a Pfc in the Engineers' Corps, said he was brown with three white spots on his head. Oscar was a very handsome puppy. When we licked the wall, we took the greatest care not to touch Oscar. When we thought that Oscar was bored, the engineer drew a cat he could chase.

"Where are we going?" asked a little seventeen-year-old infantryman who had gotten both legs crushed.

"Home, my boy," whispered his buddy, an NCO with a head wound.

"Did you hear that?" cackled the Black Sea sailor, a fellow with a smashed hip bone. "We're going home! What is home, you stupid pig? Hell? Heaven? A green paradise valley where Adolf's angels, with swastikas on their foreheads, are playing 'Horst Wessel' on a golden harp?" He guffawed and jeered at the thousands of ice crystals on the ceiling. They gleamed back indifferently.

The train took off again. The emergency auxiliary field hospital train, made up of eighty-six ice-cold, filthy cattle cars, filled with heaps of human misery called soldiers—wounded for their country, heroes! And what heroes! Hundreds of coughing, slobbering, cursing, weeping and deadly frightened poor devils, writhing with pain and moaning each time the car gave a jolt. The sort of wrecks never alluded to in heroic accounts of combat or on recruiting posters.

"Listen to me, Desert Rambler," Tiny whispered loudly to the Legionnaire. "Now, when we come steaming into this stinking hospital, I'm first going to get roaring drunk. Yes, once more I'll get properly stoned, and afterward I'll take care of three little carbolic pussies all at once." He looked dreamily at the ceiling and snorted blissfully, licking his frostbitten lips. "You bet, I'll give it to them for all I'm worth." His eyes shone with expectant rapture. It would be the first time in his life he'd ever been in a hospital, and he imagined it as a sort of brothel with a quite extensive service for the clients.

The Legionnaire laughed. "You'll learn, my boy. First, you'll be cut up so drastically that you'll have something else to worry about during the first couple of weeks. You'll be sweating steel splinters from every pore. They'll shoot syringes into you all over so you won't conk out on them, because they can still use you for cannon fodder."

"Stop it! I don't want to listen," Tiny shouted, white with terror.

After a few minutes' silence, he asked guardedly: "Does it hurt very badly, you think, when those field surgeons cut into you?" –

The Legionnaire slowly turned his head and looked closely at the big rascal. Every feature of Tiny's oafish face showed fear of the unknown ahead of him.

"*Bon*, Tiny, it hurts, it hurts like hell. They tear and pull the flesh into shreds and tatters so you gasp and groan. But cheer up; it hurts so much you won't be able to utter a sound, not a squeak. That's the way it is," nodded the Legionnaire.

"Oh, Jesus Mary," Tiny gasped. "Holy Mother of God."

"Once they have me patched up in the hospital," I thought aloud, "I want to find a mistress, an expensive, attractive mistress in a long mink coat—a real trophy with plenty of experience."

The Legionnaire nodded.

"I know what you mean, a prize piece." He clicked his tongue.

"What's a mistress?" Tiny bungled in.

We conscientiously explained to him what a mistress was. His face lit up.

"Oh, a whore to keep at home. One of those free-lancers. Oh, Christ, if you only could hunt up one of those!" He closed his eyes, dreaming up whole battalions of gorgeous girls. He could see them walking in a straight line down a long street, wiggling their well-shaped posteriors.

"How much does one of those cost?" Not to let the dream girls entirely out of his sight, he contented himself with just opening one eye.

"A whole year's pay," I whispered, forgetting the pain in my back at the thought of the mistress in a mink coat I was going to have.

"I had a mistress in Casablanca once," the little Legionnaire mused. "It was just after I'd become a sergeant in Number 3 Company of 2nd. A good company, a nice boss, no stinking pile of shit."

"To hell with your boss. We want to hear about your broad, not your damned bosses."

The Legionnaire laughed.

"She was married to a dissolute shipowner, a real old goat. The only thing she saw in him was his dough. His fortune ran to a nice string of O's. Her favorite pastime was buying lovers and then discarding them when she had worn them out."

"Were you thrown out, too?" asked Tiny, who'd become attentive.

The Legionnaire didn't answer, but went on with the story of the shipowner's wife in Casablanca who bought good love.

Tiny obstinately persisted in butting in. Finally he let out such a roar that the other wounded passengers in the car started bawling him out.

"Did you also get the boot, Desert Rambler? I'd like to know if you were kicked down the kitchen stairs."

"No, I wasn't," the little Legionnaire yelled, annoyed by the interruptions. "When I found something better I cleared out."

We knew it was a lie, and the Legionnaire realized we knew.

"Her complexion was olive yellow," the Legionnaire went on. "Black hair, always up to some trick. Her underthings, *mon dieu,* were a treat like a bottle of Roederer Brut 1926. You should've seen them and touched them, *mon garçon!*"

The NCO with the head wound gave a low laugh. "You must be quite an epicure. I wouldn't mind going out with you some evening and taking a look at your girls."

The Legionnaire didn't even bother to look at him. He was lying with his eyes closed, a gas mask container under his head.

"Women don't interest me any more. I only speak from old experience."

"Tell me a little more about your Casablanca girls, Desert Rambler. Where actually is that whorehouse, Casablanca?"

The Legionnaire gave a hollow cough.

"Evidently you believe there are only two things of importance in this world, whorehouses and barracks. Casablanca is no whorehouse, but a lovely city on the west coast of Africa. A place where Legionnaires of the second class learn to eat sand and drink sweat and where you can order a complete Turkish band. In Casablanca, too, those asses who imagine they're going to have a glorious time with the Legion find out they're swine, because they're born of swine ..."

"...and made by swine," added a voice from the darkness that had gradually fallen on the car.

"Quite true," the little Legionnaire nodded, "they are made by swine like you and me and all other joes in this world."

"Long live the swine!" someone yelled.

"Long live the swine!" we roared hoarsely in chorus. "Long live the stupid swine for the Nazi piles of shit to push around!"

"You scum, you nasty rabble!" It was Hitler's sergeant who'd cried out; he was quite indignant. "God help you, you rats, when the attack will roll forward again! Field Marshal von Mannstein will soon cross the Lowart and storm toward Moscow."

"In that case, it'll be in a transport train bound for Siberia with prisoners," someone jeered.

"Onward, grenadiers, saviors of Greater Germany!" the sergeant bellowed frantically.

"Haw-haw, you self-made Adolf, were you in action at Velikie Luki?" Tiny inquired. "Since you speak so warmly of Lowart!"

"Were you?" asked a Pfc with only one arm, which was festering with gangrene.

"You bet I was. The three of us sat in the stronghold with the 27th. Any objections, you dirty bastard?" All at once Tiny confided to the whole car: "As soon as I'm out of the hospital I'm going to beat up a QMC officer. I'll thrash that common thief till he doesn't know his ass from his elbow. I'll slash him across the jaw so he'll have a grin stuck on his face for the rest of his life."

"Why're you so mad about QMC officers?" asked the one-armed private.

"Did you leave your brains in your lost arm?" Tiny exclaimed. "You ass, have you never gotten dripping wet under one of our rain capes? You see, those QMC fellows get their cut on everything we use. Every rain cape is made in such a way that the rain sloshes through. Don't you see the trick? Since the QMC makes a fat profit from every rain cape, and big fools like us throw away the first two in the hope of getting something better, you can plainly see what the gimmick is."

"A prize stunt," the Legionnaire remarked. "If only I could get into the Quartermaster Corps and sell raincoats to those officer thieves! Should this befall me, Allah would indeed be wise and good."

"What about that broad you were telling us about?" Tiny cried. He'd forgotten about the QMC officers.

"Mind your own business," the little Legionnaire snarled. A little later he spoke to himself: "Mohammed and all true prophets, how I loved her! Twice after she dismissed me I tried to break into Allah's garden."

"But you said you threw her out," Tiny guffawed.

"So what?" the Legionnaire shouted. "I don't give a damn about the bitches, those short-legged, wide-hipped, jabbering creatures! And to think a man should be stupid enough to chase after something like that. Take a look at her in the morning, eyes swollen and her whole face puffed up and smeared with lipstick."

"Thank you," said a voice from the interior of the car. "That's what I call a compliment to the fair sex!"

"He's right," came from somewhere else in the darkness. "You lose your appetite when you face one of those with metal curlers in her hair and down-at-heel slippers, and stockings dangling about her shanks."

Through the noise of the train we could make out the drone of an airplane. We hushed up and listened, like wild animals when they scent the death song of the beaters.

"Yabos*," someone whispered loudly.

"Yabos," repeated several others.

We shivered, not because of the cold, but because death was there in the car with us. Yabos....

"Come now death, come!" the Legionnaire hummed.

The plane swerved and roared in a steadily growing crescendo. With a zooming roar it swept along the train. The blood-red star glared coldly at the numerous cattle cars with the cross of mercy on their roofs. The plane wheeled skyward, then swooped back down like a hawk upon a young hare.

Tiny got up, supported himself on his muscular arms and roared at the doors: "Come on then, you red devil, grind us to hash! But get it over with!"

As if the pilot had heard and wished to do his best to fulfill the request, the bullets pealed through the walls of the car and rapped against the other side. Scores of little peepholes appeared at the top of one wall in neat rows.

Some screamed. Others let out a rattle. Then they died.

The locomotive blew its whistle. We drove into a forest. The pilot returned home for tea and eggs, sunny side up.

---

* Fighter-bombers.

It was such a nice morning, with clear frost. The pilot must have enjoyed the beautiful landscape from up there.

The Legionnaire said, "I could fancy having a sausage. Not just an ordinary sausage, but a sausage made of pork meat with a tang of smoke and strong as black pepper. It must have a whiff of acorn. This it gets from the pig running loose in the woods."

"You can get typhoid from eating raw clams," announced an infantry color guard with a smashed kneecap. "If I could only have a whole basket of typhoid-infected clams when I go back to the front again. Every time I go back to the front."

The wheels rumbled along the rails. The cold was relentless. It burst in through the holes left by the Yabos bullets.

"Alfred," I called. I hadn't spoken the name of the little Legionnaire for a long time, if I'd ever done so.

He didn't answer.

"Alfred!"

It sounded silly. "Alfred, did you ever yearn for a home? Furniture and that sort of thing?"

"No, Sven, I'm past the time for that," he answered with eyes closed. His mouth was set in a sneer.

How fond I was of his drawn face.

"Now I'm past thirty," he went on. "At sixteen I went to *La Légion Etrangère*. I lied that I was two years older. I've been a swine for too many years. The dunghill's my home. My hut down there in Sidi-bel-Abbès, smelling sour from the thick coat of sweat thousands of men have left behind and no fumigation can remove, that hut will be my last."

"Do you regret it?"

"You should never regret anything," the Legionnaire answered. "Life's good. The weather's good."

"It's damn cold, Alfred."

"Cold weather is good, too. All weather is good as long as you breathe. Even a prison is good as long as you're alive and forget about how well off you could be *if*. . . . It's this 'if' that drives people mad. Forget this 'if' and live!"

"Aren't you sorry you're wounded in the neck?" asked the man with gangrene. "You may get a stiff neck and have to wear a steel collar to support your head."

"No, I'm not sorry about it. I can live even with a steel collar. When this is all over I'll take a depot job in *La Légion Etrangère* with a twenty-year contract. I'll be able to drink a bottle of Valpolicella every night and carry on some small trading on the black market with unclaimed depot things. Forget about tomorrow. Kick a priest in the pants when I'm drunk. Visit the mosque twice a day and say to hell with everything else."

"I'm going to live in Venice when Adolf's been laid out," the infantry color guard cut in. "Saw it with the old man at twelve. First-class city. Has anyone here been to Venice?"

"I have," came softly from the straw in the corner.

We were horrified when we discovered it was the dying airman. He didn't have a face any more. Burning oil.

The infantryman piped down. Without looking at the dying man, he said, "So, you've been to Venice?" He said it in Italian to please the airman.

Long silence. Everyone felt the rest of us should keep quiet. To hear a man so near death talking about a city was a rare privilege.

"Canale Grande is most beautiful by night. Then the gondolas look like diamonds playing with pearls," the airman whispered.

"St. Mark's Place is fun when the water rises and floods it," the color guard said.

"Venice is the best city in the world. I'd like to go there," said the dying soldier, knowing full well he'd die in a cattle car east of Brest-Litovsk.

"An old soldier is always gay," the Legionnaire said, apropos of nothing. "He's gay because he's alive and understands what this means." Glancing at me, he went on: "But there aren't so very many old soldiers. Many call themselves soldiers, but only because they have their stripes on. You're not a soldier till the Man with the Scythe has shook hands with you."

"When I'm settled in Venice," the infantryman mused, "I'm going to eat cannelloni every day. I'll have crab served on the shell. And I'll be damn sure to have sole, too."

"*Merde!* Clams are also good," the Legionnaire said.

"But they give you typhoid," a voice warned from the other end of the car.

"I don't give a damn about typhoid. When Adolf has been strangled, we'll all be immune;" the infantry color guard said confidently.

"I forbid you to speak like this about our divine Führer," the artillery sergeant shrieked. "You're a bunch of traitors and you'll swing!"

"Oh, shut up!"

The brakes squeaked. The train moved in short spurts. Then it accelerated slightly and braked again. It went slower and slower till finally it came to a halt with a long wail. The locomotive blew off steam and drove off to get water and the other things a locomotive needs.

From the noise outside we could tell we were standing on a
station. Trampling of boots, shouts, screams. Some people
were laughing loudly and defiantly. We noted one person's laughter in particular. We lay there getting furious at
him. Only a Nazi pile of shit could have a laugh like that.
No honest beat-up guy would laugh that way.

"Where are we?" the engineer Pfc asked.

"In Russia," came the Legionnaire's laconic answer.

"I don't need to be told that, damn you!"

"Why the hell do you ask then, you fool?"

"I want to know in what city."

"What's that to you?"

The sliding door was ripped open. An MC noncom fixed
us in a dim-witted stare.

"*Heil,* comrades," he whinnied.

"Piss me in the eye," Tiny yelled aggressively and spat in
the direction of the Aesculapian hero.

"Water," a voice moaned from the filthy straw.

"Have a little patience," the NCO answered, "and you'll
get water and soup. Is anyone here especially sick?"

"Are you crazy, of course not—we are as healthy as new-
born babes! We've come to play soccer with you," the infantry color guard remarked dryly.

The NCO took off as fast as his legs could carry him.

An endless time passed. Then a couple of POWs turned
up with a militiaman. They lugged along a pail of soup
and began to scoop it into our greasy and incredibly filthy
mess tins. One scoop for each. The soup was lukewarm.

We drank and became even more hungry. The militiaman
promised to bring more, but he didn't come back. Instead
there came a new batch of POWs. Under the supervision of a
sergeant they started hauling out corpses. Fourteen corpses.
Nine of them were the work of the fighter-bomber. They
wanted to take the airman along too, but he managed
to convince them he was still alive. The sergeant got peeved
and muttered something, but left him behind.

Late in the afternoon a reserve doctor came, accompanied
by a couple of MC noncoms. They glanced quickly here and
there. To everybody they said the same thing: "It'll be all
right, it isn't really bad."

After repeating the same formula to the airman, they
came up to Tiny. The fun started. Before they had a chance
to open their mouths, he flared up: "You dirty finks! Look
how they've messed me up! But that's not really bad, is it?
Just lie down, you quack, and I'll tear off one of your buttocks. Then you can tell me if it's bad!"

He grabbed hold of the doctor's ankle and toppled him over in the stinking straw.

"*Attention! Attention!*" the Legionnaire yelled.

"Good, old Tiny, that's the way," rejoiced the man with the bleeding arm and flew at the doctor. The rest of us followed suit and in a moment we'd given the doctor a coating of blood. After his two NCO's had managed to extricate him, he looked menacing.

"Not so bad," we sneered in chorus.

"You'll pay for this," the shocked doctor threatened.

"If you dare, come on once more," Tiny laughed.

The doctor and his two attendants jumped down from the car and slammed the door.

The train didn't take off again till next morning. But they forgot to bring us breakfast. We cursed.

The airman was still alive the next morning, but someone else had died during the night. Two guys were fighting over his boots. No wonder, they were a fine soft pair of boots. No doubt a pair he'd had custom-made before the war. They were too long by regulations. They were lined with light fur. A sergeant from the railroad artillery got them. He gave his rival, a chasseur NCO, a smack on the jaw that made him forget about the boots for a while.

"A damn fine pair of boots," the sergeant cried jubilantly, holding them up so all of us could enjoy the sight of them. He moistened them with his breath and rubbed them down with his sleeve. "Christ, how I'll march in these!" he beamed, caressing the good boots.

"You'd better slip your own on the dead guy," someone warned. "Otherwise you might run the risk of losing them in a hurry."

"What d'you mean by that?" the sergeant gaped, hiding the boots under the straw. "I'd like to see the fellow who dares!" He resembled a dog guarding his bone.

"Well, in that case just forget about putting the boots on the dead man and you'll find out there are some who dare," the same man laughed. "The head-hunters* will pull off that fine pair of boots for you and then string you up for looting. For that's what it is, looting. It's even been called corpse robbery. You see, I've been with the flying drumhead court-martials. I know the score."

"Oh, damn it all!" the sergeant protested. "He won't need those boots any more."

"You won't either, brother," came soberly from the drumhead man. "You have a pair from the Army."

---

* Military Police.

"That's just crap. Those rotten dice boxes aren't fit to walk in."

"Tell that to the head-hunters," the other laughed. His face was pale, with bloodless lips and cold eyes. "They'll beat you till you admit in writing you've received from Adolf the finest pair of boots in the world."

The sergeant didn't say any more. He had come to his senses. Cursing, he slipped the old dice boxes on the dead man.

An hour later the dead man wouldn't have been able to recognize his outfit. It had been replaced with all sorts of unfamiliar things.

Huhn, the NCO with the abdominal wound, again asked for water. The Legionnaire shoved a lump of ice toward him. He sucked it greedily.

My feet had begun to burn. Pains were shooting through my whole body. It felt as if flames were gnawing my bones. The second stage of frostbite. I knew. First, the pains. Then the pains recede a little, and a bit later your feet start burning and go on burning till they're numb. This numbness is the sign that it's all over. Gangrene is in full swing and your feet die. The pains move up. In the hospital a stump will steam under the surgeon's knife. Terror gripped me. Amputation. God, anything but that! I whispered my fear to the Legionnaire. He glanced at me. "Then the war will be over for you. Better the feet than the head."

Yes, then the war will be over. I tried to console myself, but the chilling terror stuck in my throat. I tried to imagine I'd been lucky with my feet. It would've been worse had it been my hands; but terror didn't loosen its grip on me. I saw myself on crutches. No, I didn't want to be a "peg-leg."

"What's the matter with you?" the Legionnaire asked, surprised. Without knowing I had cried out "peg-leg."

I fell asleep. The pains woke me up, but I was happy with my pains. My feet hurt, but there was life in them. I still had my good, wonderful feet.

The train stopped twice. Both times a medic looked at my feet. Each time the same: "Not too bad."

"By Mohammed, what's really bad then?" the Legionnaire fumed. He pointed at the maimed airman, who had just died. "Isn't that bad either?"

No one bothered to answer him. The emergency auxiliary hospital train continued west.

On arriving in Cracow sixty-two per cent of the wounded were unloaded as cadavers after a twelve-day transport.

"You're a flock of blubbering old women," roared the army chaplain, Colonel von Zlavik, when we moaned. He was greatly annoyed that we betrayed our pain. "You implore the Holy Father to help you, but the Lord will have nothing to do with a pack of good-for-nothings like you."

He ordered us to stop our wailing. He threatened to lock us up till we'd rot. God was exceedingly merciful, he told us in confidence, but only to decent people and good soldiers, not to a gang like us, the most hideous dregs of society. He raised the crucifix to a kind of Nazi salute, then commanded the orderlies to remove two corpses wrapped up in sheets. A little later, the sheets were brought back and prepared for the next.

The Colonel-Chaplain spat and left us.

The same afternoon he fell down the stairs and broke his arm. He broke it in three places.

"He whined like all of you put together," grinned the nurse, sister Monica, who needed a man twice a day to keep her spirits up.

"Well, there are all kinds," the little Legionnaire said. He turned on his other side and praised Allah. In a low murmur he told us about the holy man who climbed up into the barren stony wastes of the Rif Mountains, alone.

chapter ii

Death's Depot

IN THE 3rd Reserve Field Hospital, located in a former Polish theological seminary in Cracow, mute physicians and their aides were playing around with the wounded. The operating room had once been the president's office. The good parson could hardly have foreseen that so many were to die in his office. In peacetime, the deaths in this one room alone would have kept several homicide squads busy.

I was lying on a low stretcher which felt like corrugated iron. Someone with a head wound was under the knife. He died. A fire-team leader with an abdominal wound was put on the table. He died. Three died. Two came out alive. Then it was my turn.

"Save my feet," was the last I remembered saying before going under the anesthetic. The surgeon said nothing.

My feet were still with me when I woke up later in some ward. The first hours were pleasant and quiet. Then pain set in. Unbelievable pain. Others were no better off. When darkness had mercifully fallen upon the ward, which gave off a heavy stench of carbolic acid, a vague murmur filled the night. It was the wailing of the tortured, the unending song of the damned.

A nurse bent over me, felt my pulse and vanished. My temperature rose. Fear of death came slithering over me. It crawled like a snake, winding its coils around my body. I couldn't clearly make out anything. There was nothing but a haze and disconnected images. Most distinctly I could see the Man with the Scythe over in the corner. He was swinging his leg impatiently. The gray man with the black cape and the scythe seemed to be very busy.

"You've had good hunting, haven't you? Damn good hunting. You pile of shit, you stinking pile of shit! D'you think I'm afraid of you? I've seen more dangerous things than you. Far more dangerous. Should I be afraid of you? Hah!"

Of course I'm afraid. Hell, I'm scared stiff.

Again the nurse was there.

"Scram, carbolic bitch. Leave me alone. Just you wait till the Muscovites are coming, then you'll get busy, you Nazi pot-swinger. Then you'll see something."

"No, come back, please come! God, how scared I am." But she'd gone. The Man with the Scythe grinned. Through the moaning of the others I could distinctly make out a hoarse gurgle. He swung his leg a bit faster. His patience was nearly exhausted.

The Legionnaire hummed, "Come now, Death, come." I stopped my ears, I didn't want to listen to the damned song; but thousands joined in: "Come now, Death, come!" Again gurgling laughter from over in the corner.

The gray man passed his finger probingly along the edge of the scythe, the bright glittering scythe. He nodded with satisfaction. It was sharp. Sharp like the large guillotines in Plötzensee and Lengries. Like the knife that sliced Ursula's head from her slender neck I wonder, are there guillotines in Kolyma? What's wrong with you, you stupid pig? I thought you'd said good-bye to that love you had once in Berlin, the Jewish girl who slept with the SS because she had a sense of humor! A lovely girl. A gorgeous piece. Don't blubber, you sissy! Once you wanted to be an officer. You wanted to be a soldier, you blockhead. And what are you now? A little shit in the reserves scared of the Man with the Scythe. What do you have to worry about? Close up your bellows and stand down. Whom do you have to worry about but yourself, you dimwit? Isn't it strange! Not a single soul will think of you when you've pulled over to the side. Come on, then, you ox, take me with you across the Styx. D'you imagine I'm afraid of you?

The gray man got up and wrapped the cape about him. With measured steps he came toward my bed. I let out a loud piercing scream.

The nurse came once more. She wiped my forehead with something which felt deliciously cool. It was raining. A monotonous soothing patter. The Man with the Scythe had gone. He'd taken along two from the ward.

Seven days later I was transferred to the ward where Tiny and the Legionnaire were lying. Tiny had saved up two weeks in the can for himself, which he'd serve as soon as he'd recovered. As the head nurse and three other nurses trooped in the door, he'd shouted: "Hurrah, here come the broads! To the bunks, boys!"

A terrific uproar followed. It ended an hour later with the medical officer giving him two weeks. Tiny just couldn't understand why. He couldn't be made to see that the army hospital wasn't a brothel. Wherever he saw women, Tiny saw brothels.

"All sorts of things are happening here," the Legionnaire grinned. "Some of the nurses are dying for someone to sleep with who has brass on his chest. Staff Corporal Hansen over there has been here for seventeen months and has the dope on everything. He says sister Lise had taken it into her head to have a boy as long as there's still time. She's tried a whole pack of men, but so far no boy. But she hasn't given up hope yet. She's going as strong as ever. She sees it as a national duty."

One day the Legionnaire and I were bundled up in some blankets and carried off to a spot from which we had a view of the glittering waters of the Elbe and could observe the tugboats working their way upstream. Shortly we were joined by Tiny, who was also placed in a chair. For a whole hour we sat there, listening to the boom of the riveting hammers at Stülckenwerft.

A nurse taught me to walk. My legs were paralyzed. The last grenade splinter had struck the spinal column as we clambered up the cliff. Gradually I learned how to walk. It cost me torrents of sweat. That nurse was exceedingly patient. Though old and ugly, she was devoted.

I've forgotten her name. Those who help us are very often forgotten, enemies never.

Tiny thrust his big fist under the nose of each of our ten fellow-patients in the ward. "This is no lady's hand. You'd do well to realize that from the very beginning."

"It reminds me of a funeral chapel," Stein mumbled with a scowl.

"That's the way I like it," Tiny said. "Your words show you've been to school. I don't mind if you sit around on the beds—but listen to this! When I say, 'Fetch beer!' you'll put your pennies together and run like blazes to pick up beer for Tiny. And God help you should you try to dilute it! If I only get enough beer I'll be silky as a kitten, make a note of that. But if I'm out of beer"—he made a long pause and looked about him ominously—"may God Almighty have mercy on you!"

chapter iii

Dictator Tiny

RUSSIA HAD been forgotten. What we knew of Russia, that is: the Eastern Front. A name, my dear, which comprehends a worse hell than any described by the priest, even that of a

23

sect founded solely on man's fear of the unknown. The most inventive missionary of such a sect wouldn't be able to conjure up a hell that could even faintly compete with the hell we learned to know on the Eastern Front—a hell-peopled with devils in khaki and green, experts in sadism.

At present we were remote from this hell. We were wounded, ill, lecherous, drunk. We didn't give a damn about anything. Just live and forget. Tomorrow you'll die.

We had ended up in a good army hospital in Hamburg, with a sympathetic head doctor, good and bad nurses. The operations were past. They'd cut us up a little in Cracow, a little more in Berlin, and now in Hamburg they cut us up still a little more. We weren't confined to bed and could take walks outside the hospital grounds. Though liquor was banned, we drank anyway. We spent our time whoring, getting into fights, frequenting saloons, and fornicating with the girls and wives of other soldiers.

The little Legionnaire couldn't fornicate any more, thanks to an SS-*Unterscharführer* in Fagen concentration camp who amused himself with amateur surgery. Since he couldn't cheer himself up by breaking the Sixth Commandment, he had to find other means. Alfred Kalb, former corporal in the 2nd Regiment of the French Foreign Legion, drank slowly, single-mindedly and uninterruptedly. When someone said, "The Desert Rambler is slightly drunk," he was very drunk, so drunk it would make anybody else conk out.

Tiny provoked fights wherever he went. He let on to everybody he'd come to Hamburg to kill someone, preferably a soldier from the sticks. He trounced one of the bouncers on Sankt Pauli because he suspected him of mixing water in his beer. When the manager asked him to pay his bill, Tiny tossed him into the arms of the chorus girls. A horse was walking around between the tables and was given beer by the guests. Tiny took it along with him and left it in the hall of the nurses' residence, where it created a wild uproar. When the head doctor, Dr. Mahler, heard about Tiny and the horse, he chuckled:

"What's the harm, let them have their fun."

Dr. Mahler, Head Medical Officer, was the most unmilitary army surgeon imaginable. For many years he had practiced in the British colonies. His specialty was tropical medicine. After the attempted assassination of July 20, the Nazi authorities had him arrested. It was rumored he barely escaped hanging. He was somehow mixed up with Admiral Canaris, the leader of the German resistance. How he got off alive was never explained. When questioned about it, Dr.

Mahler would shrug his shoulders and say: "Rubbish." He still walks the rounds in his fever-ravaged army hospital, accompanied by the head nurse, sister Emma. Thousands of people are alive today because of the devotion of this physician.

But there were bad physicians in the hospital also, useless Nazis whose greatest amusement was to detect "truants" and malingerers. Dr. Frankendorf, for one. He was constantly persecuting flak private George Freytag, who was afflicted with a strange fever no one could make head or tail of. They were continually making blood tests, but every test came out negative. Just when they believed he'd been cured, the fever would set in again. Under the leadership of that bandit Dr. Frankendorf, blitz raids were carried out to check whether George possessed benzine-soaked sugar or similar fever-inducing agents. They found nothing. Frankendorf held interrogations, cajoled, threatened, cursed, but every time he walked away defeated and deeply disappointed.

Whether it was convenient for Dr. Frankendorf or not, the fever of flak private George Freytag persisted.

With Dr. Frankendorf, all the other patients in our ward were convinced that George was shamming. For a whole afternoon and evening straight till midnight, Tiny was making the most fabulous offers to George in return for his secret. Tiny's motive was somewhat different from Frankendorf's. To him it seemed that George had found the perfect disease. George shook his head:

"Believe me, pal, my fever is real."

Tiny made no bones about his disappointment. He yelled and threatened to punch him in the face. In his fury he kicked a water basin out the window, but to no avail. George kept the divine secret to himself.

All in all, George was a strange boy. He neither drank nor gambled, and he showed no interest in women. All he did was to take a stroll when the fever would permit it. George was a pretty boy, a good boy. He used to do things for the nurses, from all of whom he received the affection of a child—which he actually was.

We sat in Number 72 with a view of Reeperbahn and the Palace of Justice, which loomed menacing at the end of Glacis Chaussée. From the Sankt Pauli Brewery came a whiff of beer.

The Legionnaire pulled a bottle from under his mattress, a big bottle of Kümmel. It passed from man to man. Tiny

belched blissfully and had two swigs. He glanced about him
to see if anyone objected. Heinz Bauer was already a bit
fuddled. This annoyed Tiny, who happened to be in his
"sensitive" mood.

"Some real swell girls have been cooled off lately," Paul
Stein said. He was thinking of the three women who'd been
murdered in Hamburg in the course of a couple of weeks.

"That murderer must be nuts," Tiny said, and belched
once more after a long pull at the bottle. "The last one he
strangled with a stocking and then cut her up."

Paul said that first the girls had been strangled with a
stocking or a piece of underwear; afterward they'd been raped
and mauled with a knife. The murderer's gratification seemed
to depend on the girls being strangled with an intimate article
of clothing. At this stage the police were nearly throwing fits
from frustration.

"Maybe Dr. Frankendorf is the sex killer," Tiny suggested,
his face lighting up. "Damn it, boys, what if Dr. Frankendorf
would get his nob lopped off!"

"*Bon Dieu*, that would be great," the Legionnaire exclaimed. In his mind's eye he saw the bovine head of Frankendorf drop into the basket.

"Have you seen the photographs posted in the glass case
at the Davidstrasse police station?" asked Mouritz Klokyty, a
volunteer from the Sudeten. We couldn't stand Mouritz.
"There ought to be a law against posting things like that,"
he continued. "God's wrath will soon be upon them, upon us
all."

"What d'you mean by that?" Tiny asked and sent a gob
of sauerkraut after him. He'd stuffed his mouth from an
emergency pot he kept in a cardboard box under his bed.

Mouritz grew solemn: "But don't you realize all that scan-
dal will lead to a bad end? Thunder and lightning will strike
you."

"I can quite see that God might get worked up a bit over
some females getting ripped up from top to bottom," Tiny
answered good-naturedly between mouthfuls of sauerkraut,
"but that's no reason why he should punish me, the Desert
Rambler, Sven, or the Schupo's* in Davidstrasse. It wouldn't
occur to any of us to chop up broads. We'd prefer to give
them the old-fashioned treatment."

"Almighty God," Mouritz cried in indignation.

"You shouldn't curse," Tiny admonished, threatening with
his finger.

---

* *Schutzpolizei*—the Civilian Police.

Mouritz couldn't be interrupted. He turned to the rest of us:

"You're blasphemers, devil's brood. God's arrow will strike you, since you refuse to see the coarse morals around you."

Like a priest excommunicating his congregation, he pointed at Tiny, intoning: "You are the tempter, the vessel of evil, but the good will crush you."

Tiny had been struggling with a piece of pork he had a tough time biting in two. He stopped chewing. He pulled the whole chunk out of his mouth and glowered at Mouritz: "What am I, did you say?"

"The vessel of evil," Mouritz intoned. "Life is a thorny path, bestrewn with vices, and you are one of these prickly vices." This made Tiny, who was sitting cross-legged on the floor with the pork in his hand, gape in astonishment. Mouritz made a threatening gesture in his direction: "But you won't tempt me, you devil. Tempter and seducer, I say 'No Admission' to you!"

Mouritz was interrupted in his excommunication by the Legionnaire, who shouted laughingly: "*Voilà*, that's enough somber talk."

Tiny had gone back to chewing on his pork. Slowly, he got up. From his throat came a growl. "You ought to be a bit careful about abusing Tiny, you prune. Apparently you're not aware I'm saved, that I'm now a pious person who's bought absolution. Would you like to hear the price, you who have sold your piety to Adolf, you Czech Judas? Five quarts of vodka, a quart of cognac, and two hundred makhorka cigarettes I risked my life stealing from the QM sergeant of 27th Panzer—and then a squirt like you says I'm ungodly!"

He pulled the pork out of his mouth again and slapped Mouritz in the face with it. Mouritz was reclining on the edge of his bed. His face had gone green with fright.

"Louse of Sodom," Tiny remarked. He spat at Mouritz, lying now as if stone dead and staring with glazed eyes at Tiny, who had renewed his battle with the pork. Mouritz's mouth opened and shut like the mouth of a codfish in a fishmonger's box just before its head is cut off—to prevent the customer from discovering the cod is half dead. Tiny belched himself through the pork, which stubbornly remained in one piece.

"Get out of here, you Nazi fink, and try to walk across the Alster on a nice little prayer, just like Moses when he crossed the Suez Canal." Tiny's concepts of Biblical history were somewhat confused. He smacked Mouritz straight in the face with the tough piece of pork. With a shriek Mouritz fell under the bed. Without removing his boots, Tiny flung himself on his own bed and continued his efforts to best the pork.

A nurse's aide poked her head into the ward, to see only one thing: Tiny on the bed with his boots on. Delighted, she galloped off to announce the unheard-of infraction of regulations to the universally feared matron, sister Emma, who was nicknamed "the Battleship."

Without a word, the Legionnaire pitched the bottle of Kümmel across to Tiny, who caught it without getting up. He gargled down the drink conscientiously as he lay on his back with the pork in one hand. This is how the matron found him. For half a minute she was speechless. With glazed eyes she fixed the human gorilla who was preening himself on the bed, displaying a pair of infantry boots on the blue-and-white checkered cover.

"Have you gone out of your mind?" she asked, pointing a pudgy finger at the black, polished boots. Tiny removed the bottle from his mouth, spat over the foot of the bed and hit a bowl a couple of yards away. The nurse's aide barely escaped being spattered. Tiny cleaned his nose by snuffling inward loud and forcibly.

"What do you want, you fat sow?" he asked.

We caught our breath. We hadn't noticed it, but Tiny was drunk, and in that condition he could take it into his head to do anything. Some time ago he had quarreled with a girl in an apartment on the third floor. The girl had wanted Tiny to go and bathe first. By way of protest he threw the bathtub out of the window. The racket was such that the people who were around thought a bomb had fallen in the yard and started walking to the cellar.

The eyes of "the Battleship" vanished in her fat face.

"How dare you?" she hissed, bending down over Tiny who was resting quietly on the bed as before. "You call me a sow?"

Tiny answered nothing and continued chewing the pork.

"Get up, you pig, or you'll find out whom you're dealing with," the giant woman growled ominously. As she bent even lower over chomping Tiny, her dress pulled up and revealed the huge hollows of her knees.

"Save your powder, Fatty, I know you. You're head nurse in this institution, and I've been told you're called 'the Battleship' because you're so fat and ugly. I call you 'Tub of Lard' myself. Bah, that's that, now scram!"

A flush spread over the woman's round cheeks like a thundercloud over a sunny village. "Get up, you crud," she hissed, caught Tiny by the shoulder and, to our astonishment, lifted him off the bed. In the next moment she flung him to the floor, where he landed with a crash. He stared at her with deep admiration. Up to then he'd never been thrown out of bed by anyone.

The Battleship straightened out the bed, threw the bottle of Kümmel and the big hunk of pork into the trash can and sailed out of the room without another word.

"Holy Mother of God, that's a woman for you," Tiny mumbled, rubbing his shoulder. "Damn me if I won't get hooked up with her. Just imagine the close action."

"She'll choke you like a duckling," Heinz Bauer remarked.

Tiny grabbed a drinking glass, crashed it against the wall and roared: "I'm going to rape that pig, you bet I am!"

The door opened once again. As she stood there sucking a piece of candy, the Battleship filled up the doorway. She glowered at Tiny, but her stares shattered against him.

"Quit showing off, you ox," she spat out in her deep, masculine voice. "Your bawling disturbs the other patients. You're in a hospital now and not in your barracks. If you make any more trouble, you'll have to answer to me."

She slammed the door with a crash, showing no concern for the peace of those other patients that just now she had been so worried about.

"What a little rascal," Tiny cried jubilantly. He fished the bottle out of the trash can, finished it off, and flung it out of the window into the garden of the Meteorological Institute. Then he went hunting for the pork in the trash can—it had gotten mislaid among other delicacies—picked it up, brushed it off a little, and again settled down to chew it.

"A gorgeous piece," he belched and threw himself on the bed, but oddly enough he removed his boots first. He began bawling a martial song that unknown soldiers had improved.

> *Wirsind die Panzerjäger,*
> *die Hungerkünstler der Nation,*
> *Für Dörrgemüse und für Käse.*

Swinging the pork in one hand, he swelled his voice to a fantastic volume.

> *Vorwärts, dumme Schweine,*
> *im Kampfe sind wir stets alleine,*
> *denn die Scheisshaushingste*
> *fahren mit den Autos hintendrein,*
> *dann verleihen Euch was die Nazis.*

"Beer," he said, turning to no one in particular.

"Do you imagine you're in a saloon?" Paul Stein asked.

In one bound Tiny was on his feet; he grabbed Stein and swung him over his head. "You miserable lump of snot," he cooed endearingly, gradually tightening his grip on his victim. "So you imagine you can annoy Tiny? You dare to forbid me quenching my thirst! You may go to get beer now. For every darn penny you've got. And right now, you flatworm!"

He tossed the terror-stricken Stein to the wall like a discarded bottle cap, spat after him and yelled, "Make it snappy. I'm in a hurry, I'm thirsty."

Getting up, Stein mumbled something under his breath and scowled at Tiny, once again settled on the bed and indifferently chewing his everlasting piece of pork.

"You're going to break your neck with your boorishness some day," said the Legionnaire in a gentle, almost gingerly voice. He occupied the bed by the window, the best bed in the room. With his strategic eye he had confiscated this bed as soon as he entered the ward. By rights it belonged to Mouritz, the Sudeten Czech. Naturally, Mouritz had made a stink about it.

"That's my bed, buddy. You must've made a mistake."

By way of answer the Legionnaire had merely given him a lofty look. Mouritz repeated his protest. The Legionnaire put away his paper and slowly raised himself on the bed.

"*Merde, c'est possible, mon camarade.*"

"What are you saying?" Mouritz looked dumbly at the Legionnaire, who'd returned to his paper. A cigarette hung at the corner of his mouth.

"Nothing, nothing at all, *mon camarade.*" He made a gesture of dismissal, as if pushing away something bothersome. All at once he shot up like a tightened steel spring and bellowed: "*Allez!*" Mouritz didn't understand French. He merely stood there glowering. He just couldn't believe it was all real. The rest of us said nothing. We knew what was coming. A fight, a glorious nerve-drugging fight!

Tiny got to his feet. He moved toward Mouritz like a bear smelling honey. Mouritz, whose back was turned, didn't see the signs of the hurricane that was brewing to crush him. The Legionnaire turned down his thumb and whispered smiling: "*C'est bien ça!*"—the signal for Tiny. It had cost the Legionnaire hours of patient labor to hammer this signal into Tiny's thick skull.

Suddenly Mouritz was in the grip of an iron claw. He was

swung aloft and carried across the ward to the bed by the door, the poorest bed of all. Its occupant had to turn the lights on and off and was constantly disturbed. Tiny put Mouritz down very softly, as if he were made of fragile glass. Then he took a step back and observed him closely.

"You're a swine," he confided to Mouritz, "a common stupid swine who brown-noses the Nazi shit-piles. Now, tell me what you are!"

Tiny slapped him with the back of his hand. Quite loving-ly, he thought. To us it looked like a volcanic eruption.

"Now tell us what you are, you chicken coop."

"I'm a swine," Mouritz stammered.

Another slap.

"Didn't you go to school, you fathead? Can't you learn something by heart? What are you?"

"A stupid swine," Mouritz whimpered, "who brown-noses the Nazi shit-piles."

"A pretty good answer," Tiny acknowledged. He pointed at the bed where Mouritz was lying. "You requested this bed, didn't you?"

"I did," Mouritz answered, surrendering.

Tiny raised his eyebrow. "Hell, what did I hear?"

Mouritz hastened to add, *"Herr* Corporal!"

The gorilla nodded his head with satisfaction.

Everybody had witnessed this scene. It established Tiny as absolute dictator of the ward, a dictator who brutally and without scruples exploited his subjects. An Adolf in minia-ture.

This was the reason Paul Stein now obeyed Tiny's com-mand and was quick about bringing some beer from the Sankt Pauli brewery. Without a word, he placed all ten bottles in the cardboard box under Tiny's bed.

Tiny ordered Mouritz to sing for him. It came to a hymn, a sad hymn about the salvation of the world. Tiny mean-while interrupted his beer drinking and listened politely straight through the nine stanzas. His only comment was to dispatch a gob of spit after Mouritz. He ordered him to go to bed and rest, but not till he'd said a prayer for Tiny's soul.

When all orders had been duly carried out, Tiny drank a bit in silence. Eventually he had passed the stage of being simply "very drunk." He started bellowing a song. The tune hadn't yet been okayed by the historians of music, and the text was such that it could have brought a charge of high treason on his neck.

Auf der Strasse nach Moskau
marschiert eine Kompagnie,
das sind die Reste
von Adolfs ganzem Heer,
Sie konnten schon Josef sehen,
und mussten wieder stiften gehen,
wie einst Napoleon.

For a moment he was silent. Then, with renewed vigor, he roared to the same tune:

Hurra, wir haben den Krieg verloren.

"Anyone here itching for a fight?" he queried into the darkness. A moment or two passed; then he added: "If so, I'd be glad to give your hides a tanning."

No answer.

He flung the bottle out of the open window. It crashed against the street. A rasping voice rebounded from the walls by the Zirkusweg intersection. We could observe rapture in his face as he listened. Staggering to the window he neighed in anticipated triumph: "Lock your jaws, you jackasses! Can't you see you're sailing past an army hospital? We must have quiet here. We're sick people. Heroes! Don't disturb the sick! If you do, I'll come down and thrash you!"

A male voice huffily took up the challenge and egged him on. It reverberated profoundly in the watchful silence of the night.

"Holy blazes," Tiny yelled, making ready to jump through the window.

In the next instant three or four of us were on top of him. We held him down firmly.

"But he talks back, don't you hear?" Tiny was outraged. He shouted out of the window, "Just wait, you beggar, till I'm free. We're fighters here. Defenders of our country. We're heroes. What ideas can such a, such a . . ."

The Legionnaire had to knock him out with a stool.

Night came on and the ward was still.

Aunt Dora thought of everything in terms of money. She stood behind her bar counter with the stuffed swordfish and supped akvavit with angostura bitters. Her eyes measured up all who entered by the revolving door.

The Legionnaire sat on a tall bar stool across from her drinking pernod. This beverage, which looks innocent enough, tastes like licorice, is poisonously green and turns white when mixed with water.

"Pernod is invented by the devil," he said, "but you don't know till the eighth glass." Laughing, he handed the ninth to the girl.

She undressed in one of the tiny niches. Her underthings were pitch black, quite sheer. Only her panties, which she refused to take off, were red, coral red. When she removed them upstairs, only Stein and Ewald, Aunt Dora's assistant pimp, were watching.

chapter iv

Aunt Dora

WE OFTEN went to "Wind Force 11" behind the Central Station. More correctly, we *always* went to "Wind Force 11" behind the Central Station.

Aunt Dora, the hostess of this ritzy saloon, was an unfeeling ugly woman. She measured everything in money. Some people, perhaps most, thought it was disgusting. To us, Death's grooms, it seemed wise. Money can get you anything. "For money you can buy eternal life at the seat of Allah in the blue valleys," the Legionnaire said and piously bowed his head to the southeast.

"Money can buy any amount of female meat," Bauer said.

"Money can buy a whorehouse," Tiny said. With his glance he undressed a girl preening herself on a tall bar stool.

33

"Money will admit you to Aunt Dora's." I laughed and blew her a kiss.

"And allow you to get cuckoo on stuff you can get nowhere else in the Third Reich," Stein grinned. He flushed down a large glass of gin and ordered a refill.

"You're a herd of dirty pigs," Aunt Dora insisted, "but as long as you can pay you're welcome in Wind Force 11."

We had plenty of money. We had been away at the front for very long. Most of us had a knack for business and knew how to procure merchandise. The black market in Hamburg was the best in the world, the little Legionnaire declared. Anything could be bought and sold there, even a corpse.

The light in Aunt Dora's saloon was red, very soft. There was a law against dancing, in force now for almost three years. But at Aunt Dora's they danced anyway. The police and their stooges came around frequently, but Aunt Dora, a demon in petticoats, said: "The best way to keep your friends is to know something about them." And she always managed to find out something about them, enough to make them close their eyes to anything unlawful in Wind Force 11. In the reports on public sentiment filed at the Secret Police, Wind Force 11 figured as a nice place with a regular clientele and without political significance.

In Wind Force 11 more rules and regulations were broken than anywhere else. Ladies would come there to experience the forbidden, though at the last minute they might chicken out. Other people would come there to get drunk and then shoot themselves—or they'd get their throats cut and be thrown into the Elbe. By and by they would be hauled in with a boathook by a revenue vessel at Landungsbrücke.

A girl in a knee-length dress asked the Legionnaire for a dance. He didn't even bother to look at her. He sipped his vodka and took a long drag at his cigarette, then slowly let out the smoke through his nose.

"Would you like to dance, little one?" the girl asked a second time. With greedy glances she surveyed the stringy figure with the brutal face, its long knife-wound gleaming fiery red.

"Go to hell," the Legionnaire snarled through the corner of his mouth.

The girl exploded. She was terribly offended. A lanky young fellow came sliding up to the Legionnaire's stool. He reached out for the throat of the little soldier, but in the next instant he found himself on the floor. A kick in the face and a murderous blow at the larynx. Then quiet once

more. The Legionnaire sat down again and ordered another
vodka. Aunt Dora gave a sign to the doorman, a big Belgian.
He grabbed the lifeless figure like a big bag of flour and
chucked him through a doorway. From there others continued
the transport to some place sufficiently distant from Wind
Force 11.

The girl was soundly whipped in a little room behind the
kitchen. She didn't cry. A soiled quilt covered up her head,
as with so many other women who'd been brutally punished
in that room behind the kitchen. The quilt choked her cry.
The person in charge of this business was Aunt Dora's
right-hand man, a former pimp. He had placed the girl on
a table specially made for the purpose. He beat her with a
short Cossack whip he'd bought a long time ago from an SS
man who had two of them to sell. Ewald, Aunt Dora's executioner, bought one, a police detective the second. The
detective thought it might help get confessions.

In all other respects this criminal detective had been very
correct in his work. But he didn't produce enough confessions. Among themselves his superiors had a kind of saying,
that he would profit greatly from a trip to Russia. That was
the reason he bought the Cossack whip. He immediately became a police sergeant; some said he even did better.
For now he was no longer correct, and he got plenty of confessions. A dictatorship can't use correct people. What it wants
is results.

Ewald flogged the girl twice. Then he slept with her.
Those who knew said he always did that.

Next evening the girl went back to work at Aunt Dora's.
She took home thirty-five per cent of her earnings. Never
again did she ask the Legionnaire to dance.

Two ladies sat down by the Legionnaire. They were well-
dressed, arrogant ladies, no common barflies. One of them
gave the Legionnaire a quick glance. She crossed her legs and
her skirt came up above her knee. There was a hint of a
flaring white petticoat. The two ladies drank champagne.
The best, they'd ordered. The Legionnaire lit a fresh cigarette with the butt of his old one and squinted at the champagne. Pointing at the filled glasses, he asked:

"*Chateauneuf, est-il le meilleur?*"

The ladies pretended they hadn't heard.

His face distorted with haughtiness and expectant victory,
the Legionnaire bent over to the dark lady, called Lisa by
her friend. The other's name was Gisela. "How about a
throw for a hundred marks?"

The lady answered nothing, but her cheeks flushed. It

could have been the champagne. The Legionnaire laughed. Aunt Dora stood with her back to the counter, but she could see the whole thing in a tiny mirror among the glasses. She laughed. I laughed. Bauer laughed. Tiny was drinking, cursing, and babbling wildly about girls.

"Do you want to come upstairs and play a little? I'll give you two hundred marks and a new pair of panties," said the Legionnaire in an undertone.

Aunt Dora laughed over her bitters. With Danish schnapps she used only angostura. It cleansed the soul, she used to say. A pastor had once told her that her soul would be hard to wash clean. That's why she drank the hot stuff.

"You should be ashamed of yourself," Lisa said, turning the Legionnaire down. She had almost emptied her glass in one swallow. She must have done it by mistake; her friend Gisela had only sipped at hers. Laughing softly, the Legionnaire ordered a refill for her from Trude, a waitress from Berlin helping out Aunt Dora at the bar. He winked at her. Trude understood.

Madame Lisa's glass received a couple of dashes from a special bottle. Aunt Dora alone knew the contents of this bottle. Whatever it was, a few drops mixed in a girl's drink always produced results. Lisa was completely unsuspecting and picked up her glass. Turning around from her glasses, Aunt Dora poured out a drink for the Legionnaire and told him, stressing every word: "You are a filthy swine. But good luck. Filth makes money, my boy."

The Legionnaire laughed.

"Madame, four hundred down and new undies from France," he wheedled, then went back to blowing smoke rings.

Trude moistened a perfectly clean glass with her breath and polished away as if trying to wear it out. A smile hovered about her lips. Like all of us she was excited, because she knew the Legionnaire couldn't have anything to do with women and didn't want to, either.

"You're repulsive," said Lisa, demonstratively turning her back on the cruelly grinning Legionnaire in his black panzer uniform with small silver death's heads on the lapels.

"Sacre nom de Dieu!" the Legionnaire exclaimed, feigning surprise.

Aunt Dora stuck a long cheroot in her mouth and turned to the Legionnaire. "Give me a light, you African bastard."

The Legionnaire obliged and rubbed his nose. "What d'you think, should I hire that lady for a turn in bed?"

"Now shut up, you swine, and leave the lady alone. She

wants none of you, and you of her. You know that well
enough."

She sat down on a tall chair across from the Legionnaire,
who turned again to Lisa. "You have beautiful legs, madame.
Mon Dieu, you've got damn beautiful legs. I wouldn't mind
undressing you. Six hundred in cash if you'll let me undress
you! How about a dance, madame?"

"No, and do leave me alone. I'm not what you think I am."

The Legionnaire raised his eyebrow. "You don't say so!
What a shame."

Aunt Dora blew smoke in the Legionnaire's face. Her brutal mouth smiled.

"What did you take the lady for?" Bauer asked.

The Legionnaire smiled, pulled his nose and took a swallow from his glass.

"A distinguished lady looking for adventure, not a cheap
slut going out in her mistress' clothes."

Lisa sprang up. In the next second the Legionnaire's cheek
resounded with a slap. With lightning speed he caught her
by the wrists. He twisted his lips to a snarl, showing a row
of pearly white teeth.

"*Merde*, so the little thing is showing her claws? Tiny, *c'est
bien ça*. Madame would like to dance."

Tiny slid heavily down from his bar stool and slouched up
to them like a gorilla.

"Brassy fellow, I don't want to dance," Lisa snorted.

"Of course you do," the Legionnaire decided. He nodded
to Tiny.

She tried to free herself, but the sinewy fingers of the Legionnaire locked her wrists like a steel trap. A heavy gleaming gold bracelet jingled faintly like little bells. Without a
word Tiny caught her round the waist and swung her onto
the floor. He yelled to the pianist:

"Alois, thrash away, you piano-puncher. Tiny's going to
crank up a whore."

At the little tables in the niches the guests were snickering.
The girls whinnied, gloating over the elegant lady who got
herself into a scrape. They looked upon Wind Force 11 as
their beat, exclusively theirs. All strange women to them
were like rags to a bull.

A savage tune was struck up on the grand piano. The
other guests stepped down from the little dance floor behind the curtain. Tiny geared up and rolled out on the floor.
He braked with a jolt, slid sideways in small crow steps,
stopped and howled, swung Lisa above his head and spun her
around. Then he declutched and glided through the room in

waltz time, with no regard whatever to the music. All at once he felt like an apache, flung his lady into a corner and spat on the floor. But he had her in his grip again directly —even before it had dawned on her that she'd just torn right through the room. He let out a loud roar and danced a solo round his partner, who had gradually gone half mad. Fists on hips, he circled about her in rocking motion like a rooster doing a mating dance, humming:

> This will soon be over,
> There's an end to everything.

Alois, the pianist, forgot to play. Grabbing Lisa, Tiny flew past the grand piano at top speed, but he managed in passing to butt Alois in the face.

"Get a move on, you shrimp, what do you imagine you're here for?"

With exemplary zeal Alois started banging the keys. He beat out a spirited Hungarian waltz, Tiny meanwhile having switched over to a tango. Neither let himself be disturbed by the clashing rhythm. Paying no special attention to the music, Tiny did as he pleased, off and on twirling the helpless Lisa in the air like a propeller. She had lost a shoe. It was lying in the middle of the floor, blue and forlorn.

Lisa wasn't dancing any more. Her legs had given way while they were doing a rhumba. Tiny continued dancing solo, meanwhile turning her around on his shoulders. Suddenly, he came to an abrupt halt and glowered round the room. "Is someone spoiling for a fight?"

No answer. He nodded, content. "I hope not, for your own sakes."

The Legionnaire chuckled. "Come, put your lady on the counter."

Puffing, Tiny chucked the semi-conscious Lisa onto the bar. He sat down beside her friend Gisela.

The Legionnaire looked at the panting woman in front of him on the counter.

"Trude," he commanded for no apparent reason. "Madame needs a tonic."

Another glass with a dash from Aunt Dora's bottle.

Presently poor Lisa was again on her feet. She'd gotten drunk. Quite suddenly. Aunt Dora's drops. She let herself go, forgetting all about her dignified arrogance. She danced with Bauer. She danced with Stein. She danced with an infantry sergeant.

The sergeant didn't get to finish his dance. Tiny knocked him down and the Belgian threw him out in the back where others continued the transport further.

She danced once more with Tiny. She drank with the Legionnaire. She became very drunk. She threw her clothes into one of the small curtained-off rooms.

Aunt Dora's subtle drops made people forget about regulations. An avalanche was in progress.

Lisa asked the Legionnaire if he'd bring her home.

"You're a slut," he said, and took another sip of vodka.

She cried a little bit. The Legionnaire didn't pay attention to her any more. He told Aunt Dora that women who came to her dive to have an adventure were a bad lot. He told her about the women in Casablanca and Rabat. About women who loved and died. About men who were noiselessly murdered in a narrow passage between white houses. He related this jerkily, in a soft murmur.

Aunt Dora listened, her eyes screwed up. The smoke from her long cheroot bothered her.

Gisela attempted to leave. She'd suddenly been hit by an overwhelming desire for fresh air. The Belgian at the door —a revolving door—smiled amiably, but he shook his head. "You don't leave a party this way, madame!"

He led her back to the bar.

A shrill laugh from Lisa struck the red lamps in the ceiling. She took another sip from her glass. Gisela didn't drink. She was smoking, feeling very hot. She sat down beside me. I proposed we should take a trip upstairs together. I, too, had gotten a little drunk, and I felt like emulating the Legionnaire. I knew very well I didn't behave nicely, but so what? Tomorrow we may die.

She shook her head and waggled her foot in a pink little shoe.

She must be rich, I thought.

"Oh, go to hell," I said.

She pretended not to hear.

Tiny was yelling for whores. No one took any notice, because he was always doing that. He wanted to fight the doorman, who'd been a wrestler, but the Belgian had no desire to fight Tiny. One night they had fought. It lasted for more than an hour. When finally it was over, Tiny looked awful. The Belgian looked awful. Tiny told Dr. Mahler he'd been run over by a carriage in the port. Dr. Mahler pretended to believe him. One must pretend to believe many things when men from a penal regiment come to a big city with girls and schnapps after a long stay at the front. The grooms of

death must live as they think they ought to. Death may
come tomorrow.

Gisela vanished, but I had her handbag. Her identification
card was in it, with her address. The Legionnaire carefully
examined the contents. Then he returned the bag to me,
after helping himself to a hundred marks.

Her name was something with "von" and she lived on the
Alster. So, she was rich!

"She should be whipped," Ewald said. He licked his lips.

"And you should have a bayonet in your belly," the Legionnaire smiled amiably.

Ewald was about to say something, but Aunt Dora removed
the cheroot from her mouth and snarled a warning. "Shut
your trap, you brute!"

Ewald said nothing. The Legionnaire hummed: "Come now,
death, come!"

Ewald gave himself a shake as if he were cold. Aunt Dora
felt nauseated by the cheroot and looked at the Legionnaire
out of the corner of her eye. The scar from his knife wound,
running from his temple to the edge of his collar, shone
pale blue.

"Oh, cut out that damn song," she whispered in her hoarse
voice.

"Scared of death, my girl? Death's my friend."

He laughed harshly and started playing with his battle
knife.

Tiny startled. Making no attempt to cover up, he felt for
his own knife, hidden in a secret pocket of his boot.

"Would anyone care to be sliced up?" he grinned, sticking
his mouth out toward Ewald, who was eager to get away.
A brutal punch tumbled him back against the bar.

"You stay here," Tiny warned. "I might feel like making
a few gashes in you. You're a filthy bastard. Now, tell me
what you are."

Ewald let out a forced laugh. His small cunning eyes
rolled in his head.

Tiny drove his knife in between Ewald's fingers, but without giving him even a scratch.

"What are you, you whoremaster?"

"A filthy bastard," Ewald stammered, looking with glassy
eyes at the quivering knife. Once this knife had belonged
to a man from Siberia. The man had been kicked to death
at Cherkassy for gouging out the eye of a lieutenant in the
104th Rifleman Regiment. Tiny had taken the knife from
the leg of his boot. The knife had been made specially to

· slash the throats of other men. It was a good knife, and Tiny had learned to use it with amazing skill.

One time in the East we were going to reconnoiter at the far end of a bridge. It was an old and decayed bridge, be-·cause no one could be bothered to take care of it. Wood-and-iron bridges have to be taken care of to look nice.

We stepped briskly across the bridge. Our boots rang against the iron. The river grinned up toward us between the cross ties. It chuckled with suppressed laughter because it knew something we didn't. It held a surprise for us.

As usual we were jabbering away. Tiny was walking at the very back. He was peeved because we had been without food for three days and because he was dead set on getting permission to rape one of the women rifle soldiers we had captured during the night.

"She won't give a twitter," .he promised. "No one will know anything about it. A panty soldier like that, would it really matter?"

"I'll shoot you like a dog if you hurt any of those women," the Old Man threatened.

This was the reason Tiny walked across the bridge a little behind the rest of us. He kicked spitefully at a lump of clay, which enraged him by getting stuck on the toe of his boot. He kicked out several times, but the lump stuck. Red with rage he bent down, tore off the lump and hurled it far into the grinning river. By now he'd fallen even further behind. Morose, hateful and bloodthirsty, he slouched behind the pa-trol, which had vanished into the mist and was audible only as a pleasant buzz of murmured words.

Suddenly he stopped, gaping. Out of the fog, across the rail of the bridge, there emerged a figure, a lithe figure. With the nimbleness of a cat he glided after the patrol. Tiny speeded up. He seemed transformed. The gorilla had turned into a black panther. Both vanished in the fog.

A gurgling shriek cut through the clammy air and sent the patrol flying for cover. The buzz of their chattering had died away.

Groans and blows could be heard through the fog. Then footsteps clanked against the iron. We caught a firm hold on our sub-machine guns. The Old Man slit his eyes. The Legionnaire cocked his gun. Porta pulled the pin of an egg grenade. True to pattern when something special was up, Stege trembled slightly.

Where the gray curtain parted, Tiny appeared, dragging a lifeless figure behind him. He threw it down before us in the middle of the bridge, like an angler who's caught an unusually big pike he'd like to show off a bit. He grinned:

"Seen the like of this before, eh?"

The throat of the dead Siberian soldier gaped red and made sucking motions like the gills of a big fish. The blood muddied up the iron of the bridge.

Using his sleeve, Tiny wiped some black blood off his face. It was from the foreign soldier, whose blood had spattered Tiny as he slit the soldier's throat from ear to ear.

Tiny grinned apologetically. "Look how this pig messed me up when I knocked him off."

The Old Man drew a deep breath. "How did you find him?"

"He came up from the river, was going to play a trick on you, fellows. Haw-haw, I was too bright for him and made a slight gash in the Stalin beggar."

"You've saved us," the Old Man said, holding up a couple of high-explosive charges he'd found under the oilskin uniform of the enemy soldier.

"A suicide rifleman," Stege shuddered and stroked his sub-machine gun.

Porta whistled long and pointedly.

"Tiny," the Old Man said. "You saved our lives. If that fellow had caught us by surprise, we'd have been blown sky-high like a well-oiled rocket."

Tiny was in contortions from embarrassment. He wasn't used to praise.

"I lunged my knife straight at his face and just gave a pull. It sank in so easily and gently, then he was dead. He yelled only once. And, d'you know, half his yell came out through the hole I'd cut in his throat."

"You're good with the knife," the Legionnaire nodded proudly. He was Tiny's teacher in using the knife properly.

Tiny swelled with pride and joy. He looked at the Old Man, narrowed his eyes a little and bent his head to a pleading angle.

"After this, may I rape the rifle girl with the fat ass?"

The old man shook his head, slung his sub-machine gun across his shoulder and continued across the bridge. The rest of us followed in silence. Tiny shouted more loudly than necessary. His voice penetrated deep into the fog and must've been heard both by the Russians and by our own troops far on the opposite shore.

"Christ, I'll do it anyway. I saved you, and she isn't so very tender, you know."

The Old Man stopped, swung his sub-machine gun under

Tiny's nose and said quite low, but with so much weight that no one could mistake him, "You stay away from the flint-lock girls, including the one you're so sweet on. Otherwise you'll go straight to hell and I'd be sorry to have that happen. I mean it, Tiny."

"Turds," Tiny growled. He sulked again like an offended child. He didn't get his hands on those flintlock girls. But he became even more proficient with the knife. The Legionnaire was proud.

Neither Tiny nor the Legionnaire used the steel sling. They used only the knife. The rest of us preferred the sling; it was noiseless. But Tiny didn't at all mind their screaming. He said that they seemed more dead when they'd screamed first.

Ewald well knew Tiny's skill with the long battle knife. But Ewald, too, was handy with a knife. His own weapon, however, was a switchblade knife, of the kind fancied by the Portuguese and by pimps in Marseille. Sailors coming to Marseille from Oporto and Lisbon made good business with these switchblade knives. Ewald had received his from a sailor who'd gotten very drunk. It was on account of this sailor that Ewald, the pimp, served his twenty-first prison term. Something or other—it could never be established with certainty precisely what—had saved Ewald from the liquidation camps for habitual criminals. When questioned about this, Ewald sensibly kept quiet and casually shrugged his shoulders.

Criminal Secretary Nauer at Police Headquarters, Stadthaus-brücke 8, had torn off one of Ewald's ears and broken his toes. Not because of the murder of that sailor. That was of minor importance. He wasn't the only sailor who was killed during that time. The mortuary chapel for unidentified persons had space for a great many cadavers, and as long as they didn't have to be piled on top of each other there was no reason to make a fuss. But Herr Nauer at Police Headquarters believed that Ewald had some dope on *Rote Kapelle*, the large underground Communist organization. The dream of Herr Nauer was to be transferred to the Communist Section of the Secret State Police. This section was headed by *Kriminalrat* Kraus, the greatest criminal who ever held public office. But Kraus was a fine police officer, at least by the standards of the Third Reich, or even by police standards anywhere.

Kraus was hanged in 1946 in a cell in Fuhlsbüttel. It was raining. The weather was really dismal that day. He squeaked like a drowning mouse and looked like one, too. He had to be carried to the hemp rope, which smelled pleasantly new—that is, if you can stand the smell of a rope.

He was supported by two young men as he stood on the stool under the steel pipe in the ceiling to which the rope had been fastened. He jumped up and down on the stool like a rubber ball, sobbing: "No, no!" But Fate said, "Yes, oh yes!" The stool was kicked out from under his thick feet.

He gurgled a little. Sort of long and deep, like sour milk that can't quite make it out of the neck of a bottle. His neck stretched and his eyes popped out of their sockets.

One of the young men let out a mere "Damn it!" in his native English and went on his way. The other stayed behind to take a snapshot. Since this was prohibited by law, he had to make haste, but it was "a damned good souvenir," he later told his girl friend in Harburg. She was a nice girl who happened to love that sort of photograph. Her father was shot in the back of his head with a Nagan pistol somewhere in the East. Not because he had done anything, but because somebody had to be shot in the back of the head with Nagans now that the war was over. But at that time the girl didn't know this.

The picture showed clearly *Kriminalrat* Kraus' tongue hanging out of his mouth. Large, strangely swollen.

Laughing, the young man said to the girl from Harburg: "He doesn't want to have anything to do with us. He sticks out his tongue at us."

The young man didn't know that *Kriminalrat* Kraus, from Gestapo's department 6C, the so-called Communist department, would've sold his own mother, wife, and children to get into the secret service of his own country. Kraus had volunteered his services. He had talked and smirked every day for an entire year, and now he stuck out his tongue, like all snakes.

Ewald, pimp, murderer, sadist, and lady-killer, managed to get out of Police Headquarters without becoming acquainted with *Kriminalrat* Kraus. Dumpy Kraus. How? He was said to have talked both plenty and long, lies as well as truth.

Aunt Dora had taken some unusually powerful puffs at her cheroot and said: "None of my business. But if that swine starts speaking to 'Lange Nauer' about anything that concerns me, then . . ." She smiled and winked. Whether the wink was caused by the smoke from her perpetual cheroot, or by the necessity of signaling to someone in the soft darkness around the little tables—that couldn't quite be determined.

Now, Ewald stood squeezed between two bar stools, afraid of what might come.

Everything about Ewald recalled a jackal. For one, he had all of the jackal's cowardliness.

Tiny grinned as he played with his knife. He tossed it in the air and caught it again. He did it again and again. Ewald's face bobbed up and down as he followed the knife with his eyes.

Tiny looked at him. "Would you care to fight Tiny, my lamb?"

Ewald shook his head.

Tiny leaned back and chuckled. "You're a turd, Ewald. And no one fights a turd. It's only good for spitting at."

Tiny spat at Ewald. Ewald wiped the gob off his face with the back of his hand, then rubbed his hand clean on his trousers.

Aunt Dora was picking her teeth with a fork and looking from one to another. "No rumpus, boys. If you want to kill that swine, do it outside. But don't play any pranks here."

Ewald again made an attempt to get away, but Tiny tripped him up. He toppled over and slid some distance along the floor. When he got up and was about to run, a knife whizzed right past his head. It imbedded itself in the door of the room where he used to flog the girls.

He pulled up with fright and whispered hoarsely, "I haven't done any harm to you."

"We damn well hope you haven't—for your own sake," Stein grinned.

Tiny motioned Stein to lay off and called quite loudly: "Come over here, you louse, we would just love to have a little talk with you. Come!"

Ewald walked slowly up to the bar, followed by all eyes. The girls nodded with expectant pleasure, gloating over Ewald's unhappy predicament.

Tiny patted him lightly on the cheek, but finished it off with a terrific slap in the face which made Ewald topple over.

"But good Heavens, what are you doing to baby-boy?" Stein said, pretending to be shocked. He made as if to help Ewald get up from the floor, but suddenly the terrified Ewald was sent flying through the air by a judo grip. He crashed to the floor and lay there unconscious.

Tiny thought he owed him a last greeting. Big and heavy, he got up and bent over the curled-up figure on the floor. He squinted at the Legionnaire, who gave him a secret nod as he was taking a sip from his glass. Tiny winked and gave Ewald a kick in the groin. He doubled up like a sandwich that's been lying around for too long.

We left Wind Force 11 proud of our work.

"You are a business commodity," said Brandt, the cross-country truck driver. "Every Jew in Himmler's camps becomes a first-class object of trade."

"That isn't true," cried the old Jew in the striped prisoner's uniform.

Brandt laughed. Heide laughed. All of us laughed, but joylessly.

"You and all of you Jews will never be anything else than what you are right now—and have been for thousands of years—a plain commodity, a trump held by the rulers which they play or don't play, depending on the needs of their tawdry market," Brandt continued.

Stege nodded. "There's something to what you're saying. At the moment we are the big joes. Later, when the war's over, you will be. The whole thing works like a dial, with 'sun' and 'rain' as on the old barometers. Today, we're in the sun and you in the shade. But soon the situation may be reversed. At the moment, in any case, the Jews are one of the best items on the political market."

The old Jew sat listening with open mouth. Despair shone in his hollow eyes.

"It isn't true," he whispered. "The chains will soon be broken, as when Moses brought us out of slavery in Egypt."

The old prisoner let out a tired laugh.

"That was possible a couple of thousand years ago; it isn't today. Some of you'll escape the gangs of Himmler, but on the other side there will also be Himmlers, and they'll know how to use you to their own advantage. You are and will continue to be a mere object."

"No," said the old Jew. "A new age will come."

Bending toward him, Porta gave him two hundred marks.

"This will give you a start in the new age you're talking of. When you've found it, be sure to send us a postcard."

Loud laughter.

The Jew gently passed his hand over the bills. He looked at Porta with a feeble smile. "What address should I send it to?"

Porta shrugged his shoulders. "Who knows?" His voice

47

*softened to a confidential whisper: "If you notice a rusty
steel helmet on the ground, knock at it and ask: 'Who is
rotting here?' When you come to mine, I'll answer: 'One
of the stupidest swine in the whole German army.' Then
you just place your postcard under the helmet and I'll pick
it up at full moon."*

chapter v

The Jew

"I LOVE YOU," I told her, and at the same time I thought: I
have said that so many times. I wonder if I mean it this
time.

She laughed softly. The crow's-feet around her eyes displayed their finest texture.

"We aren't likely to have much luck at it," she said, putting her arms around my neck and kissing me.

We sat down on the sofa and looked through the window
out upon the Alster. A boat was sailing out there, an old
boat loaded with people. She passed a finger along my broken
nose.

"Did it hurt very much when your nose was broken in
Torgau?"

"Nah, but it bled like a fountain."

"Didn't it hurt at all?"

"A little, maybe—well, yes, afterward it hurt quite a bit."

"Your eyes are cold, Sven, even when you laugh. They are
hard. Try to make them kind!"

I shrugged my shoulders. "That's my eyes. Can one's eyes
be changed? Yours are brown and gentle. Mine are gray
and evil. I'm evil because my work demands it."

"No, not evil. You're not evil."

"Oh, yes, I am. I am one of Hitler's soldiers and must
be evil."

"Nonsense. You're not a soldier and certainly not Hitler's.
You're a boy who has been slipped into an ugly uniform
with tin on the breast. The war is evil. Not people. Kiss me
once more! Hold me close. Tighter. Tighter! Ah, now. Now
I'm comfortable. It's so lovely to feel safe. If one only could
be safe always."

Instead of answering I kissed her. We lay down on the

sofa - and fixed our eyes on the rosette on the ceiling. In the street some people were quarreling. A trolley braked with a grating noise.

"How do you look in civilian clothes?"

"Oh, go to hell. Worse than a fool," I assured her.

"You use ugly language."

"I know, but it belongs to my trade."

She raised herself on her elbow and looked into my eyes, as if trying to see to the bottom of a well. She looked at me for a long while.

"You're afraid of yourself," she said and pressed her lips to mine. Hot lips, a taut body—for a moment they kindled something in me which resembled tenderness. A soldier at war is not accustomed to being loved for his own sake, only for his body and his uniform—and because there is no one else.

Rot, I thought and again looked indifferently at the ceiling. We were both lying on our backs again, resting our eyes on the rosette in the ceiling and letting our minds wander.

"How I should love to go hunting for a spell," I broke the silence. "Duck-hunting," I added after a moment. "The ducks are lovely around this time. They come from the east, big and fat."

"My husband - and I often went duck-hunting," she said absently. Then she pinched her lip because she'd said something about her husband.

"Where's your husband now?" I asked, though I didn't care at all where he was.

"With his division in Russia."

Christ, what's that to me, I thought, and still I listened to her soothing whisper.

"My husband is a colonel. He received the oak leaves."

I smiled. "We call it vegetables. Is your husband a hero? I should imagine he would be, with his iron and vegetables!"

"You're mocking, Sven. Now you're cruel."

"No, I'm not. Is your husband, the colonel, a hero?"

"No, he is a reserve officer like you."

"Hell, I'm no reserve officer. Good Lord, no!" I ejected the words with a grimace, as if I had swallowed something nauseating.

"I mean, he is like you. He can't stand either the war or the Führer."

"It's a mystery to me why you meet so few people who like Adolf. How the hell did we get stuck with him?"

"Weren't you ever for Hitler?" she asked, getting up on her elbow. She looked closely at me.

I turned my head and looked out upon the Alster while I examined the devious maneuvers of my brain.

"Weren't you ever for Adolf Hitler?" she repeated.

"Yes, Gisela, a long time ago I was for him and believed in him." I let out a shrill laugh. "Great God, fancy believing in that absurd figure!"

"Did you say absurd?" she asked incredulously. "Can you really see anything absurd about him?"

"Nah, when you stop to think, he's quite the opposite of absurd. Anyway, now I don't believe in him any longer. What of it? Tiny simply says: 'He's a stupid swine.' Was your husband, the colonel, also for him at one time?"

"Yes, he believed he'd save Germany."

"What was he to save Germany from?" I asked.

"I don't know, but it was understood he'd save Germany. Everyone said so. Didn't you, too, believe he'd save Germany?"

"No, never. I believed he'd give us food and work."

"Well, didn't you get it, Sven?"

"True, but as time went on the food became slightly rationed and the work, you know, wasn't quite what we'd bargained for. But shut up now, you bitch, I can't stand talking about it any more."

"Sven, you're impossible. You'll never be fit for decent society. A person simply doesn't use the word 'bitch' to someone he loves. He doesn't use the word 'bitch' at all."

"Is that so? All women are bitches and nothing else. They're whores, too, all of them. Didn't you come to Wind Force 11 to play at being a whore?"

"It isn't true, Sven."

"Hell it isn't! You wanted to see whores. You wanted to see sex-crazy men. You wanted to see sex, feel sex. That's why you went to Wind Force 11 with Lisa. Lisa got what she wanted. You chickened out, like the amateur you are."

"You're disgusting."

"Perhaps I am. Would you expect anything else? You think perhaps we were taught good manners in Hitler's barracks yards and on the Eastern Front? We're the filthiest pack of hired killers that ever existed. I feel sorry for the society that'll have to readmit us sometime!"

She threw her arms around my neck and kissed me so hard that I tasted blood on her lips. Then she relaxed again.

"I think there's going to be a thunderstorm," she said drowsily.

It was very muggy. She was lying in her slip. Lilac with

wide lace trimming. The slip of a whore, I'd said. One of the expensive ones.

The street echoed with the noise of many people and frequently stopping streetcars. Number 12 in particular made a racket. Number 12 was altogether a stupid streetcar.

I'd thrown my tunic on the floor. It looked abandoned as it lay there on the red carpet. Black and ugly. One death's head was grinning fatuously at the ceiling. What ass invented those death's heads, only God knows!

Far away a siren started hooting. It rose to an infernal howl. We glanced out of the window. A lady in a lilac slip and a soldier with a broken nose.

"Air-raid alarm," she said and glanced up at the cloudless sky, tinted red from the sunset.

"To hell with the alarm. Come here and let's spend the time together as best we can."

"You're horrible!"

I pulled her down on the sofa and forced her to lie back.

While death dropped on the streets below us, our two bodies met and for a few moments we forgot everything else. Two wasted aimless people who didn't know what else to do with themselves. Her slip tore. It only goaded us on to greater frenzy. She screamed. We forgot everything.

Far above the big bombers were drawing their white lines.

"You're a whore. One of the expensive ones," I whispered.

"You think so?" she laughed.

"And I love you. I'll stay here with you. To hell with everything else."

"And everybody else?"

"Well, everybody else, too. You . . ."

Bombs were falling, but far away. Probably somewhere around Kaiser Wilhelm-Strasse.

She sighed and hugged me tight. I felt her tensing her slender body against mine. It was smooth and supple and gave off a scent of freshness. Not the stale and foul smell of a soldier, that peculiar dusty smell that sticks to all soldiers. God, how it had filled me with loathing throughout these years. I could never get used to it. Her nails were polished blood-red. She held up a foot and I could see the red toenails through the sheer texture of the stocking. Her legs were long and well-shaped.

With my hand I traced the curve of her leg, from the ankle over the knee to the roundness of the hip.

"If your husband came now he'd shoot us," I said.

"My husband won't come. He's with his division. A storm division."

"In what division is the heroic colonel?"

"Drop it, will you. Horst is in the 28th Chasseur Division. He's commander of a regiment."

"I know that division. It has a falcon for its emblem. We call it the Falcon Division. We fought side by side with it at Gomel and Nikopol. A real butcher division. You'll never see your husband again!"

"Don't say a thing like that."

"Are you thinking of him now?"

"Maybe," she said, her eyes assuming a far-away look. "Is it possible to love two men at the same time?" she asked a bit later.

"I suppose so. I don't know."

She started crying, mutely, quietly. The tears wouldn't stop flowing.

I stroked her naked body, not knowing what to say. I stroked her hair like you stroke a cat.

"The war's to blame for everything," she said.

The all-clear was sounded. The street noises of the warm evening again came back to us. People laughed again, relieved. It was only a light attack. Just a few hundred dead and wounded.

We drank tea with rum and then we climbed the mountain together. The ever young and lovely mountain where everything is new and where oblivion lies waiting at the summit. We were skilled mountain climbers familiar with every crater and peak, and yet we felt our way with wonder. We were explorers with a truly oriental verve. Then we grew weary and fell into a delicious light sleep. With peace.

"Tell me something of what goes on out there," she said all at once.

I tried to ignore it, but she kept pestering me. She insisted. I couldn't understand why she wanted to hear about what was going on out there.

"Is it true that people are killed because they are of another race? I mean Jews?"

"You can take it from me it's true. Killing people is only part of it. You can buy a sack of Jews or gypsies for fertilizer."

I took a bite from an apple.

"Who knows? Maybe I'm right now eating a Jewish child. Because the ashes are also used for fertilizing fruit trees."

"I don't believe it."

"No? And that's not all. You have no idea. . ."

"Why do people hate the Jews so much?" she said.

"I don't know. Personally I have nothing against Jews or

other races, but I've often met people who do. And they weren't even Nazis. On the contrary."

"They must be mad," she said.

"Of course they're mad. We're all mad. Completely crazy. And those who're not mad are locked up behind barbed wire and prison walls. The world has turned upside down and only madmen have a right to exist. I've seen so many things I can never forget. Like the time we ran into a Jew when we were hunting partisans."

"Tell me," she said and stretched drowsily.

"It's a long story. Are you sure you really care to hear it?"

"Why not. Tell it."

"We were hunting partisans in the Czech mountains. A nice job, really, because we were free to look out for ourselves and roam around in small patrols with little or no control. Now and then we fired in the air to make it sound impressive. As expected, the invariable upshot of these immense losses of ammunition was that our reports of the great partisan battles we'd become involved in were credited. As a matter of fact, we hardly ever saw or heard anything of the partisans. They avoided us and we avoided them.

"We always managed to find something to eat and drink, and if we didn't have anything, Tiny and Porta went out hunting chamois bucks—in bowler and top hat and armed with sub-machine guns."

"Did Porta wear a top hat?" Gisela asked, surprised.

"He did. Porta had once won a silk top hat playing cards in Rumania. This was before we went to Russia. He always wore it, just as Tiny always wore a bowler he'd picked up in a home for the aged."

"That must've looked comical," she laughed.

"That's not the word, but it is a relief to be able to turn Adolf's damned war into a joke. He wouldn't have been very happy to see what fantastic quantities of ammunition these hunting expeditions cost the German Armed Forces. It was seldom they returned with a chamois buck or deer. More often it was a pig or a calf, which were easier to shoot since they were tethered.

"One evening shortly after sunset we reached an abandoned mountain cabin and decided to settle there for the night."

"Who's we?" she interrupted.

"You don't know them. A gang of devil-may-care professional killers in one of those regiments with one foot permanently in the grave.

"The inmates had evidently managed to take in a good

meal before they had to run. The delicacies were still standing on the table. It was like a luxury hotel in some place where war was unknown. Pork, a roast goose.

"We would've enjoyed the meal even more if we hadn't noticed a strange, sweetish smell from the very moment we entered the house. While we were eating, this stench seemed to become increasingly stronger. Porta went upstairs to check if the stench came from there. In a little while we heard him call. As he appeared on the landing, he was wiping off his top hat on his sleeve.

"'There's a fellow up here who's croaked in his bed,' he said. 'That's where the stench comes from.'

"Heide grinned. 'Imagine him lying there popping off in his bed—it's an insult to the war and to Hitler's call for heroism.'"

Gisela had gradually dropped off. I, too, had grown sleepy, speaking to deaf ears. We dozed a little, but I couldn't dismiss the thoughts of the night in the ski cabin.

All twelve of us went upstairs to take a look at the man. He was an old man resting nicely in his white shirt.

"That pig has shit in his bed," said Porta, who'd lifted up the heavy peasant quilt. "What an old pig. The nice bed we were going to sleep in."

"Phew, how he stinks," Stege said, crinkling his nose.

"So, our student can't stand the odor?" Porta asked. He prodded the corpse with his bayonet.

"See he doesn't spring a leak so the corpse gas seeps out," the Old Man warned. "Then we won't be able to stand it here any longer." Surveying the room and pulling his nose—which he was in the habit of doing when faced with some problem —he went on: "Instead, we should get him buried."

Tiny and Porta each grabbed one end of the sheet and carried out the corpse. But it was impossible to dig a grave; the ground was too hard. So instead they buried him in the dunghill. It was considerably easier to get to.

When the burial was over we again went on eating, drinking and playing blackjack.

"There is a puttering noise from somewhere in this damn cabin," Heide growled, glancing around the room where we were sitting.

The kerosene lamp smoked and cast a murky light about us.

"Cut out that crap," Porta hissed impatiently. "Either play, or clear out and join the old codger on the muck heap where you belong."

"What the hell do you mean, you red brute?" Heide was getting worked up. He pushed over his chair.

Broad and large, Tiny got up, shoved back his bowler and wiped his nose on his fingers. Then he grasped the heavy oak table with plates, meat, bottles, cans, weapons and all the rest and put it aside to make room for Heide standing pale and furious at the other end. With a snarling grin Tiny slid across to the brawny Heide.

"Why're you poking your nose into this?" Heide yelled. "This is a matter between Julius Heide and Joseph Porta. It's nothing that concerns you, you stupid gorilla."

Tiny grunted, swung out his fist and hurled Heide to the floor with a resounding slap.

The table was put back again and the game went on. But it was hard to concentrate on it. We strained all our senses to listen. Heide had only cried out about what worried us all. Our primitive instincts had been aroused. Somehow we were warned. Something was wrong in that cabin.

We could have been playing about half an hour or so when suddenly the Old Man threw down his cards and bellowed against the ceiling: "If someone is there, come out!"

Silence. Gloomy silence. Not a sound. And yet, there was something. All of us knew that by now. And it was something alive.

Heide, who had come round, had again asked for cards and was playing. He sat there scowling with slit eyes, fingering his storm carbine.

"What the hell is wrong?" he whispered.

"Someone is hiding," Stege muttered, drawing back to the wall, his sub-machine gun held against his hip. His lips twitched nervously.

"Maybe we've landed in a partisan nest," the Old Man mumbled. "Then good night, girls!"

Tiny pulled out one of those sticky-bombs he always stuffed his pockets with and threw in the most unlikely places.

"Shouldn't we send the whole rotten pigsty to hell?" he asked, about to ready the charge.

"Just restrain yourself," the Old Man said. "Let's get this stable searched so we can play undisturbed. If not, we'll go completely nuts."

Huddled together we crowded up the stairs. We had all our weapons cocked and were ready to mow down everything that got in our way.

Porta kicked the door open with a crash, then rapidly ran for cover while the little Legionnaire sprayed a full magazine of bullets into the pitch-dark room. Heide hurled a hand grenade into the room beside it.

"At the devils," Porta roared as he sprinted along the balcony that ran around the entire house.

Storm carbines and sub-machine guns flashed vicious blue flames into the darkness. It was like fighting windmills.

"Vive la légion!" the little Legionnaire yelled, swinging his sub-machine gun over his head. With the leap of a tiger he rushed into a room he had already razed with a hand grenade.

A stupendous riot broke loose in there, as if he were engaged with several partisans; but it took only a couple of minutes till we realized what the battle was all about. He had jumped straight into a clothes cabinet and it had fallen on top of him, catching him as in a trap. He bawled and thundered to get out.

After a quarter of an hour the second floor was wrecked so thoroughly that a typhoon would have appeared like a puff of air by comparison. Down and feathers from heavy peasant quilts that we'd torn apart in our fright and fury sifted down like a fine snow everywhere.

Quiet as mice we stood listening by the landing. Darkness everywhere. A soft rustle reached us from the lower floor.

"Mon Dieu," came softly from the Legionnaire.

Fear tingled along our spines. Heide was the first to lose his head.

"Who's there? We have a bead on you, you devils!" he roared, making the quiet house tremble.

His roar was followed by a profound silence. Again we stood quietly listening for a few moments, convinced we were not the only living beings there.

"Shouldn't we get out?" Tiny whispered, moving over to one of the windows.

Again a rustle downstairs.

"Stoy!" Porta called and sent a shower from his sub-machine gun into the darkness of the ground floor. "Halt!"

Tiny let out a howl and jumped out through the window, bits of broken glass flying about his ears.

There was a general panic. We couldn't stand the uncertainty any longer. Everybody tried to get out. It was as if Tiny had taken our courage along with him.

There was a hitch in the loading mechanism of Heide's sub-machine gun. He shied the gun after the unknown thing in the dark.

Somehow all of us except Stege managed to get out of the house. He had remained inside.

"We must go and get Stege," the Old Man said. Once more we pushed our way into that damned house.

"Hugo, where are you?" the Old Man called in a low voice.

A match was struck and the kerosene lamp on the table was lit.

In the smoky glare we made out a tall thin figure in the striped costume of a concentration camp. The Old Man was the first to recover from his surprise.

The horribly emaciated figure drew himself up in a military manner and reeled off a report, his glance rigidly fixed on the Old Man.

"Herr Sergeant! Security Prisoner 36789508A reports being separated from his unit, Kz-Railroad Construction Detail 4356 East!"

"Holy Ludmilla!" Porta exclaimed. "What a mouthful. You didn't learn that one in Sunday school."

"Anyone beside you here, zebra?" Tiny asked.

"No, Herr Corporal," the zebra man answered.

"Cut that out," exclaimed the Old Man, annoyed.

"Oh, well!" said Tiny, who felt flattered being addressed with service rank and "Herr." It had never happened to him before.

"Shut up," the Old Man ordered. "Find Stege so we can go on with our game." Turning to the *Konzentration* prisoner, he continued: "You'd better find something to chew on. You look as if you need it."

The old zebra man looked about him nervously. He kept standing rigidly at attention in the middle of the floor, his fingers glued to the seam of his trousers. "Sit down, old geezer," Porta grinned, pointing invitingly at the table. "Get yourself a bit of bread and a piece of meat. There's plenty of it. You'll also find a spot of bug-juice to rinse your gullet with."

The old prisoner moved his jaws in convulsive spasms.

"Herr Staff Corporal! Security Prisoner No. 36789508A requests permission to make a statement."

"Spit it out, brother," Tiny growled, pushing his light-gray bowler over his forehead.

The old Jew didn't say anything. He seemed to be searching for the right words. He knew the deadly danger in saying something displeasing. A misplaced word could mean death. Despite our armbands with the skulls and bones and the expressive *Strafabteilung*, he saw in us his enemies.

"Hey, you zebra! What did you wish to whisper to us?" Porta barked. With a dirty finger he poked the tall skinny figure with the yellow-gray face, caked with month-old grime.

Wearily the man moved his bloodshot eyes from one to another of the government-sponsored killers.

"Well, what did you wish to say?" grinned Brandt, the former cross-country truck driver. He sucked vehemently at a hollow tooth that was always giving off a frightful odor. He didn't dare go to the dentist; he preferred to suffer the ache. Eventually we had put everything into that tooth, from gunpowder to hydrochloric acid. Even dried bird shit had gotten into it. That was Porta's idea.

"Say something," I said, smiling to the man in the striped rags.

"Can't you shut up for once, you fools!" the Old Man snapped. "Don't you see you're driving the man nuts with your stupid questions? Can't you tell by just looking at him that he's half dead from fright? If you looked at yourselves in the mirror, you'd get a shock, too. The devil is a beauty compared to you."

He walked over to the old Jew and placed his arm around his shoulder. Scratching an eyebrow with the tip of his pipe, he said in his own peculiar manner: "You shouldn't be frightened of us, my friend. We aren't as bad as we look. What was it you wished to say? Just spit it out! If you think we're a pack of stupid swine, say so. Because that's what we are."

The prisoner took a deep breath and looked at the Old Man's small, compact worker's figure with its bearded, good-humored face underneath the black panzer field cap. Their eyes met. The almost black eyes of the prisoner and the Old Man's clear blue ones. We could feel these two men finding each other.

"Herr Sergeant! Taking something here is looting. I've been in hiding in this house for three days, but I haven't touched a thing."

The Old Man shook his head, laughing.

"Forget that rubbish. Sit down at the table and rake it in. What's looting today? What's rape today? A joke, just a joke, that's all." He turned to Heide. "Get some more food and booze!"

Heide stood gaping at the prisoner as if he had caught a glimpse of something unnatural, something far beyond the scope of his understanding.

Tiny bent over him and let out a shout that could be heard for miles: "Go and get some grub, you dung beetle, or you'll get a fist through your teeth!"

Heide startled. He walked reluctantly to the kitchen to carry out the Old Man's order.

Porta and the Legionnaire had gone upstairs to look for Stege. They found him lying unconscious in the corridor. When we revived him we discovered that in the mad rush of getting out of the cabin he'd bashed his head into an open door.

"Where have you slept the three days you've been here?" the Old Man asked the concentration camp prisoner.

"On the floor in the kitchen, Herr Sergeant."

"Cut out that rank crap! I can't see why you didn't lie down in one of the many beds standing around."

"That's because I have vermin, and besides I didn't want to mess up those nice beds."

"Holy Mary!" Porta cried, bursting into a roar of laughter. "Everybody should be that considerate. Then the war would be a ball."

The Old Man shook his head and laughed. "Some angel you are, brother. The couple of bugs you've got won't make much difference once we have had a snooze here, not to mention what our brothers on the other side will do when they come. They and we are hardly as considerate as you, whom they call the scum of the earth."

Heide entered with his arms full of schnapps and smoked fat, which he tossed on the table with a clatter.

Stege pulled a book from the shelves and held it out to the Old Man. "Our hosts are people with foresight," he laughed. "They'll obviously take care to jump off the bandwagon at the right moment."

We glanced at the book: Karl Marx.

"That would be just the thing for the Gestapo," Heide grumbled.

"Dry up, you ass-kisser!" Porta snarled. "If not, we'll carve the phonograph out of your throat so you'll blare into space for the last time. We haven't forgotten you squealed."

Heide scowled angrily at the gangling Porta and his top hat, but the sub-machine gun, tilting seemingly by accident in the red-haired soldier's hand, made him keep shut. He still remembered the trip through the forest.

"I'm sorry for the nice table," the old prisoner remarked as the Legionnaire began chopping up fat on the table top.

"The table isn't yours," Brandt brushed him off. He set about slicing bread with his battle knife in the same manner.

"Things should be protected," the prisoner said doggedly.

"Dry up, sheeny!" Heide roared, foaming at the mouth.

We waited in suspense for what was coming. Knowing Heide we sniffed trouble.

Porta was brushing his topper with his sleeve. He grinned

fiendishly. Stege was playing with a hand grenade. The Old Man eyed the ceiling and shuffled the cards in silence. Tiny was noisily sucking a goose leg. Brandt was scraping out a jar of jam with a slice of bread. Krause, a former SS man who'd come to us on account of cowardice and political un- reliability, was picking his teeth with a bayonet. His small green, vicious dog's eyes were bent on Heide, who had dared to enter one of the most hazardous areas in the laws of a penal regiment; attacking a prisoner.

Heide took a swig from a bottle of schnapps. He held it slightly away from his mouth and shoved his head all the way back, making the colorless liquid stream down his throat in a long jet. His Adam's apple bobbed up and down with the gulps. Part of the schnapps overflowed the corners of his mouth and ran down his neck.

He dropped the bottle on the table with a heavy thump. The schnapps spilled out. Bending forward, he, brought his face close to the old prisoner's. His eyes, bloodshot from drink, were set in a malevolent stare. He belched convulsively.

"Huh, zebra! I, Julius Heide, noncommissioned officer in the 27th Panzer Penal-Regiment, tell you that you are a stink- ing, lice-infested Jew swine!"

Heide looked around triumphantly. "What do you say to that, sheeny?"

The old Jew sat on a stool at the table. He looked listlessly at the drunken Heide. He didn't seem to understand it was he who was being treated like dirt in this way. All the filthy taunts were lost on him. He had heard them too often. They didn't get through to his brain any longer. He had become immune to obscene words.

Heide shook his head like a bull just before it gores the bullfighter.

"I mean you, you rotten corpse!" He hissed it out through the corner of his mouth. "You are a Jew louse! A piece of stinking Jewish shit!" He leaned back his head and roared with laughter at his own wit. Cackling, he repeated: "Jewish shit!"

He kept on repeating it, alternating it with "shit-house," "dunghill," and many more vocables of the latrine which he didn't forget, even for a moment, to combine with "Jew." He warmed to his subject. He stepped on the gas. His tongue ran away with him. He howled and screamed.

The rest of us sat silent. The old prisoner was eating and didn't pay the slightest attention to him. He seemed to be sitting in a room completely by himself, not hearing the stream of dirty words.

Porta grinned expectantly. Tiny picked his nose. The Legionnaire whistled: "Come now, come now, death."

The Old Man dealt the cards, slowly and deliberately. Stege was chewing on a stick. Krause was catching lice.

All at once a 7.65 pistol was in Heide's hand. He released the safety-catch with a click, which to us sounded like a crash.

"Now, Jew, I am going to blow out your shit-brain!"

He grinned fiendishly, slowly raised his pistol and took precise aim at the old man's head.

For a moment there was an ominous silence. Then the old Jew lifted his head and looked at Heide with a pair of strange dead eyes.

"You want to shoot me, *Herr Unteroffizier*? There is nothing to be done about that. Whether you shoot me or a dog matters nothing. The only difference is that the dog is afraid of death, if it knows what's coming. I'm not. I have expected it every day for years. Go ahead and shoot me if you like, but let's go outside. Otherwise we'd make a mess on the floor in here."

"Cut out that crap," Heide hissed. We saw him bend his finger and pull the trigger tight.

The Old Man alone didn't look up. He turned up a card in his solitaire, "Black Sarah."

"Put away that pistol!" he hissed like the crack of a whip.

Heide sat there as if stupefied.

"I hate these damn Jews, and I've always wanted to plug one."

"Put away that rod, and right now!"

Tiny got up and flipped open his battle knife.

The Old Man looked up. "Julius Heide, put down that gun!"

The Legionnaire hummed: "Come now, death."

Slowly, imperceptibly, Heide lowered his hand. The pistol clattered on the floor. Terror glittered in his eyes. The superman who had just shown his big snout had been transformed into a cringing cur, crestfallen with fear.

Heide gave a prolonged hoarse squeak like a rat that's been squeezed into a corner and sees the bared fangs of a terrier flashing over it. He wanted to scurry off, but the Legionnaire tripped him up. He fell and slid along the floor.

Tiny grabbed him by his feet and swung him gaily around. His head hit the wall with a smack. Tiny, who by now had worked himself to fever pitch, let out a roar, raised his knife and was going to stab Heide in the back. But he was stopped by the old Jew, who caught his arm: "No, no, comrade, don't kill him!"

We were astonished to hear Heide's victim appear as his de-
·fender, but even more astonished to hear the word "comrade"
spoken by someone who up to now had addressed us as if we
were gods.

Tiny flung away the unconscious Heide and gaped at the
old Jew who was clinging to his arm, deathly pale and
trembling all over.

"What the hell?" he said, perplexed. "Why shouldn't I
knock that skunk cold? He stepped on your toes, you know."

The old prisoner shook his head.

"No, comrade, he didn't insult me. After all, I'm a Jew.
Those other things he didn't mean at all. He's sick. It will
pass when the world gets well."

"Sick?" Porta sneered. "That damn well beats everything.
Heide is the healthiest rotten bastard in the world. He deserves being butchered."

Tiny nodded rapturously and shook off the Jew.

"You're right, Joseph Porta. Maybe Tiny should see how
deep he can sink this knife into his throat?"

The prisoner caught Tiny's hand, kissed it and begged: "No,
no, leave him alone! After all, I'm the principal party!"

The Old Man waved his hand in protest.

"Don't be so bloodthirsty. Let that swine lie where he is,
and sit down so we can get the game going."

We sat down, though a bit reluctantly. The Old Man dealt.

"Would you take a hand in a game of blackjack?" he asked
the old prisoner.

"No, thank you, Herr Sergeant."

The Old Man shook his head despairingly and flung up his
hands. "God almighty! Can't you even say 'comrade' to me?
You do to Tiny, that big bull-necked fool!"

The old prisoner nodded and opened his mouth. A moment
passed before the words came: "I'll try to say 'comrade,'
but it is somewhat difficult."

We played a little in silence. Then Brandt threw down his
cards.

"I've no patience any more. Doesn't someone have a story?"

"You're a stupid swine," Porta said, throwing down his
cards.

"Anything else?" Brandt asked, cocking his head like a bull
ready to toss someone.

"I'll smash your ugly face," Porta flared up. He hurled a
bottle after Brandt, who lightning-quick ducked his head as
the bottle crashed against the wall in a shower of fragments.

"It's a pity you are messing up the house this way," the
old Jew whispered.

"What's that to you?" Brandt shouted angrily. "It isn't your house."

"Precisely because of that," the old one said. "If it were mine, it wouldn't matter. But I'm sorry on behalf of the people who own it. They have two children to hand it on to."

"How do you know?" Brandt asked.

"There are children's clothes in the closet," the Jew answered.

"Did you have a house yourself?" Brandt asked.

"Did have, yes. Now I have nothing. The house was taken away a long time ago."

"By whom? The bailiff?" came naively from Krause, the SS man.

We laughed till we coughed.

The old Jew nodded. "The bailiff? You might call them that."

"I suppose you snatched your house from someone in the Weimar period?" Krause said.

"Not that I know of," came rather pointedly from the old prisoner.

"How did you get into the cage, zebra?" Porta asked, sucking at his only tooth with a smacking, sputtering sound, while he wiped his top hat with a fragment of old newspaper. The headlines still spoke of victorious advances for the German army. When he had finished with the hat, he blew his nose on the victorious army and tossed the thousands of heroes into a dark corner by the old stove.

The old Jew took one more piece of meat and stuffed it into his mouth. He still looked hungry.

"Don't eat too quickly," the Old Man warned. "It takes less time to overeat than to die from hunger. Rich food is not for you." Kindly, the Old Man thrust a piece of lean meat across to the prisoner.

"How did Krause's friends get their hands on you?" Porta asked, scratching the red jungle of his thick mop of hair with the point of his knife.

"They're not my friends," Krause flared up.

"Close up your bellows," Tiny snarled, cracking a louse. "When Porta says they are your friends, then they *are* your friends!" He didn't forget to score the table for the dead louse. He had a bet with Porta who had the most.

Heide groaned and got up from the floor. His face was caked with clotted blood. One eyelid was closed and terribly swollen. He spat out a tooth and wiped his mouth with the back of his hand; a thin streak of blood still trickled out.

Porta looked at him out of the corner of his eye, put the cracked monocle in his eye and clicked his tongue.

"Bumped your noodle a bit, Julius Jew-eater, eh? Baby-boy seems to take after his great namesake, Streicher, eh, you slum lout?"

Heide didn't answer.

Resting his chin on his hand, the old Jew began talking. It sounded like he was talking to himself. Talking as only those can talk who've been locked up in an inferno of silence for a very long time. They don't really talk. They cough and hawk the words out. They dream aloud that they have a cold.

"It was in '38 they caught us. I got away because I had connections."

"You desert camels from the 'Holy Land' always have connections," Julius scoffed from the floor. He spat out the name "Holy Land" with contempt. His hate was so big he wouldn't even stop at risking his life to get it off his chest. He snarled like a vicious dog, lips curled up and teeth bared.

"You should be up there swinging, sheeny!"

The old Jew went on unwincingly. The hellhound who sat barking noisily at his feet didn't exist for him.

"I was living in Hamburg, in Hoch Allee by Rothenbaum, a lovely place," he dreamed, and sighed with longing for Hamburg in sunlight, when it smells of salt, sea, and smoke from the ships, and when laughter floats from the small boats on the Alster. "I was a dental surgeon. Had many friends and nice patients."

"I bet they were hook-noses like yourself," Heide cried.

Tiny threw a big hunk of pork at his head. He toppled over, but got on his feet again, though with some difficulty. He growled spitefully. "To be at table with a Jew dog," he lisped and squirted a jet of blood and spit at the prisoner.

"I was lucky enough to get my passport stamped by the Party and left Hamburg by steamship. I planned to go to China by way of the Soviet Union." He rocked his head. "By way of the Soviet Union—what a cursed idea!"

"But they're your friends," Heide sneered. "Jew friends in Moscow. The devil only knows why you didn't become a commissar, with a Nagan for neckshot liquidations."

The Jew looked up.

"There is a lot that you and the devil don't understand." He looked at Heide with an inscrutable expression in his eyes. "Over there, too, we Jews are hunted."

The Old Man gave a tired laugh. "Yes, you're also hunted in the Soviet Union. You were hunted in Poland. You're hunted almost all over the world. The devil knows why."

Turning to Heide, he continued: "Heide, you ought to know why, you who so faithfully follow your namesake!"

"Jews are swine and crooks," Heide barked. "The Talmud is the proof."

Julius Heide hated Jews because the most gifted boy in his class at school was a Jewish boy called Mouritz. Little Mouritz helped big Julius. He whispered to him and wrote small slips-of paper for him. As the years passed, Julius felt each whispered word and each slip of paper like a stinging defeat. His hate swelled, grew inward. On Crystal Night, he participated with enthusiasm in the window-breaking. Together with other young Nazi hopefuls and the rest of the riffraff, he tore hooting·and howling through the Jewish quarter of Berlin. The whole thing was so deliciously safe for this gang, which was under the direct protection of the authorities. For the rest, Julius Heide didn't understand race hatred any better than the other twelve of us. He had learned by heart long periods from Julius Streicher's inflammatory paper.

We played for a while in silence, but the game bored us. Porta pulled out his recorder, cleaned his nose on his fingers, spat over Tiny's head and began playing. He started several times as if searching for a piece that was acceptable to him and finally switched over to "Eine kleine Nachtmusik." He improved as he went on, and soon he cast a spell over us with his playing. Into the dark mountain cabin he lured the beauty of spring in the warbling of thousands of birds, a faraway, carefree world. He transformed the cabin into a crystal hall where ladies and gentlemen in silk costumes danced a minuet. He leaned back his head and pointed the flute skyward. It sounded like a full orchestra of two-hundred-year-old instruments, directed by a court musician.

The old Jew began humming the tune. He hummed in a deep hoarse voice. Then he fell into a reverie. Cheerful safe rooms from a time hundreds of years ago—before 1935, when the world all at once reversed and became evil and cruel. A woman in light blue, a fascinating woman, quiet and gentle. The woman he loved. His Anna. How she could laugh! With such real heartiness, her mouth open and her white teeth flashing like fresh-caught herring glinting in the August sunlight. She always had a kind answer. Anna, his beloved Anna, who was killed in a gateway because she had committed "racial outrage." The killers were laughing young men in brown uniforms. He remembered it as if it were yesterday. They'd been to the theater to see *William Tell*. It was only ten o'clock as they were walking home. He wanted to get a pack of cigarettes from a machine. She walked ahead a bit, slowly, on tapping high heels. Suddenly, the taps were drowned out by the trampling of iron-studded boots. She screamed twice. The first scream was long and tinged with horror. The second died away in a rattle. Paralyzed, he stood there watching them butcher her. Again and again fell their hard deadly blows. A shortish SA man, with ash-blond hair and the sort of open laughing face that no mother could help loving, split her head with a board. It happened on June 23, 1935, diagonally across from Dammtor.

Before that day they often had musical evenings. He played the bassoon or violin, and she the piano. It was almost always Mozart. Anna played with the same deep insight as the filthy, red-haired corporal with the tall, bulging hat.

The little Legionnaire pulled out his harmonica and joined in playing a piece of music that was almost unknown to us. But it made us dream. Suddenly they switched over to a whirling Cossack dance. In the same instant all melancholy thoughts were swept away. We went wild, just like the Cossacks must have done in their villages when this dance was struck up.

Stege, beating time against the table, represented the drum row. Tiny and Brandt jumped to their feet and let out a long-drawn Tartar yell. They leaped high in the air and tapped their bootlegs with their hands. Their feet moved like a drum roll as they whirled along the floor. The rest of us got roused and followed them. The whole house rocked. During the intervals we drank as if possessed.

The old Jew laughed. He also was drunk. He had forgotten the wife they'd killed in a gateway. The strong vodka blotted out the house that had been confiscated. He had forgotten the thousands of blows received from young men in elegant, impeccable uniforms with the death's heads on their caps. Forgotten also was the rope which had dangled hungrily from a rotten beam. He wanted to dance. He danced with Heide. They shouted. They drank. They sang:

Who will foot the bill?

They bellowed with all their strength:

Who can afford it?

Accompanied by Porta's laughing flute, we caroled the old carnival song in rapturous chorus:

And who has a pile of money?

"I don't have a shilling," roared the old Jew, cutting the most ludicrous figures as he danced around with Heide, who had forgotten that he hated Jews. They pounced at each other and rocked their hips.

Heide wound a blanket about him, fitting it coquettishly like a dress.

Porta switched over to a Spanish peasant dance. For castanets Stege was hammering with a couple of plates. We danced something we imagined was a flamenco.

The Legionnaire roared ecstatically: *"Ça, c'est la légion!"*

Exhausted, we sank down on the chairs. We drank some more. We played. We drank once again. We blazed, red and hotly drunk. The maundering talk of drunken men flowed like a nondescript porridge whose ingredients no one could determine. But we didn't care about that.

> Tomorrow we shall die.
> Oh, come now, death!

Heide wept on the Jew's shoulder and received one long pardon after another. He swore by many strange saints that he would slash the throat of every SS man he ran across. In a whisper he confided to the old Jew that he, Julius Heide, was a slurping pig. He demanded he give him a box on the ear. It turned out a tiny one, a mere breath.

"Harder," Julius hiccuped, offering his cheek.

Tiny had watched the numerous mild attempts of the old Jew in silence. Finally he lost patience, stood up, and hit Heide over the head with a wooden ladle.

With a gurgle he rolled over. The last thing he managed to say before he slipped into unconsciousness was: "Thanks, pal, it was lovely to get a regular thrashing."

There was a lull. For a short while we sat drinking in silence. Then, quite of himself, the old prisoner again returned to his story. He hiccuped a little.

"It was in a dirty little village that my journey to China was interrupted." He raised his cup. "Your health!" Half of what he drank splashed over at the corners of his mouth. "My name is Gerhard Stief—presently, since we are with the colors, ex-Lieutenant of the infantry, Gerhard Stief." He chuckled and screwed up one eye as if he'd told us an unbelievably funny joke.

We grinned. We slapped our thighs and roared with laughter. Tiny pretended to fall off his chair and to go into convulsions of laughter. He threw up and turned around in his vomit. Brandt poured a pail of water over him. Not for Tiny's sake, but because of the stink.

The old Jew continued, undisturbed. "I was in the 76th Infantry Regiment, Altona. They wanted me to enter the Guards at Potsdam. I snapped my fingers at the Guards. Grenadiers of the Guards with white insignia! No, thank you, I preferred the men of the Altona 76th. I went home every evening to eat meat balls. I love meat balls and potato pancakes.".

Porta, who was cleaning his ear with the point of his bayonet, glanced at the Jew.

"As soon as we've rested a little, I'll make a stack of pancakes for you," he promised.

"I'll help you," Tiny said and pulled his nose.

Heide turned around on the floor and muttered, "Down with Adolf. Long live the Jews!"

Porta spat at him.

"I was demobilized in 1919," Stief continued. "Then I studied again. In Göttingen. A glorious time," he added and drank a bit more.

"Yes, it's nice in Göttingen," the Old Man nodded. "I was apprenticed there to master joiner Radajsak in Bergstrasse. Do you know Bergstrasse, zebr——?" He checked himself, blinked self-consciously, and corrected it to "Gerhard." He laughed. "Do you, Gerhard? You don't mind my calling you Gerhard? Do you, Herr Lieutenant?"

We laughed. Gerhard laughed. The Old Man slapped his thighs and laughed very loudly. He filled his old pipe. This pipe had a lid. He had made it himself.

"Do you know Bergstrasse?" the Old Man went on. "There's a fine tavern on the corner. 'Holzauge' it's called."

"I know that one. There was a girl there named Bertha," Gerhard cried in a voice which was breaking with enthusiasm at the thought of the girl named Bertha.

"Was she fat?" Porta asked with interest. He licked his lips at the thought of "a girl you can feel."

"Nah," Gerhard said. "She was slim as an eel."

"Ugh, what a yellow piece," Porta said. "Those narrow boards are nothing for me. I love to drown in rolls of fat. You want something you can put your hands on, boys. To feel the meat with your fists, there's nothing to top it!"

"What happened in the transit town where you were caught?" Brandt asked. He spat at the snoring Heide, who protested aloud in his sleep. He must have been dreaming he'd become a duck, for he was making quacking sounds.

"I was called to the counter where the NKVD people were

sitting. A nice little man took me to his office, where he told me with a smile I was detained as an espionage suspect.

" 'But everything will be all right,' he said laughing, as if it were a huge joke.

"He meant of course that whether I was shot or buried alive in Kolyma I would in either case be all right; and, granted, that is also a way of being all right. Why all that bother with long drawn-out lawsuits? A printed form that can be filled out by one man is considerably simpler, you know. I saw quite a bit of the Soviet Union, unbelievably much I saw, but through barbed wire. The first Russian word I learned was *davay*, faster. I remember it, because it was beaten into me with rifle butts. Comrades, there are two colors I have come to hate. The NKVD soldier's green and the black of the SS guard."

The Old Man nodded, removed the pipe from his mouth and puffed out a cloud of smoke.

"Gerhard, friend, we understand you. A fur cap with a green cross can give us the shivers, too."

The Old Man leaned back in his chair, put his feet on the table, closed his eyes and went on smoking in silence.

Stief continued: "At Boritsov we were supposed to procure food for ourselves. There was plenty of fish in the river running through camp."

"Where's Boritsov?" Stege asked.

"Boritsov is far east, almost where the sun rises, in China." Gerhard thought a moment and passed his fingers through his tousled beard. "It *is* in China. A small wretched Soviet Republic."

"If there was enough food it couldn't have been so bad," Brandt said. He took a big bite from a salami sausage.

Stief gave him a long look. He took a deep swig from the bottle of schnapps.

"So, that's what you think? Are you familiar with the red fish?"

The little Legionnaire leaned forward on the table and looked intensely at Stief.

"The ones that give you worms?"

"Yes, those that give you liver worms."

The Legionnaire gave a long and pointed whistle.

"They are damned sophisticated over there in Boritsov. So, you have liver worms, Lieutenant?"

Stief nodded. "Yes, and it hurts. You're eaten up slowly from the inside. Those pills you get just prolong the pain.

"After those red fish we got to the salt mines in Yazlanov. You know, those large salt wastes further down in Asia.

From there we were sent to the Urals, to the locomotive works
in Matrosov. Suddenly one day all the Germans, Austrians,
Czechs, Poles and many more of Hitler's children were assembled and sent to the distribution prison in Gorki. After a
few days halt the westward journey continued. In Lvov we
had the greatest surprise of our lives. There the SS and the
NKVD had arranged a first-class barter in men. With yells
and derisive laughter all of us from the East were handed
over to the SS and all from the West to the NKVD. My
friends, have you ever had the experience of sitting on your
haunches for hours at a stretch?"

He took a cigarette Brandt flipped to him. He sucked the
smoke deep down into his lungs. You could see how he enjoyed it. He closed his eyes a moment, then continued.

"Have you been packed together in steel cars so tightly
that half the car got suffocated? Have you experienced how
soft a corpse is when you've stood on top of it for hours?
This is the modern method of conveying living meat."

We nodded. We were familiar with it, and we knew Dr.
Gerhard Stief from Hamburg, ex-Lieutenant of the infantry,
didn't exaggerate. Torgau—oh, yes, we were familiar with it.
Lengries, Fort Plive. We, too, had experienced the educational
methods of dictatorship.

Stief drank again. We all drank.

"Hell!" he cried. "I had the Iron Cross from 1914 and
the Hohenzollern family order. An SS *Hauptsturmführer*
grinned at me and said I could wipe my behind on Kaiser
Wilhelm's crap. Despite the fact that he wore both orders himself."

"He must've been an ass," the Old Man remarked.

"Of course he was," the Legionnaire said. "Or he wouldn't
be in the SS."

"Before I came to the *Baukommando* I spent a long time
in Stutthof and Majdanek," the old Jew went on. "And now
I'm here with you."

"Did they treat you badly in Majdanek?" Krause asked,
as if he didn't know.

"They're cruel in Majdanek. They are in most camps and
prisons."

"Aren't they the worst in the Soviet Union?" the former SS
man wanted to know.

"Not really. Actually, the same kind of people are guards
and prisoners in both places. In Camp 487 in the Urals we
got *balanda*, prison camp soup. The same kind that people used
to get in prison camps hundreds of years ago. Rotten, salty,
stinking. The fish *tiulka*, which stinks even alive. That fish is

born rotten. In Majdanek we were served bread filled with
worms, iron and splinters of wood. Many prisoners choked on
the things the bread was stuffed with. The NKVD whipped us
with rifle butts and jabbed at us with bayonets or just used
the *nagayka,* the horsewhip. The SS guards whipped us with
the cat-o'-nine-tails and rubber truncheons. Both parties used
a thin steel chain to break the kidneys. The NKVD mostly
performed their executions by firing a Nagan at the nape of
your neck. The SS were fondest of using a piece of rope on a
butcher's hook, with your toes just touching the ground. As
you can see, you SS man, there isn't a very great difference."

He said this with a smile which betrayed the refined physician he once had been.

"I am not in the SS," Krause protested.

A slight touch of sarcasm insinuated itself into Dr. Stief's
dignified smile. "Many will say that when sometime here or
in the hereafter accounts are to be settled."

Porta growled ominously. "All SS men and NKVDs have
volunteered. The fact that they later got cold feet is no excuse." He pointed at Krause. "You'll always be an SS rat. The
only reason we didn't plug you a long time ago is because
we're going to give you up to see you broken on the wheel
when we have our revolution. We've told you once and for
all that you're a swine, tolerated among decent people only
because we have to tolerate you."

Stief shook his head. "Why so bloodthirsty? He's sure to
be haunted by bad dreams when he gets old sometime . . ."

"*If* he gets old," Porta cut in, giving Krause a dirty
look.

". . . and is sitting alone. That's far worse than getting
hanged."

"Allah is wise. Allah does what's right," the Legionnaire
chanted, bowing toward the southeast.

"*Voos is baschjot,*" Dr. Stief mumbled like an echo.

"At Fort Plive we had to sit on a long board when we took
a crap," Brandt said. "Anyone who fell into the pit would
drown in his own and others' shit. Many got drowned. The
SS and the head-hunters made bets among themselves how
long you could hold out before you sank."

"There's a board like that in Majdanek, too," the old Jew
nodded. "Many are getting choked to death also in *that* pit.
A person who falls into it sinks slowly, as in a swamp. He
vanishes to the gurgling sound of small air bubbles. When
he's gone it looks like boiling porridge."

Tiny spat out part of a goose leg and took a slug from a
bottle of Prague beer. "In Brückenkopf 3 below Torgau

we had to piss at each other when we shit in our pants. The black beets gave us diarrhea."

We looked at Tiny, astonished. It was the first time we'd heard a single word about his time in prison. We had no idea what he'd done or where he'd been.

He took a bite of the salami sausage, spat it out again quickly, dipped the sausage in a bowl of wine and stuck it in his mouth. He continued talking with his mouth full, which made it difficult to understand what he was saying.

"An *U-Scharführer* from Totenkopf broke my arm in three places."

He began picking his teeth with the point of his bayonet and spat out capers in all directions. Then he drank a little from the bowl in which he had dipped the sausage. "He tore off my little toe with a pair of pincers, a brand-new pair."

Tiny drank a little more Prague beer. He got up, picked up a big armchair, lifted it over his head and banged it on the floor four or five times until it smashed to pieces. He kicked the broken bits. "That's what I'll do to that SS *U-Scharführer* when I find him. I know he's on duty in a camp on the Weser."

He broke into a grin which boded no good for that particular SS man from *Totenkopfsverband*.

"In Lengries they bastinadoed us," I said. I recalled a Christmas Eve long ago under bare poplars and screeching crows, with SS *Obersturmführer* Schendrich commanding: "One, two, one, two!" in a shrieking voice which broke with rapture when someone fainted. I didn't say what I would do with Schendrich if we met. I hope we won't ever meet.

"In Fagen some of us were castrated for fun," the little Legionnaire said, clenching his fists around the handle of a hand grenade, his eyes flashing like the Moor's when revenge is just around the corner.

"In Gross Rosen 367 Jews were hanged head down," Stege said. "One of them had his nose cut off and given to the dog Max. That dog just loved human flesh. While he was eating the nose we had to sing: 'Darling—I'll see you no more.'"

"When I returned home from Fort Zinna I tried to hang myself," the Old Man said.

We sat for a moment in silence. We knew from before that the Old Man had wanted to hang himself. His wife managed to cut him down in time. A clergyman friend took him in hand. The Old Man didn't try to take his own life again.

"When the war's over," Gerhard Stief said, "I'll invite you for beer to 'The Half Rooster' on Hansaplatz."

"Great," Brandt cried. "We'll meet in 'The Half Rooster' and we'll all of us stand beer!"

"Dortmunder Export, a pump barrel for each," Stege laughed. "Yes, a whole barrel," he added excitedly.

We could almost smell that beer. We slapped each other's shoulders and burst into an ecstatic yell over the Dortmunder Export we would drink in "The Half Rooster".

"Do you know 'The Green Goat' in Albert Rolfgasse in Hamburg?" Stief shouted enthusiastically above the uproar. "There you get the best meat balls and the best sauerbraten in the world."

"No, we don't know that place," Stege laughed, "but if you'll promise to show it to us, in return I'll show you Lili's saloon, the best birdcage in all Hamburg. One of the girls can do everything—just like a fakir girl. She's said to have studied whoring at the Punjab pagoda in Raipur."

"We'll wind up at Lili's," the Old Man decided.

"Any whores there?" Tiny asked through the noise.

"Oceans of them," Stege affirmed.

"Ah, if only the war was over," Tiny sighed, "so we could set out right away."

"Afterward we'll hit the town and raise hell," Porta shouted jubilantly. "We'll pick a fight with every lousy bum we meet and have a crack at all the girls."

Stief said: "We only have to watch out we don't get stuck at 'The Half Rooster'. It's so scandalously pleasant there, and after two Dortmunders you know you get thirsty."

"Let's have a game of *mariage* or blackjack," said Bauer, the big butcher from Hanover who always was afraid before an attack. He said one should carefully avoid taking any chances. Chance was a stupid swine. He claimed he had lost out on a lot of things by becoming a soldier.

"I don't want any cross," he said, "gold, iron or wood. Ten hours of work in a good sausage factory under a reasonable foreman, a good piece of nookie at night, and a game of *mariage* and beer with a couple of chums after knock-off time, that's all I'd ask for."

We played for about a half hour or so. Gerhard Stief won a couple of hundred marks. We made him win. He pretended not to notice.

"You sure are a tough one, Gerhard," Porta laughed. "You're giving us all a beating."

In order that all fourteen could participate we switched over to banker. Whenever Gerhard turned up the right card our enthusiasm knew no bounds.

"Hell, Gerhard, you'll be a rich man. Maybe you'll get to

be our boss when we're no longer busy with this war,"
Brandt said.

"Yes, but let's make sure not to forget that our revolution
has to be settled before we close up shop and go home,"
Porta warned. He blew his nose on his fingers. A lump of
snot hit a panel, where several other lumps testified to the
diligent use of fingers for handkerchiefs.

Brandt shoved the bottle across to Gerhard. "Have another swig, Herr Lieutenant."

Gerhard drank and put the bottle away, as we did, with a
resolute thump. This thump was very important. It showed you
were on easy terms with the bottle. You shouldn't just *set*
down a bottle, as a housewife does after she's poured out a
few drops of vinegar on the headcheese. You plunk down the
bottle, as if saying: "Look, that's where you stand, Comrade
Green! Damn it all, you and I can boast of a few things
neither God nor the Devil knows." A servant girl places a
bottle. The snotnoses who want to show off pound the bottle
on the table, whereas men from the port and the front, from
the large trucks and the factories, put the bottle down with
precisely this thump, which signifies that they come from the
shipyard with its plates and steel. It stamps them as adults.
These are the sort who grin at what others gape at, and the
bottle says: "Hello, you old sot!"

Unteroffizier Heide had again got back on his feet. Brassy
and provocative, he squeezed himself between Krause and
Gerhard. For a moment the situation was explosive. Calls and
yells. After a string of scorching curses, Heide was seated beside Gerhard, in the place Krause had occupied. He grinned,
drank a couple of glasses of schnapps and clicked his tongue:
"Cards for Julius Heide!" He looked sideways at Gerhard.
"Let's clean out those stinkers!"

Gerhard nodded. We played in silence. Gerhard won all
the time. Heide acted offended. "You lucky swine," he cried.
"Now I'll soon be on my ass. If this goes on for long I'll be
settling down as a gigolo when the war's over."

"That certainly wouldn't be much of a change," Porta observed casually. "You were one already before the war."

Heide said with resignation, "Broke!"

Gerhard laughed quietly.

"You may have credit from me."

"How many per cent?" Heide sneered.

"At the rate charged by sixty-percenters when the party in
question is a shady character," the Legionnaire decided on
Gerhard's behalf.

"That'll be 250 per cent," Porta yelled, slamming the ace of spades on the table.

Porta took the whole pot. Three hundred and seventy marks and four opium sticks.

All together we pounced on Porta's ace of spades and examined it thoroughly. Quite obviously he had cheated.

Heide and Brandt borrowed on sixty-percenters' terms.

"You're smart," the Legionnaire scoffed. Pulling his nose, he scowled at Porta, who'd sat down on top of all his money.

"And you'll be gracious enough to shut your trap, Desert Rambler," Porta threatened. Again he hauled in large winnings. He lent them to Krause at 275 per cent. To invest them in Krause was a very poor use of the money, as he was an SS man and sentenced for cowardice. Two different camps had it in for him, and fate could catch up with him at any moment.

"We'll arrange a first-rate cock-fight in Hamburg," Bauer cried excitedly, "and you'll be our boss, Lieutenant."

"Yeah, we'll rent *Planten en Blomen*," Stege laughed.

"Christ, what a cock-fight we can put on there," Tiny roared. In his mind's eye he saw the cocks killing each other —while we were cheating the players.

Outside, a big round moon was shining. It seemed to laugh at us, at all fourteen candidates for the grave.

The Legionnaire swept the cards off the table and kicked over his chair.

"I'm bored. Let's have a fight instead!"

In a moment everything had been prepared. Tiny and Heide were going to have a boxing match. Braids from sofas and chairs were twined together to mark the ring. The two husky fellows stood there ready, dressed in underpants and infantry boots. Dressing rolls were used for hand bandages. We didn't have any boxing gloves.

"I'll batter you to snot!" Tiny said, getting worked up.

"I'll kick you in your belfry," Heide cried.

"It'll be a good fight," Porta vowed.

The Legionnaire nodded.

Tiny grinned and began swinging his arms. "Jesus, how I'm looking forward to knocking you cold."

The Legionnaire held him back.

"No punches till I give the word. And you'll go on punching till one of you's KO'd."

"Quite right," Tiny cried. He was stalking noisily about the room in his infantry boots.

Heide slit his eyes and looked angrily at Tiny.

"Remember, you bastard, I'm city champion! You're going to whimper!"

The Legionnaire pounded on an empty gas-mask container with a hand grenade, the signal to begin the fight.

The two boxers jumped up and started stalking and dancing around each other. They both acted professional, but we knew from experience that the professional bit would soon wear off. As soon as one of them should happen to hit a bit hard, a regular fight with all the meanest street-fight tricks would develop. This was what we were looking forward to.

Throughout, Heide went after Tiny with his chin resting on his chest. He resembled a young bull set on chasing all other bulls to the ends of the earth.

Tiny walked backward and growled like a polar bear threatened with being deprived of his piece of meat. Both men were constantly muttering curses at each other.

All of a sudden Heide raised his right and planted it three or four times in Tiny's face. Tiny's head flew back like a coiled spring. He yelled from rage and frantically lashed out with both fists, but without hitting the grinning Heide, who evaded every murderous blow. He was excellent at defense and knew the art of keeping his guard up.

After three rounds Tiny's face was badly decorated. Heide became presumptuous. After the tenth round he hammered a left against Tiny's ribs. A blood-red stain appeared.

Tiny snorted up blood and roared balefully.

"Now Tiny's mad," Stege yelled joyously. "If he catches Julius he'll kill him."

"It beats all the bullfights in Spain," came the Legionnaire's fascinated whisper, as Heide's iron fist landed with a hollow smack in Tiny's stomach, making him gasp for breath.

"At him, Tiny!" Porta cried. "He said he can beat you as easily as a little Harlem bitch!"

Tiny stopped and glowered at Porta.

"Did that pig say that?"

Porta nodded with a grin. "Oh yes, and more."

Heide seized his chance at once and drummed away at Tiny's diaphragm. At the same time he kicked him in the wrist.

Tiny bellowed with pain and boiling rage. He lowered his head like a ram and charged forward. With his speed he flung the Legionnaire out of the ring, tore the ropes to bits and hurled a stool after Heide, who'd leaped for cover behind us.

From deep within Tiny came strange animal sounds. He

was almost totally blind, since the flesh around his eyes had
swelled up terrifically. Heide kicked him in the stomach and
butted him in the face—the Danish kiss.

They rushed in circles after each other. Heide jerked his
left shoulder and hit Tiny a stinging blow across the neck.
It brought him to his knees.

Like a weasel Heide was upon him. They bit, snarled,
kicked, and spat. Then both of them were again on their
feet. After all the thrusts and hits Heide had managed to
place, Tiny's face was twice its normal size.

"My knife," Tiny yelled. "Get me my knife."

He searched for it blindly. Heide gave him a kick that sent
him smack on his face. For one second Heide forgot to look
out. That second decided Heide's fate in this as in countless
earlier fights. Tiny got hold of his ankle, got up roaring like
a sick gorilla, seized both of Heide's kicking legs and pounded his head against the floor till he hung in his fists like a
sour dishcloth. Then he threw the limp body into a corner,
cashed in his prize for the scuffle, slumped down and slept.

In a little while the rest of us also went to sleep, huddled
together like puppies in a cold stable.

Outside, the moon, suspended, shone down among naked
frozen trees. The ominous stillness of the mountains fell upon
fourteen candidates for the grave, in a cabin where formerly
merry tourists had rested after skiing.

Tiny was the first to see them. They were walking in single
file. They strode quickly down the mountain, where a fallen
rock lay like a natural gate.

Tiny's grunting brought us all out. We were cold. They
outnumbered us by far. They had flame-throwers, three heavy
machine guns and one of the new stovepipes.

The sun, which had just given the mountain a good morning kiss, flashed with inexplicable cheerfulness on their silver
death's heads.

Through the Old Man's field glasses we could see that an
SS *Obersturmführer* led the way. Stege was probably right
thinking it was a full company.

"That guy in front looks like a bloodhound with a cold,"
the Legionnaire said and spat out beyond the stone curb.

The Old Man lowered his field glasses. Without looking
round, he whispered hoarsely: "Get Gerhard out of the way!"

"Where?" asked Gerhard Stief, who was standing in the
door looking over Porta's shoulder.

Yes, where? We looked at each other in despair. Where?

Tiny and Heide turned their bruised faces toward the sun and blinked their eyes. It was an evil morning.

High up there on the narrow path someone stumbled. We could faintly hear him being bawled out by an SS *Oberschar-führer* who was swinging a sub-machine gun and rushing around the company like a sheep dog.

"That guy up there is a crap-pile," Heide grunted, feeling his swollen eye.

"Let's set up our light machine gun and plug the whole pack," Porta grinned, curling his narrow lips to a snarl like a dog ready to snap.

"A great idea, and afterward we'll cut their throats!" Tiny suggested, flinging his long Siberian knife into the air. It twinkled as it twirled about and then ended up in his fist again, as if a rubber band had been attached to it.

"Shut up, you fatheads," the Old Man exclaimed, annoyed. "If we start shooting we're through. It's twenty to one. We have to deceive them."

"You don't believe that yourself," Stege mumbled. "They'll knock us cold as soon as they notice the remnants of our big feast and find Gerhard. There will be fourteen 'pops' and then the damned ravens will again have something to feed on."

"Right, Hugo," the Legionnaire nodded. "And that guy, the *O-Scharführer*, will have the job of pickling us!"

He pointed up at the tall fellow, who was again bawling out one of the SS riflemen.

The SS company disappeared slowly behind some spruces. In about a quarter of an hour they would emerge on the other side, and then they would soon be upon us.

They emerged like a bombshell. Stege started chewing and cocking his tommy gun.

The Old Man raised his eyebrow and signaled a warning to us. Tiny stood shifting his feet.

The weapons of the SS company clanked harshly, like the instruments of a sailors' dentist just before he extracts the tooth of a stoker in filthy donkeyman's trousers and torn tropical undershirt.

Krause, the SS man who was with us because of cowardice, gave a hollow cough. "Let's get out of here!"

"Afraid of your brothers?" Porta inquired sweetly.

The SS man winced nervously and didn't answer. The Legionnaire whistled. *"Mon Dieu,* now we're going to see something."

The SS *Obersturmführer* at the head stepped along briskly.

His sleeves were rolled up, making the thick black hair on his arms visible.

We had a foreboding of death. Our nostrils dilated as on game flushed by far-away beaters.

Gerhard walked into the house. Tiny and Bauer went along.

They were sweating when they reached us, with the SS *Obersturmführer* in front. They were all very young. Fine fellows in good condition.

"Company, halt! Order arms! Left turn! Stand at ease!"

The command was cold and sick, like the rest of the morning.

The Old Man blinked at the SS officer with the death's head cap and the long black hair on his arms. Their eyes met. The Old Man walked slowly across the fabulously green grass. The grass the old Jew loved so much.

The little Legionnaire slouched behind. As if accidentally, he swung his sub-machine gun into firing position and slipped for cover behind the stack of firewood.

Porta sneaked into the house. In the little barred window behind the rafters one suspected the presence of a blackish blue muzzle. The Old Man was covered by the two best killers on the front.

The SS officer hitched up his wide belt, weighed down by his Mauser.

Plates and bottles clattered in the house. The SS men craned their necks. The bottles made such a pleasant, familiar sound.

The report which the Old Man delivered was short and non-cooperative. He gave patrol and unit. Thirteen men, not counting the zebra man. He underscored the false communication by declaring in an exceptionally loud voice: "Nothing particular to report!"

Glasses and plates clattered again as if protesting against the Old Man's report. They seemed to be calling: "Come inside, SS *Obersturmführer,* and you'll have a surprise!"

The slim SS officer gazed with raised eyebrows at the open door. He walked towards the house with slow steps, uncannily slow. His new high boots and leather things creaked loudly. He stopped for a while at the chopping-block, picked up the axe and cut a heavy stick in two with one stroke. That axe had been ground by an expert. He kicked at the split stick and laughed gently. His face became hard. He turned to the Old Man.

"Sergeant, assemble your men and get out of here quick!"

As he raised his arm to the perfunctory salute of the SS, a heavy gold watch gleamed on his wrist.

The Old Man made us fall in.

Porta emerged. The Legionnaire got up, surprising the SS officer a bit. He pushed back his crumpled cap and whistled between clenched teeth.

The sergeant in the Old Man came out. He called very loudly: "On the double, you bastards!"

Sullenly and reluctantly we fell in. We jostled each other and squabbled. Tiny, Heide and Bauer came strolling out of the house. Tiny with his long Siberian knife in his hand.

"Shoulder arms! Rout step, forward march!" the Old Man commanded with a voice so loud it cracked.

We walked right past the SS men, who grinned and spat out their contempt at us. "Shits," one of them crowed exultantly.

Tiny was about to yell something but the Legionnaire and the Old Man were at his side, keeping him quiet.

There were amazingly many horseflies out that morning. They bit us viciously, always at the very edge of the collar.

We walked between the spruces without looking back. We came to a halt only when we'd gotten as far down as the old bridge across the dried-up river. Without a word we flopped down in the brush and glanced up toward the mountain cabin, which was steeped in the sharp morning sun.

The SS *Obersturmführer* stepped into the house, followed by two SS men. One of them was the tall *Oberscharführer,* who was carrying his sub-machine gun like a riding whip.

They were inside for a long time, but we didn't hear anything. Some of the SS men had thrown themselves on the green grass, where they were playing craps and cards. They seemed to be waiting for a late train.

"Our friend, Lieutenant Stief from the 76th, has hidden himself well," Porta nodded.

"Let's hope well enough," the Old Man said nervously. He was chewing on his lidded pipe.

"We'll soon see," the little Legionnaire said. "Allah knows. Allah knows everything."

Tiny passed around his canteen. He had had enough foresight to fill it up with schnapps. We drank in big gulps. Porta and the Legionnaire had also filled their bottles. We finished them all off. We became braver. We wanted to see blood. Tiny spat on a leaf.

"Dogs, stinking shits!" he cursed. "Let's plug 'em." He tapped the magazine of his tommy gun. Stege started chewing.

"Let's do it, Old Man," he said hoarsely.

The Old Man was sucking at his pipe.

A long wailing scream cut through the dewy morning. Instinctively we wormed our way to safer cover. Tiny was licking the empty canteen.

"The old Jew didn't hide well enough," Stege sighed.

There was another scream. Each of us knew that scream from prisons and camps.

"I wonder what they're doing," Brandt whispered.

"Killing him slowly," came brutally from the Legionnaire, who pulled the flame-thrower into position and started adjusting the sprayer. "In the Rif Mountains we always took revenge when the blacks cut up our joes." His eyes probed the Old Man, who was lying behind a bush staring at the cabin.

The Legionnaire wanted to say something more, but he just reached the first syllable.

They came out with Gerhard Stief. He crawled on all fours in his zebra togs. He was moaning all the time. They kicked him. On such a cold morning all sounds are amplified. They borrow volume from the fresh vigor of the morning and are heard pure and without intruding sounds. We heard the thuds quite clearly when they kicked him, and we could hear them breaking his arm, once, twice. And then a third time. And every time we heard only a sound like branches cracking on a winter night and a tortured soul's subdued but piercing moan.

Every detail etched itself into our hearts. With every new torture grip, we moved a little closer to insanity.

They did something to his face. Then he collapsed.

The tall *Oberscharführer* bent down over the silent Gerhard Stief. In his hand flashed a knife.

We knew what was coming. We had seen it before, and yet it always overwhelmed us—the shriek. This prolonged, indescribable shriek as the body shot upward in an arc. The nearly dead body hopped squealing along the path.

They put his head on the chopping-block. The SS *Obersturmführer* struck only twice. Blood poured out in a long spurt.

The still morning was now defiled only with their laughter and their jokes.

Then they dug a hole in the dunghill and threw the corpse and the chopped-off head into it.

They fell in. A command—and they vanished among the spruces, singing, "Jewish blood shall flow."

Stege sobbed loudly. Tiny growled, while the Old Man almost begged: "Be reasonable!"

But the Legionnaire hissed: *"Ça c'est la légion!* We'll be mad like the men in the Rif."

. His outburst of fury kindled like a forest fire. The following took only seconds to happen. The wolves would be confronted by even bigger wolves, led by a Moroccan dog-wolf.

To kill a man may have a cleansing effect.

We didn't believe it, but we tried it and became convinced.

He who was to die fell over. He scraped the earth with hands and feet. Blood mingled with earth and filth flowed down his face. He blubbered. His eyes were closed.

The Legionnaire kicked him in the mouth because he groaned out a "Heil."

Doubling up, he came to rest with his face in the dust, which slowly got caked from blood and sweat.

The sunlight crawled up the mountain slope to be a spectator at the long drawn-out murder of revenge.

Brandt tore off his ear before we strapped him to the birch tree.

The prisoners in Auschwitz would have been delighted if they'd learned how this man died.

His dead body rolled further down the slope. For a moment it settled on a ledge. We. hurled stones and branches after it to work it loose.

It rolled on. It seemed to be turning somersaults. Heaps of turf and pebbles were having a race with it. It chanced to stop in a position that would give the ravens a hard time getting at its eyes.

chapter vi

Revenge

WE HAD dug in and were waiting for Gerhard's murderers. It sounds like a paradox, but we looked forward to killing them. It was like Christmas Eve just before the door's thrown open for the big tree. Only, we were ferocious like wolves.

Stege was weeping. He was the only pure soul among us. Porta cursed savagely. Tiny described graphically and with sweeping gestures all he would do to the SS men when he

caught them. In the meantime he was cracking thin twigs
and tearing apart plants.

The little Legionnaire was muttering Mohammedan curses.

The place where we had dug in was a natural fortress, a
sure death trap for the SS men when they got there. All we
had to do was to pull the trigger and set up target practice.

"It'll be a riot," remarked Brandt, the cross-country truck
driver who was always sucking on his hollow tooth.

"I want to scalp that big SS super-shit," Julius Heide said
from his tree. He was to warn us as soon as the SS company
emerged from among the spruces.

"Nah, brother Julius, that's my job," Porta resolved, kissing his long battle knife.

"You're stark raving mad," the Old Man cried. "Can't you
grasp the consequences of what you intend doing?"

"You're a pale shit," Porta remarked. He spat down onto
the path far below. "Not one of those guys will get home to
mother and talk. Before nightfall the ravens will be lying
gasping on their backs, bellies bursting from overfeeding."

"We'll take our good time in killing them, won't we,
boys?" Tiny called cynically, putting on the visor of the
heavy MG.

"Ass," the Old Man exclaimed, annoyed. "Don't you see,
damn it, that what we're planning to do is murder?"

We gaped.

"Did you say murder?" Porta yelled, forgetting sound carried far here in the mountains. "What then do you call
what we've been doing for the last four years? Maybe you
can explain that to us, honorable Herr Sergeant?" He scoffed
and spat derisively.

"Imbecile!" the Old Man snorted. "Till now we've only
murdered enemies, not fellow countrymen."

"Enemies, did you say?" Porta roared. "Your enemies,
maybe. I've no enemies except SS bastards."

"Oh, no, you don't, do you, you stupid ass!" the Old Man
shouted indignantly, getting up from the hole he'd dug with
Stege and me. He swung his sub-machine gun toward Porta,
who was lying on the ledge above us looking down.

"You're very forgetful, my boy. If I could only put on
blinders in the same way. Let me help your memory a bit.
Don't you remember the NKVD men we butchered at Bro-
busk? Do you remember the time you, Tiny and the Legionnaire slashed the throats of the suicide crews in Kiev with
your own hands? Did you forget the Bosnians or the women
in the flame-thrower unit? Maybe you'll even tell me you've

forgot the partisan Boris and his band? But maybe they were
your friends? In that case you have a very odd way of showing your friendship! Not to mention the infantrymen at
Height 754 we all sent to hell with flame-throwers and explosives. And what about the civilians in the sewer at
Kharkov? The prison personnel in Poltava? All of them were
your friends, I suppose? Do you want me to continue?" The
Old Man's face was flaming red.

"God, how you can run on!" Porta sneered. "He should've
been undertaker in the storm troops of the Salvation Army."
Turning to Heide, he pointed his thumb at the Old Man.

"Shut your filthy Berliner mouth or I'll shoot you right
this moment," the Old Man yelled, exasperated.

He was holding the sub-machine gun pressed to his hip,
aiming it at Porta.

Silence. In the three years Porta, Stege and I had been
associated with the Old Man, this was the first time we'd
heard him threaten shooting.

Surprised, we looked at the Old Man, our Old Man, our
Willie Beier. He was breathing heavily, as if choking. Then
he began speaking in a stutter. The words came falteringly, as
if they had to clamber over an obstacle topped with barbed
wire.

"Those SS fellows are murderers, devilish brutes. They deserve every one of those things you say you'll do to them.
If anyone understands you, I do!"

He clutched his neck, sat down on the edge of the hole and
looked up toward the mountains where we could hear the
SS men sing:

> For as far as the brown heath runs on,
> It's all in my possession . . .

"But you don't fight murder with murder, don't forget that,"
came almost inaudibly from the Old Man.

Porta was about to say something, but the Old Man motioned him to be quiet.

"Do you recall the time the head-hunter lieutenant was
shot in Lvov?"

The Old Man looked at each one of us with his penetrat-
ing blue eyes and went on. "Don't you remember?"

He repeated the question four or five times before receiving an answer. But we remembered as plainly as yesterday. A lieutenant from the Military Police had been shot
in the head and killed. It occurred in Pahlevi Street in Lvov.
During the ensuing razzia sixty people were assembled and

shot outside the house where the lieutenant's fate had been
sealed. Among the sixty were nineteen children under
twelve. All the furniture in the adjacent property was
chopped to bits. A woman with a baby was knocked down
by the rifle butts of the SS.

"I wonder if the person who plugged the dirty head-hunter officer regretted it? Indirectly he was responsible for all
those people's deaths," the Old Man went on in an undertone.

He pulled off his helmet. It rolled down the crag on to
the path and continued further down the valley like a merry
ball. Heaps of little rocks rolled behind the helmet as if
playing tag with it. Indifferently we followed the ugly helmet
with our glances.

"Do you remember the two SS men you stabbed to death
in Stalino?" the Old Man persisted stubbornly. "In reprisal the
whole town of Brigadenhof was massacred. Or when they
found the *Blitzmädel*, that telephone operator on the highway and believed she'd been raped by civilian Ivans? Within
five minutes, thirty women were dragged from their homes
and children to drudge in the slave camps of the Reich."

Oh yes, we remembered. Later, the Air Force girl admit-
ted she'd not been raped. It had been mere play-acting.
They shrugged their shoulders, put her in the clink for ten
days for having made a laughingstock of the secret Military
Police; meanwhile children were starving to death in the
village and their mothers worked themselves to death in
Germany.

With closed eyes the Old Man went on giving one instance
after another while far away we heard the SS soldiers bawling:

> Red hussars are riding, riding rapidly away.
> Loveliest maiden, you cannot go their way.

Porta blinked with his pig's eyes. Stege sighed. Heide
spat. The Legionnaire hummed: "Come now, death, come!"
Only Tiny seemed to be untouched by it all.

"If you massacre those SS up there," the Old Man warned,
"you should keep one thing straight: retaliatory action will
be taken on the people in this area. And in the prisons," he
continued after a pause. "And you'll be guilty of every single
one of those murders. Every shot that's fired is yours. After
all's done, you'll be murderers if anyone is. Mass murderers!"

The Old Man again looked at each one of us in turn. He
held our eyes firmly with his own. Then he said sharply,

like a burst of machine-gun fire, "Fire away, if you dare.
But don't forget that every time an SS man dies from your
dumdum bullets, you kill twenty civilians at the same time,
with probably a good many women and children among
them. Schoolchildren. Little starving toddlers who're right
now innocently occupied with their play. Fire away, boys,
to hell with it, fire away! Release your safety catches! Blaze
away and avenge Gerhard, the Jew, who refused to lie on a
bed because he would foul it with vermin. If he could see
what you plan to do he'd spit straight at your dirty faces.
If you want to avenge him, pick up your junk and let's get
out of here. Let's tell everybody what we've seen. Cry it out!
Never forget it! Sing it out again and again! You have to
survive this war in order to blare it out everywhere. Draw it,
write it, say it again in twenty years when the world will
be spinning comfortably! No one should forget what happened to other races, to those who thought differently, and
to women and children. That will be your revenge for the
thousands of Gerhards they've tortured."

The little Legionnaire got up, seemingly dead tired.

"As always, you're right, Old Man. You're right."

Suddenly, in a fit of frenzy, he flung aside the heavy
tank of the flame-thrower, kicked it, thumped it fiercely
with both fists and cried in despair: "To hell with it all!
Our freedom's gone and our courage is useless. Any use of
arms, even by us stupid, rotten swine, is dead sure to play
into the hands of the big bastards!"

He flopped down, kicked off his boots, pulled out his
prayer rug, bowed toward the east and mumbled a long
prayer to his Oriental prophet.

Silently, we watched the man-wolf from the mountains of
Morocco, who could only snap at the knife that was to
butcher him.

One by one we got up. The Old Man started walking down
the mountain. Hesitantly we followed. From the corner of our
eyes we sent back venomous glances at the positions we'd
dug. Porta spat, gathered up his top hat, slammed it angrily
on his head, slung his heavy weapon over his shoulder
and strode after the short and broad-shouldered Old Man,
who was heading for the valley without once looking back.

The SS men sang:

> Grethe und der Hans
> gehen am Sonntag gern zum Tanz,
> weil das Tanzen Freude macht,
> und das Herz im Leibe lacht.

We clenched our fists impotently. Heide hissed between his teeth: "We could've laid them out—every one of 'em!"

"And it only would've taken five minutes," Brandt grumbled.

Porta shifted the heavy MG over to his other shoulder: "I looked forward to plugging 'em so much."

"Damn it, soon my knife will get rusty," growled Tiny.

The Old Man trotted faster. We followed him sluggishly.

Not till we'd reached the bottom of the valley did we notice the black sickly smoke rising up over the forest. Surprised, we stopped to gaze at the tell-tale smoke.

"What kind of a fire can that be?" the Old Man asked thoughtfully.

"It must be a forest fire," Porta suggested. "But it's further off," he went on after a moment. He shoved back his top hat. "I shouldn't be surprised if it was Katovi. But why the hell should it be burning?"

Stege took out his map and got the bearing of the place. "It's Tekolovice that's burning," he announced briefly.

Sweating, we struggled across rocks and mountain pastures. Like the savages the war had made of us, we naturally took a short cut.

The Legionnaire cried out, pointing southeast. Fresh smoke puffed heavy and suffocating against the blue sky.

Stege nodded meaningfully and consulted his map. "This time it's Branovice. Do you know what this means?"

"Reprisal action," the Old Man answered. "But for what?"

Brandt slung the stovepipe across his shoulder. "Let's get going so we can take a look at it. Maybe we can put a stoke in their wheel."

Porta burst into a sneering laugh. "Yeah, call up the Travel Bureau and order a third class ticket for Berlin! Or a sleeper with nookie if that suits you better. And all you have to do in Berlin is to go up and arrest SS Heinrich."

"Now, don't be snooty, you fanny with ears," Brandt cried, throwing down the stovepipe to go for Porta. But Tiny, who'd been standing behind Porta, raised his free hand and let it fall like a hammer on Brandt's head, causing him to collapse without a sound.

Porta spat at the unconscious Brandt, kicked him in the back and glanced across at Tiny.

"Pretty good. See to it that discipline is maintained, my boy. You'll get a piece of candy when I go to the store."

The rest of us hardly even noticed this everyday intermezzo. We'd discovered a new fire, this time to the south.

"I wonder what's happened. They're taking such strong measures!" Heide said.

"Just what I said before," the Old Man said. "Some bunch of desperadoes has plugged some of Heini Himmler's bandits, and now half the region has to pay for the affair."

A dog came tearing down the mountainside. Porta caught it. It was part wolf, the sort of dog kept on most farms in these mountains. The broken ring of the leash showed it had been chained. His fur was completely burnt off in several places. The dog was wild with fear and pain. That dog must've gone through something monstrous.

While Porta tried to quiet the dog by murmuring to it in a low intimate voice, the Old Man looked at it, sucking thoughtfully on his pipe. Removing his pipe, he pointed it at the dog, which was now lying whining and whimpering.

"That dog is from one of the mountain farms. Not from any of the three burning villages." The Old Man said it so confidently that no one thought of asking how he knew.

The Legionnaire scratched the dog behind the ear. "In other words, it means that they're liquidating the farms, too. What the . . . Then something big must've happened."

He opened the lock of his light MG, looked through the barrel and started an almost uncannily meticulous examination of his weapon.

The rest of us, who'd settled down on the grass, followed the maneuvers of the little desert soldier with increasing interest. What was taking place in the brain of that little scarred killer?

The Old Man rose and wanted to continue the march, but the Legionnaire asked him to wait a little. He carefully laid aside the light MG, bowed his head facing east, sat down cross-legged in the middle of the group and asked Porta for a cigarette. He hawked and spat because of the bad tobacco. At the time Porta only had makhorka.

"The Old Man has given us a long sermon, boys," he said finally. "We listened to it, we were sensible, because there were good reasons why we should be. But now it's blazing all around us. The reason no doubt is that some friends on the other side haven't been as sensible as we were. So I don't see any reason why we should go on being sensible."

"Shut your trap," the Old Man shouted furiously. "Pick up all your weapons. We have to get going!"

"Half a sec! Let's hear what the Desert Rambler has to say," Porta proposed. He kicked at a large fir cone.

The Legionnaire grinned maliciously. His eyes shone with hatred. "By Allah, let's spread out those SS sons of bitches!"

"No," the Old Man cried. "We won't behave like common murderers."

"Mad dogs are shot," the little Legionnaire yelled, "and SS Heinrich's curs are nothing more. Who's coming? Raise your hands."

Porta, Tiny, Heide and Brandt immediately put up their hands. Reluctantly, the rest of us followed. Stege was the last. He looked apologetically at the Old Man as he did it.

Only the Old Man didn't raise his hand.

"By Allah, what a feast it'll be," the Legionnaire hissed, getting up. He put his hand on the Old Man's shoulder. "We understand you, Old Man, but you have to understand us, too. The SS can't take any further reprisals. They're burning the towns already. Will you lead us as you always did at the front?"

The Old Man shook his head: "I'll go with you because I have to, but I refuse to be in charge of murder!"

The Legionnaire shrugged his shoulders. "Good, boys, follow me!"

We worked our way up through the wood lots and climbed countless obstructions. Many of them would have made *chasseurs alpins* fall back, but we had revenge to spur us on.

Hour after hour we pushed on. Cut a path through hawthorn thickets with our sharp-edged intrenching spades and pickaxes. By tying together ropes and leather things we pulled ourselves across perilous rocky ledges. We cursed, fumed, fought each other and quarreled. Sweat poured down our faces. Our hands were bloody shreds, but the Legionnaire kept driving us forward more fanatically than ever. We threatened him with our guns, but he grinned derisively and uttered his Moroccan battle cry against the blue mountain peaks.

Then we stood at the first farm. A smoking ruin with three charred bodies. Two women and one child. We said nothing. We just looked. The Old Man slit his eyes. His face was chalky white.

We weren't God's best children. We were combat swine and had knocked about a good deal. Our fists clenched tighter around our lethal weapons. Once again we rushed ahead, following the cursing and swearing Legionnaire.

An hour later we found two more bodies. Two men killed by neck-shots. The Legionnaire turned them over.

"A .38," decided Porta, probing with his finger round the point of impact. No papers were found on the bodies. Everything had been removed.

"Don't you think the partisans may have done it?" asked
the SS man who was with us on account of cowardice.

"Certainly," Bauer guffawed. All of us grinned at this
fantastic naiveté.

The Old Man glanced ironically at the SS man while he
took some powerful puffs from his lidded pipe. He removed his pipe and pointed at the SS man. "I can tell you
almost verbatim what the newspapers will say tomorrow or
after tomorrow: Peaceful peasants, women and children have
been murdered by bandits. In a bestial manner these terror-
ists have burnt down three villages and several farms. Reprisal measures will follow at the earliest possible date. And
this whole pack of lies will be signed: SS *Reichsführer* Heinrich Himmler. Subsequently, SS *Standartenführer* Blobel will
receive orders from his superior, *SS und Polizeiführer*
Brach, to carry out a few executions of hostages. As a matter
of precaution, the readers will also be apprised that the bandits were dressed in German uniforms. Oh yes, oh yes, they're
sophisticated at Central Security."

Porta probed the edges of the wound of one of the murdered. Tiny looked at him with interest. Porta sniffed his
slightly blood-stained finger.

"What does it smell of?" Tiny asked, bending over the
corpse.

"Sort of strangely sweetish, sort of rotten," Porta answered
and sniffed once more. "Something like gangrene in its first
stage."

"You mean like those yellow corpses at Dobrovina?" the
Legionnaire cut in. Porta nodded and again sniffed his finger.

"The other one has shit in his pants," Tiny said, nudging
the second body with the butt of his sub-machine gun.

"When we gassed them at Birkenau, in Auschwitz, they
always did," came from the SS man.

The effect was like a dynamite explosion. We'd completely
forgotten about the two bodies. Something new, something
devilishly interesting, had crashed down among us. As if ready
to spring on him, we glared at the big broad SS man, a man
who'd been expelled from the ranks of his like-minded fellows
and degraded to dishonorable service in one of the Army's
hundreds of penal regiments.

"What else happened when you gassed them at Auschwitz?"
Porta asked foxily.

The SS man turned pale, almost blue. What he'd kept a
secret for three long years had escaped him by a fluke. He'd
lived through anxious nights afraid that someone or other
would give him away. Someone from the office, like *Unter-*

offizier Julius Heide, who by this time had been with the platoon for a year. What a shock he'd had when Heide was kicked out of the company office and ended up here in 2nd Platoon. A couple of times he'd come close to asking Heide not to talk. He would pay him anything for secrecy. But maybe Heide hadn't read his papers. Heide couldn't possibly have kept shut for so long if he knew about it. He had tried to get away from the company, but Captain von Barring had shrugged his shoulders, with the remark: "Out of the question!" Barring was a stupid pig. Just as everyone in this lousy platoon was a stupid pig. They were traitors and should be liquidated.

Then the unbelievable happened. No one had given him away. He gave himself away. He made a silent prayer to the God he'd forsworn in 1936 when he entered the SS *Totenkopfsverband*. Eicke's cruel *Kz*-guard troops. How proud he'd been at being able to stroll down the street at home dressed in his green SS uniform with the embroidered silver death's head on the left lapel instead of the SS runes. How lovingly he'd sewn the black silk ribbon with the silver letters TO-TENKOPFSVERBAND around the left sleeve. He had laughed heartily at his mother's scare the first time he showed up at home in the feared SS skull-and-bones uniform. When his father blabbed about God's punishment because he, In-gerd, had reported to SS *Gruppenführer* Eicke's concentration camp guard, he had threatened him with confinement and flogging. How wonderful he'd felt when the street urchins at home sent fearful glances after him. All those who'd been insolent before now wanted to be his friends. When the tavern-keeper had refused him credit, he'd gotten up and flung the marks on the table. When he called out to the host: "You'll soon come and dance for me!" there was silence in the overcrowded room.

The next day he had slipped a note into the camp mail-box, the box which was emptied by Eicke personally. He had written the tavern-keeper's name and address and, in red, TRAITOR.

He observed the Stapo picking him up from the front door at his neighbor's. Three weeks later the tavern-keeper arrived in camp. The same day he was hanging over the buck as he received his first ten strokes.

True, Commandant Eicke had raised quite a stink over his failure to hand in a report, as he should have, before having a prisoner thrashed.

But that tavern-keeper was a turd. He ran into the wire

one day in January 1938. He was buried together with fifty
Jews who'd been hanged behind the stables.

The day he came to Gross Rosen as *Unterscharführer*
had been one of the greatest in his whole life, and he often
recalled it with nostalgia. He became leader of the dog team.
He just loved those dogs. But SS *Hauptsturmführer* Streicher,
who kept the records, was an ass, putting on a big show
just because one of those traitors had been lightly bitten
by the dogs. It's true that one of them conked out, but,
damn it, the fellow would've done so anyway. He'd been a
minister in the Weimar period, it was told. An old worm who
fell over each time he was hit over the head with a stick.

The *Hauptsturmführer* requested an investigation of the dog
affair. If there hadn't been a hullabaloo beforehand over
"Hoopla hop," nothing would ever have come of it. "Hoopla
hop" was maybe a bit rough. He was prepared to admit
that, even if it was used only against rotten traitors. The
Oberscharführer from Block 7, Steinmüller, had started it.
More and more things were invented that could be used for
"Hoopla hop." A couple of prisoners were placed in the large
square behind the old sheep-cotes. Cans were placed on top of
their heads and the prisoners were threatened with flogging
if they fell off. Then the SS guards would shoot the empty
cans from their heads.

Naturally, some prisoners got a bullet in the brain, or
were wounded. But it made great target practice, and it was
fun.

The prisoners picked out for "Hoopla hop" were also
forced to run races across the latrine pits, only to have the
board pulled from under them when they were at the mid-
point of the pit. It looked so funny when the striped ones
were thrashing about down there in the dung. It also happened that a couple of them choked. But then they were
only traitors and deserved no better.

How they had amused themselves in the battalion! Without mentioning the boxing matches that were arranged between the human skeletons, there were many, many other
things in "Hoopla hop." But unfortunately Steinmüller went
off the rails. He tied three prisoners naked to the radiators
in the detention bunker. He wanted to see if they were real
men.

That stupid swine Streicher found out about it. If they
only had found the person who squealed. God, what a riot
there was! But they fixed Streicher, that brute. He was
arraigned before an SS court-martial, charged with having
defended traitors and enemies to the Reich. He was thrown

out of the SS and transferred to the Air Force. There were rumors he'd been shot in Poland.

From Gross Rosen he came to Ravensbrück. Nothing but broads. Those were the days! A *Stabsscharführer* in camp with the Order of Blood from '23 was completely crazy about sex shows. What he didn't think of doing with those girls! You were completely out of it after a show like that.

The commandant in Ravensbrück ordered no investigations. He knew how that kind of riffraff should be treated.

What fun to flog those women! At times you had pains all over from thrashing away at them. But though the commandant was nice enough, he still had a narrow escape. One of those spitfires tried to inform on him because he'd played a slight prank on her and made her pregnant. But before things could come to light he took measures to put her out of the way. Thanks to his good relations with the orderly in the medical center, the cause of her death could be hushed up.

How incredibly difficult it was to strangle a creature like that! Even when you used thin twine, which was supposed to be specially effective—so Ernst had said. Ernst had tried it a couple of times. Nah, give him the benzine syringe any time. It was much better. He'd had occasion to prove this repeatedly after he came to Birkenau. Though Höss was commandant there, it was Lorentz who made the decisions. He was a tough one. Three times dismissed as commandant because of cruelty.

For three months he had been in the liquidation section. In the beginning, it's true, he got to feel slightly woozy when a thousand or so Jews were herded in to get a dose of Zyklon B. But you can get used to anything. He completely lost count of all the Jew women he had to plug with a low-caliber gun behind the wall. They were the ones who refused to take their children along to the gas chambers.

The darkest day in his life, at any rate till a couple of minutes ago, was the day he was thrown out of the *Kz*-guard service. It was SS *Untersturmführer* Rochner who did it.

It was called fraternization. He had taken part in the rape of a woman from Bucharest. It was their damn bad luck that he and his four chums were caught with their pants down.

First he was sent to the SS field training unit in Cracow, but here he managed to get to the infirmary with an inflamed foot. That inflammation had cost him a thousand marks. He thought then that the war was over for him, but he had bad luck. From the infirmary he went straight to Klagenfurt, where he was to join the SS regiment *Der Führer,* a collection of imbeciles whose highest wish was to die like heroes.

Months of sweat, despair, and fear—right up to his escape in Kharkov on his first day in the firing line.

Then came the SS court-martial. Demotion. The clink and Torgau. Afterward he shivered at the mere thought of the months spent in Torgau, in the filthy Armed Forces prison. What a terrible thing to be expelled from the glorious SS, the Guards!

And since then the days spent with the worst kinds of criminals in this disgusting Wehrmacht penal regiment.

Now, inferiors like that wanted to interrogate him, the Führer's soldier, a veteran *Kz*-guard. He puffed himself up, but when he looked at Porta, Tiny, and the Legionnaire his courage escaped like the air from a punctured balloon.

You never knew what such psychopaths could take into their heads. They got such a horrible feeling of inferiority when they came face to face with someone from the upper class. They were animals. They could hit upon anything.

He remembered Captain Meier, *Obersturmführer* Gratwohl. And what didn't that gang do to *Sonderführer* Hansen!

Icy beads of perspiration stood out on his forehead. Should he cry for help? Maybe some of his friends from the SS were nearby and would hear him. Ah, if they only were a few steps nearer. Then those swine over there would dance, penal-battalion swine! He would tell the SS soldiers everything they intended to do and everything they'd said. Some neck-shots would be fired. He cheered up at the mere thought.

But what the hell was this? Porta was getting up and starting to walk toward him: he came on very slowly. He seemed to be playing the game of jumping from flagstone to flagstone without hitting the line.

"Don't touch me, you," he wanted to shout. But not a sound came from his lips. He wasn't capable any more of breaking a silence which meant death. DEATH! He felt his tongue becoming thick, dry and swollen. He felt very warm.

The Legionnaire, Moroccan monster, that little, disgusting, scarred, inhuman thing, was coming toward him with a grin on his face.

Still this paralyzing silence. God, how vile silence can be! And then Tiny, the gorilla, and Julius Heide, the rowdy. They walked slightly stooped, as if they were about to butt someone. That common thief Brandt pulled out his battle knife.

But they couldn't possibly kill him. Oh, yes, easily. Very

easily. No, no, they couldn't. The Old Man said it was murder.

And yet! They slowly killed *Sonderführer* Hansen. It was murder. And they hanged Gratwohl. That was murder. And they shot Captain Meier. That was murder.

Devilish brutes! Traitors! He would fight. Fire with his storm rifle.

A clattering sound. He looked down and didn't understand at once. Christ! Porta had struck the rifle out of his hand. Now he would be defenseless against their knives and automatic storm weapons.

They were grinning noiselessly. With bared teeth and snarling sounds. Would he really die now? He didn't want to die. Ah, how wonderful to live! He'd only done his duty to his country. Nothing more. But did those criminals understand anything of that?

The Old Man looked at him in silence. The Old Man's eyes were dark. It was no longer the Old Man. He was his enemy. The Old Man didn't say: *It's murder!*

The circle became narrower. They stood close around him. He stood in the middle like a bull's eye in a target.

They struck. They jabbed. A searing pain tore through his body from head to foot. He screamed as Gerhard had screamed.

"Jesus Christ, help me! Help me! Holy Virgin, help me!" He fell down. "Oh, Holy Virgin," he cried, but only a gasp came out. "I'll be a priest for the rest of my life! Good God, I'll serve you and never deny you any more. Oh, help me against these devils!"

The mountains tipped over. The sky split open.

They tied him up with biting straps. They let him lie and suffer while they smoked in silent indifference.

Then the birch tree slowly slid to the earth like a catapult. He knew what was coming. He let out a savage rattling shriek. Could he be going insane?

God didn't hear him. Only the devil heard him and rejoiced.

He died with every limb, every bone, torn out of joint.

He screamed for ten full minutes before he died. Porta thought it wasn't long enough.

The Old Man said, "Swine!"

The little Legionnaire spat at him before we rolled him down a narrow deep ravine.

He was forgotten.

The patrol trudged on. By a sooty ruin, still smoking, we ran into a body of SS men. We didn't shoot. The long battle cry of the little Legionnaire, "Allah el Akbar," was no longer heard amid the mountains.

Our blood lust had been satisfied on an unknown SS man.

Gisela was sleeping. I kissed her. She woke up and stretched. She threw her sleep-drugged arms about me and kissed me passionately. She had slept long.

"That Jew you met, did he die?"

I kissed her again. Couldn't bother answering.

Number 12 rattled down the street. The panzer soldier and the girl in the lilac slip again came together in the old fourposter, while Gerhard Stief kept rotting in his grave.

The brothel had been tidied up. There was no more dust on the rafters. Fresh girls had arrived. The big fish suspended over Madame's table had disappeared. In its stead a bull's head had been hung on the wall. Someone had hung a sheer stocking and a pair of light blue panties on one of the horns. They were left hanging there like a sort of trade mark.

The Legionnaire, of course, couldn't take part in the game. When the rest of us went off with the girls, he settled down at a table with five bottles of wine and a bowl of Pein-Pein from the Chinese saloon in the cellar.

Two girls who'd been to Africa stayed behind to entertain him. You could almost smell the camels. You could veritably feel the Kabilah.

A stark naked woman was dancing on a row of tables. She twisted and turned during the dance, pushed her abdomen forward and revolved like a wheel. Colored spotlights played over her body, and the red beam always stopped at the most intimate spots.

Tiny could hardly be held back.

Finally the Legionnaire had to knock him out with a bottle.

chapter vii

Tiny Gets Engaged

I GOT back to the hospital after my nightly excursion just before inspection.

My comrades had covered for me, but as usual "the Battleship" was where she shouldn't have been. She saw me come in. I got a murderous look, while her mannish voice trumpeted through the cloistral corridors. "Get to your ward in a jiffy, you little pig!"

"Certainly, matron," I mumbled softly.

The expressions which rumbled behind me like dying thunder when I reached the ward were anything but maternal.

"Was it nice?" Tiny asked curiously. Without waiting for an answer he grinned. "I just came from a tumble myself. Three at once. Did you ever try that, boys? It's like flying straight into heaven—the heaven that Czech swine Mouritz talks about—to be greeted by harp music and songs of young girl angels in lilac ass-cases and ribbon-like tit cups with red bows in the valley."

He smacked his tongue and licked his well-fleshed lips. He was about to embroider on the night's experiences in more detail when interrupted by inspection.

Dr. Mahler stopped at Mouritz's bed, glancing at the case sheet which the Battleship handed him. As usual he was humming. Humming with his lips. He read a little and hummed again in a deep tone of voice, looking intensely at Mouritz, the volunteer from Sudetenland.

"How is our adventurer today?"

"Not so good, *Herr Oberstabsarzt,*" Mouritz shouted, just as the sergeant had taught him to do when he was in training.

On Dr. Mahler's humming lips appeared a subtle smile.

"Really? My dear friend, you are far from being as sick as you think you are."

He turned around and looked at Tiny, who lay at attention in his bed, his arms extended along his side. He looked marvelously stupid.

"The patient feels better!"

Tiny uttered a frightened gasp, but Dr. Mahler didn't hear it. He smiled and again hummed with his lips.

"The patient's general condition is excellent under the circumstances. The patient requests a discharge to the convalescence field battalion of his division."

Tiny got up on one elbow and stared at Dr. Mahler in utter astonishment. The doctor looked at the big hooligan and smiled.

"Since it is possible to grant the patient's wish, he will be discharged on . . ." Dr. Mahler counted on his fingers . . .

"Tuesday the 7th," the Battleship helped him out.

Dr. Mahler smiled his delicate pale smile and gave her a friendly nod. "Fine, matron, Tuesday the 7th!"

Tiny gaped. Terror was written in his eyes. He understood just as little as the rest of us what Dr. Mahler was up to.

The Battleship took down the dictation with a fountain

pen which scratched in protest. Her round cheeks glistened.
Tiny gave her a heart-rending, imploring look.

Dr. Mahler turned quickly to Mouritz's bed. He took the
hand of the Sudeten lad and said to our relief: "Live well! I
hope you've had a good rest with us."

Relieved, Tiny fell back on his pillow.

"The patient looks pale," Dr. Mahler said, looking at Tiny.

The Battleship snorted and handed the head surgeon Tiny's
bulky case sheet, which said more of disciplinary penalties
than sickness. He tapped Tiny's big scar and listened to his
heart. Then he put the stethoscope to Tiny's pulmonary
region.

"The patient has pronounced difficulty in breathing. Bron-
chial tubes inflamed," he dictated.

The Battleship recorded this reluctantly with her scratching fountain pen.

Tiny's face assumed an expression of boundless suffering.

"Markedly bad breath and tongue heavily coated."

Tiny's tongue hung far out of his mouth. A huge piece of
grubby meat, almost ruined by tobacco and alcohol.

"How are things otherwise, my friend?" Dr. Mahler asked
sarcastically, looking into Tiny's deeply suffering face.

"*Herr Oberstabsarzt,* when I'm lying like this I'm really
quite all right," Tiny breathed in a dying voice. "But as soon
as I'm up and about I'm no good any more." He waved his
hand in an expressive gesture. "Then I feel cockeyed, *Herr
Oberstabsarzt,* sort of woozy in my head. My paws turn to
jelly, like when you're getting back to the flea-bag at four
o'clock in the morning after hitting all the joints in town.
Rotten, *Herr Oberstabsarzt,* really rotten. Only the horizontal
agrees with me."

"H'm." Dr. Mahler nodded, while pensively humming the
Radetzky March.

For a moment it looked as if Tiny intended to join the humming, but before he managed to start, Dr. Mahler nodded.
"I understand. No appetite, only thirst?"

"No, none," Tiny groaned feebly, not having the slightest
idea of what appetite meant.

Dr. Mahler nodded with a smile and went on to dictate:
"Patient on fever diet for a week. Strict confinement to bed.
Hot pads. Warm compresses. Contrast baths. Enemas. Also,
we'd better have a test meal, with the rubber tube."

The Battleship smiled maliciously, baring her yellow teeth.
Dr. Mahler nodded to Tiny and sailed on to other patients.

Tiny didn't realize the full horror of what had happened

till inspection was all over. He cursed and swore, but knew there was no reprieve for his fate.

The Battleship was personally in charge of the enema, and she didn't handle him with kid gloves.

They shouted, growled and threatened. The two of them were only conscious of each other and of the injector. Tiny had to hold the tube. The water sloshed over. The matron fumed but refused to give in. Tiny roared he would take a crap at her and meant it literally.

"I'll let the MPs come and get you and have you court-martialed," the Battleship cried, swinging the injector. Her face was red and puffy.

"There isn't a single court-martial in the whole world that'll care whether I crap on you or not," Tiny bawled.

The Battleship howled, Tiny hissed. But he received his enema, every drop of it, though it took some time.

"Don't lose it now," the matron thundered before she strode out of the ward with the dry injector.

Knowing full well that the matron would be back to give him his injection again, he kept it for the hour, while emitting a ceaseless stream of blasphemy. Tiny was the only patient who received his injection from the matron personally. She used the oldest and thickest needle she could find for the injection and pushed it in extra slowly so she could hear him roar. To her it was a very sweet music.

She had no sooner bent over Tiny and shot the needle into his hairy behind than it happened. An oozing discharge and a couple of detonations. By comparison, an eruption of the Vesuvius was like the small summer fireworks in an allotment garden. But she held her ground, though her apron stank horribly already. Then the volcano erupted in full force. She gave a howl of terror and started back coughing, while Tiny laughed till the whole bed shook. He pulled out the injection needle and hurled it crashing against the wall.

"Disgusting pig," hissed the defeated Battleship. "You'll answer to a military court for this. I'll have you locked up till you rot."

"Shit-piece," Tiny decided and discharged a stream of tobacco juice through the open window.

Growling like an animal, the Battleship rushed at Tiny, grabbed him by both ears and pounded the back of his head against the edge of the bed.

"Merde," the Legionnaire said laconically and went on reading the Koran.

The Battleship wasn't the only one who had profited from the volcanic eruption. Lava was lying everywhere in the ward.

Even the clock on the wall ran irregularly for the next few days, a clear sign that the mechanism had been hit.

Tiny didn't receive any more enemas.

Eight days later he got prodigiously drunk and forced his way to the Battleship, who was sitting in her room reading her favorite novel, *The Wife with Two Husbands.*

There was a fantastic uproar, which nobody wanted to get mixed up with. The doctor on duty, who was new, was warned at the last moment by a nurse in the ward. He was smart enough to take her advice and avoid getting involved in the battle of the giants.

After an hour had passed there was complete quiet.

We figured that one of them had been killed. When the silence extended to two and a half hours, we started wondering if we should check what had happened. But suddenly we saw them coming down the stairs, walking arm in arm, Tiny with a black eye and an incredibly well-brushed uniform. His boots and his belt sparkled as never before.

The Battleship was dressed in a red coat fitting her like a bursting potato sack. On her head she had a blue hat with a pheasant feather in back. Without even bothering to glance at us they rumbled down the stairs and vanished on Zirkusweg in the direction of Reeperbahn.

They returned in the early hours of the morning. Tiny was impossibly drunk. The Battleship giggled like a teenager. She had a red balloon around her wrist.

Babbling away, Tiny tumbled into the wrong bed. When the owner made objections, he was hurled to the other end of the room. Tiny grinned in his sleep and smacked his lips like a glutted boar. The saloon smell penetrated far and wide.

Mouritz, the Sudeten German, was praying. Intermittently he would stop praying and curse that scum Tiny.

Tiny was in love. His behavior was peculiar. If we had dared we would have laughed at him, but we didn't dare.

It was great fun to look at him getting ready to go out. Up to now he had looked at any kind of soap as pure crap, used only by fools and sissies. A comb was a sign of far-advanced degeneration. He looked at perfume and hair tonic in the same way.

At the moment he was standing in the middle of the ward trying to part his hair in the back. But it didn't quite come off. Despite all his efforts, the cowlick still bristled up.

"Give me some perfume, or whatever the hell they use," he muttered and turned his head in front of the mirror with a helpless look in his eyes.

"Hair tonic," the Legionnaire helped him out and chucked a quart bottle to him.

Promptly, Tiny poured the whole bottle over his head. All for love. He spat on a clothes brush and tried to get the cowlick to come round by massaging with the brush, but to no avail. He looked about him despairingly, grabbed a pair of scissors and cut off the bristly wisp of hair.

He looked dangerous, even more so than usual.

After forcing one comrade to polish his boots, another to press and brush his uniform, he placed himself in front of the little Legionnaire. He resembled a slightly overgrown boy who'd been scrubbed and dressed up by his mother and then sent to a Sunday School Christmas party.

"Do I look good now, Desert Rambler?"

The Legionnaire pursed his lips and slowly swung his legs out of bed. He circled him with a scrutinizing glance, giving him a thorough overhauling.

"Hell, you look great," the Legionnaire decided and gave a nod of satisfaction. "Maybe the trousers are a bit full over your buttocks."

"You think so?" came from Tiny in an anxious voice, while he passed his hand over the great mass of excess material in his trouser-seat.

"But, damn it, that isn't noticeable," the Legionnaire reassured him. "Just take off and you'll go over big. You really look sharp. And I assure you, you have a rich fragrance."

He threw himself on his bed again, pulled a bottle from under the mattress and drank in long gulps.

"Well, I'm running up to Emma," Tiny grinned and once more adjusted his tunic.

He stopped by Mouritz's bed and pointed a commanding index finger at the horror-struck volunteer from the Sudeten.

"You lousy fink will say a nice prayer for me, or I'll break your neck, you little pig."

To underscore the seriousness of the command he gave Mouritz a smack in the face with his forage cap. Then he vanished.

A few minutes later he came rushing back to the ward like a mad bull, tore Mouritz out of bed and hurled him from one end of the room to the other. Three others took the same ride before he managed to blow off some steam.

He sat down by the Legionnaire's bed, scowling hatefully around the room.

"Lice, scab-mites," he grumbled. "A pig like that from a

ramshackle cow barn throws me, Tiny, out saying I stink like a bankrupt whorehouse!"

"You stood for that?" the Legionnaire asked, astonished.

"Only because I was surprised. I'll be damned if I'll stand for it a second time," Tiny said, urging himself on. "An overstuffed plant louse like that! Throwing me out because I smell like a gentleman—that's going a bit too far."

Tiny slumped down a bit, propped his head on his hands, and gazed up at the Legionnaire, his idol, who followed the dumbshow as he was lying on his stomach in bed.

"I'll grab her by the throat and throw her down from the third floor so she'll land in the cellar like a bomb. A real man has to show what he's good for to someone like that, don't you think? Simply as a matter of discipline. Don't you agree?" he added, with a note of uncertainty.

The Legionnaire nodded.

"Absolutely. You have to stand up for yourself, or she'll play pranks on you, like taking other tramps to bed and dirt like that."

"I wouldn't give a shit about that, Desert Rambler. That's nothing to take to heart. Everybody should have the right to amuse himself and to take the little pleasures along with the rest. And Emma isn't likely to wear out so easily. But to be snotty and use mean words—" he was getting excited— "hell, that's going too far. What a mean little turd! I knocked politely on her door and spoke to her like a well-bred and respectable man: 'My beloved Emma'—you know, just like that book you read to me about how to behave when you're cultivated, like you and me. And d'you know what that bag answers? 'Get out, you pig! Why, you stink like a corpse.' Well, I still keep cool and say, like you taught me: 'Will you permit me to sit down beside you, my beloved Emma?' The fat crab sets up a grin and asks if I've gone nuts. Then I blew a fuse in my top and forgot everything you read to me about polite behavior. Naturally I socked her one and she's still walking around sneezing from it. But she's a coarse-grained woman, a real piece of sandpaper, and you can't expect to bring her to heel simply by socking her in the teeth. 'What the hell, you're a walking cliché,' she says. What's a cliché, Desert Rambler? And then she kicked me right here, the most sensitive spot, you know, so I had to curl up. Then she grabbed my hair and, bang, mashed her knee in my face. Next I knew, I was sitting on the stairs. Thank God I didn't fall down. I could have hurt myself something terrible."

Tiny didn't stop to think how the matron would've gotten hurt if he'd thrown her down.

"Give her up," the Legionnaire recommended. "She gives you far too many worries. Women are unpredictable. Go down to the cathouse and find a whore for yourself. That's much better. She doesn't deserve you. Down there you pay and that's the end of the trouble. It's understood of course that you pay what you owe and with your own money."

"No, I'll go to holy hell first," Tiny swore. "I'm not going to give up that mare. Damn it, there's plenty of fire in her. But the fat pig will find out what I really am. I'm not going to give an inch. After all I'm a fighter."

"You're an ass," the Legionnaire said kindly. "And sooner or later you'll be sure to find it out for yourself."

"Who's an ass?" Tiny exploded and stood up menacingly.

"You," the Legionnaire smiled, "and I, Alfred Kalb, former corporal in the 2nd Foreign Regiment, feel free to tell you so."

Tiny chomped and alternately turned red and pale. Both his fists were clenched, ready to strike. His small mean fish-eyes blinked cautiously. Then all at once he went flat.

"That's what *I* am?"

With a jolt he fell down by the Legionnaire's bed and pounded the floor with both fists. He had to hit something.

"She's a dud, I swear she is," he affirmed reflectively. After a short pause he went on: "When she comes around to invite me for some sweating night work, I'll say: 'Emma, you bloated whore...'—is 'overblown whore' better?— '...you may give me a mighty kiss in the ass, I'll have nothing more to do with you, you mushroom fly."

"Are you really going to say that?" the little Legionnaire asked skeptically.

Cursing and swearing, Tiny nodded. He rumbled across the floor, kicked a wash basin, for precaution smacked Mouritz in the face, and threatened to hit Stein. Then he roared out of the window after a cyclist who unsuspectingly came down the Zirkusweg dragging a pair of tires he must have stripped off some bike.

"Are you trying to show off, you mutt?"

With satisfaction Tiny noted that his roar had knocked the guts out of the cyclist. He spat and started whistling a tune remotely reminiscent of something from "The Merry Widow." When he got it all mixed up, Mouritz was ordered to sing a hymn. The first three were turned down.

"The song is over! Another song! One, two, three, four!"
He kicked time against Mouritz's bed.

When Mouritz didn't quite succeed in satisfying the aesthetic appetite that had suddenly hit Tiny, he was chased under all the beds three or four times. He ended up in his own bed, where he bawled out his hymn in a cathedral voice. He resembled a Christian on his way to the lions.

Puffing, Tiny stuck his head under the faucet and wiped himself on the first sheet he could get his hands on. Both patient and bedclothes were dragged to the floor.

"Stein, Bauer, the two of you will come along to pound those tramps in the cathouse," he decided.

"So early?" Stein asked in surprise while Bauer started dressing without a word.

The Legionnaire chuckled. *"Bon,* let's get going. We need some exercise."

Tiny threw a boot at Mouritz's head.

"Louder, you reserve vicar. I can't hear your heavenly marching song."

In a squeaking treble the unhappy volunteer from the Sudeten mauled an evangelical hymn.

We tramped off. Walking downstairs Tiny kicked a bucket of water, making it splash over in every direction.

He raised hell wherever he went.

"You dirty fink," he yelled at the cleaning woman, who glistened all over with fat, complacent National Socialism. "You put that bucket right there so I should break my neck. I'll have you locked up for sabotage against the combat forces of the Reich!"

The woman gave him a mean look. She planted her red fists on her swelling hips and hissed, "You did it deliberate, you filthy hoodlum! What a scum! I'll get you before a court-martial and you'll swing."

"Huh, you Hitler hag," Tiny jeered and gave the bucket another kick, which sent it flying through a pane of glass in the folding door.

The woman roared and slapped her hands to her face in frantic rage.

Equipped with a steel helmet and a pistol in his belt as prescribed for NCOs on duty, the OD came rushing on the scene.

"He kicked my bucket," the woman spouted. "He insulted the Führer. He called me a Hitler hag!"

The OD was young and inexperienced. His clear blue eyes flashed ferociously, according to custom among young NCOs. He looked at the swaying bucket on the tiled floor.

He looked at the smashed pane in the folding door. He noticed the floor-cloth smiling gaily at him in the middle of the floor.

"Attention," he commanded, whipping himself up to a bustling frenzy.

Extremely slowly we put our heels together and assumed a position that could possibly be confused with standing at attention.

The cleaning woman brightened up. She wiped her hands on her dirty apron, with a pale eagle in the middle of the stomach, and clattered accusingly into the corridor.

Tiny stared stupidly and indifferently ahead of him. He tried to spell his way through a signboard about the duties of outpatients when they came for their first examination.

The OD puffed himself up before him, put out his chest and squeaked: "I'll take care of you, you pig's ear."

Tiny cocked his head and scrutinized the service-happy MC noncom with a much too large helmet as if he glimpsed signs of incipient madness in him.

"I mean you, you lazy bum."

"Me?" Tiny asked in simulated amazement, pointing at himself.

"Oh, God help us!" The OD tried to roar at the top of his voice, but it came only to a breaking crow.

"You see, sir," Tiny grinned familiarly. "According to regulations I should be addressed by my rank. Even when I'm in for some dirt." He held up his sleeve right under the nose of the MC noncom, who had to jump back a step in order not to be pushed over. "As the *Herr Unteroffizier* can see, I'm a corporal and I request you to address me as 'Herr Corporal.' "

Our faces flushed deep red with enthusiasm. No one would've thought Tiny to be capable of an answer worthy of Porta.

"Does a stinking hick like you want to instruct me?" the OD yelled. "Answer me when I speak to you!"

"You're a fanny with ears!" Tiny said in a kind, low voice.

The medical NCO jumped in the air like a mortar shell hitting rocky ground. He refused to believe his senses and glared at the grinning Tiny, who was eagerly awaiting what was to come.

"Would you repeat what you just said," the OD stammered, gaping with astonishment.

"Do you have dirty ears?" Tiny asked confidentially.

The NCO stuttered, unable to speak one clear word. With

an effort he pulled himself together, pointed at all of us and meowed: "You're all my witnesses to what this swine said."

The Legionnaire laughed softly, which caused the NCO to lose control of himself completely.

"What are you grinning at, you tramp. Don't worry, I'll take care of you, you castrated nigger!"

The smile went out on the knife-scarred face of the Legionnaire. His eyes turned cold like a cobra's. In his fury the NCO had made a terrible enemy.

Stein quickly called out, "We report to the *Herr Unteroffizier* that we can witness nothing. We've heard nothing, seen nothing."

The short NCO hopped up to Stein like a rooster thrown off while mating. Stein stood big and broad, as if carved out of granite.

"So, you're going to mutiny. To arms!" he crowed.

Rumbling like a company of armored cars taking off, ten MC soldiers came rolling out of the guardroom. Hustling and bustling, they bunched in front of the pale OD, who reviewed his army with satisfaction. Indicating us, he screamed to his housecarls: "Arrest them!"

Nobody reacted. He pointed at the guard. "I've ordered you to arrest them!"

"We can't," an old corporal answered in a drawling Hamburg accent.

The OD gave a start as if hit on the head with a club. Some time passed before he could collect himself sufficiently to repeat the order.

"Arrest them! Lock 'em up!"

"We can't," came promptly from the old corporal, who looked as if he were a longshoreman before the war.

"Mutiny, mutiny," yelled the OD, by now totally bewildered. He was darting around like a cat who's jumped on a red-hot kitchen range.

The old corporal winked at us. We stood there following the course of events with thinly veiled enthusiasm, hoping for the worst.

After an assortment of gurgling sounds the OD came back to himself. He turned with a hiss to the uniformed circle around him: "Think of what you've done! Come back to your senses! You may have to pay with your heads for this." With a gloved hand he made a whistling movement through the air like the guillotine in Plötzensee. "I'm a Hitler Youth *Führer*, my words carry weight!"

"We thought you were a *Sanitätsunteroffizier* in the Army,"

Stein remarked gently. "If you're a Hitler Youth *Führer,* then we don't belong under your command."

He was about to leave, but the NCO jumped on him like a wild beast, tore his heavy .38 out of his holster, cocked it and squealed with spluttering mouth: "In case of attempts at escape I use my weapon! You're all arrested in the name of the Führer and you're going to be beheaded!"

"To have that kind of power is really something," Bauer laughed. "Arrest, prosecution, sentencing, execution. The whole music in two minutes."

"Don't you grin!" bawled the OD, who'd been brought to the point of explosion. "You'll swing, you louse! You'll all swing," he threatened, waving the pistol over his head.

Then of course happened what always happens in atmospheric disturbances of this kind. The pistol went off. Not just one shot, but two. The little potswinger with the steel helmet got so frightened with the first shot that his hand cramped and he squeezed the trigger again. Another thundering shot shook the silent corridors with their many doors. He threw down the pistol. Tiny courteously picked it up and handed it to him, but not till he'd blown into the muzzle in the Texan manner and informed the NCO there were four shots left.

The cleaning woman slipped off in fright at the row she'd caused. She didn't forget her pail and floor-cloth.

First Sergeant Domas strode into the corridor, still greasy about the mouth from his breakfast. In a flash he summed up the situation. The pistol in Tiny's hand on its way to the OD. Two distinct holes in the lab door, from which a couple of fresh young maidens were peering out, sure that the tide of revenge of the Revolution was near their door. He noticed the guard standing in an uneven column and dressed contrary to regulations—some in steel helmets, others without them; three with rifles, one with a sub-machine gun; the rest without weapons and in unbuttoned jackets. He saw water on the floor and the smashed pane of glass. And before all he saw us, the old gang, in a strange posture of attention.

He looked reprovingly at his OD, who managed to pull himself together sufficiently to deliver a report, a very long report, in which words like "mutiny," "execution," "sabotage," and "insubordination" occurred several times. The army hospital sergeant was still making a little snack from the fat glistening on his lips, remnants of the stolen pork he'd put away five minutes ago.

"Are you sure this report is right?" he asked, drumming

the topmost button but one on the OD's tunic, while the latter was standing as straight as a pillar.

He didn't wait for an answer, but rapped out sharply: "Who fired?"

"I did, Herr First Sergeant," barked the little man in the large steel helmet.

"Well, I'll be damned," the Sergeant said and again licked his thick lips. "And who was the intended target? Because I gather nobody was killed?" He looked around with a searching glance to make doubly sure that a couple of corpses weren't lying around on the shining tiled floor. That would have disturbed his sense of order as an army hospital sergeant.

"I was the intended target," Tiny trumpeted loudly. The OD opened his mouth to say something, but the Sergeant patronizingly signaled him to keep silent.

"Well, in that case there certainly shouldn't have been any trouble aiming," he muttered. "But that's the way it goes when lazy bums want to shoot." He started buttoning his tunic. The situation was too serious, he thought, to be dealt with in an open coat. In a subdued, threatening voice he questioned the OD, who resembled a wet hen as he stood there with his pistol in his hand.

"Why did you fire, *Herr Unteroffizier?*"

He strongly emphasized *Herr* and *Unteroffizier* to show his contempt.

No answer from the officious Hitler Youth *Führer* who had chosen to serve his fatherland by carrying pots for nurses.

"Now, then, you *Unteroffizier,*" the MC sergeant smirked with deadly sweetness. "Why all this artillery fire? I see no one killed, and still I did hear a tremendous barrage—unless my well-developed sense of hearing has been damaged."

The hospital sergeant admired himself. He pointed accusingly at the two 9 mm. holes in the door panel leading to the laboratory, where the flaxen-haired Teuton girls had now fully emerged. Courage was again blooming in their protruding bosoms.

The Sergeant strutted with delight. He enjoyed the feeling of being the center of attention. He was master of the situation. He could crush that louse of an NCO. He smacked his lips with relish, narrowed his eyes and looked ferocious. Already he had court-martial, incarceration, and head-hunters on the tip of his tongue, but decided to hold these delicious words in reserve for a while yet.

"What did you say about sabotage, *Herr Unteroffizier?*"

The OD again spluttered out his report, to him of equal

importance to an attempted assassination of the Führer. But he was brutally interrupted by the Sergeant long before he could finish.

"You must be insane, man! A thing like that doesn't happen in my hospital. Simply can't happen. Are you seeing things? Hearing things? Do you have blackouts, *Unteroffizier*, eh? Would you like to receive a one-way ticket to the front?"

"No, Herr Sergeant," crowed the OD, suddenly becoming eager.

"What do you mean by 'no'?" the Sergeant inquired. He placed his fists at his sides in Prussian style and planted his feet, legs wide apart, solidly on the floor. "Are we then agreed that the sort of nonsense you're trying to put over on me cannot occur in my hospital?" He put special stress on "my." "Because I can't imagine you'd care to disagree with me, *Herr Unteroffizier?* Well, answer, and don't give me such a stupid look!"

"Herr Sergeant," began the confused OD, unable to keep pace with the tactics of the experienced first sergeant.

"Yes or no, none of your long speeches, you gasbag." He licked his still slightly greasy lips and hungrily tasted the word "gasbag."

"Certainly, Herr First Sergeant."

"Certainly to what, you comic worm?" the Sergeant exploded.

To his immense chagrin Dr. Mahler, the head surgeon, then appeared. With flapping arms and white coat fluttering, he came walking along in his round-shouldered, unmilitary way. He stopped before the disturbance on the stairs. Nonchalantly waving his arms, he said with quiet authority:

"This place needs tidying up, First Sergeant. It really looks terrible. Like a bombed-out depot with refugees." He glanced at the five of us. "If you have permission to go out, get lost, won't you!"

He pointed at the folding door. "That pane of glass will have to be replaced. We can't have a mess like that around. When off duty, the guard should stay in the guardroom and not dance ballet in the corridors. This is a hospital, not a circus ring!" To the great annoyance of the war-happy, Dr. Mahler always said "hospital," never "field hospital."

He cast a short, disapproving glance at the many women who'd gathered on the stairs and corridor. "I dare say my female co-workers must have other things to attend to than listening to soldiers' stories on the landing."

Mahler nodded and wobbled off. Nurses, cleaning women

and receptionists buzzed eagerly back to work. The guard rumbled off to the guardroom. The rest of us disappeared through the revolving door. Tiny demonstratively stepped on the bits of broken glass, making as much racket as possible, while he openly grinned at the OD.

The Sergeant snarled at the defeated NCO: "The two of us will settle this later. The court-martial is itching to teach you a lesson, you skinny bastard. I'll soon have you locked up."

He shouted "locked up" so loud that Dr. Mahler turned around at the other end of the corridor, asking, "Did you say something, First Sergeant?"

A booming barracks roar: "No, *Herr Oberstabsarzt.*"

As soon as we got to the whorehouse, Tiny began, true to form, to turn the whole place topsy-turvy by refusing two airmen admission to the anteroom. To ease control we had to show our papers and register in this room.

Naturally, the airmen couldn't be turned away from the lovely birdcage just like that. They were combat fliers and had long ago learned that if you wanted to get even with hoodlums you had to be a hoodlum yourself. The entire Third Reich consisted of hoodlums. The roughnecks of the Thirty Years' War were like Sunday School children by comparison.

They slit their eyes and thrust out their jaws. They punched Tiny in the throat and gave him a kick in the belly at the same time. A hollow grunt escaped Tiny. Then he got up steam and went for the pilots ruthlessly, air brakes released. With a murderous stroke he broke the jaw of one and knocked out the other with his bayonet.

With a roar of laughter he rushed as fast as his legs could carry him into the anteroom, where an ugly fat woman sat behind a counter awaiting customers for her girls. On the wall behind her hung a yellow sign which said in large Gothic letters that the MPs and the flying squad could be reached at 0001, but in an emergency the number to call was 0060.

The sight of Tiny's criminal face seemed to make the flabby woman immediately decide in favor of 0060.

Tiny bent intimidatingly across the tall counter. He drummed on the registration record with both fists, leaving two large greasy spots.

"Do you speak German?" he addressed the woman.

"Of course," she answered amazed, since German was the only language she knew and she had never dreamed of learning any other.

"Fine, then listen to me, you swag-belly pig."

"Who're you calling pig?" the lady yelled.

"You, .you old triple whore," came promptly from Tiny. "Pull your thighs together and perk up your ears!" His voice swelled to unprecedented power. "Get your goods together, have them line up for parade, and order them to throw off their rags. And lose no time about it, for Tiny is ready for a great bunk battle. That peasant bitch Emma has cheated me and your pack will have to bear the brunt."

He grinned, drew himself up to his full giant height, wiped his mouth with the back of his hand, cleaned his nose on his fingers and blinked expectantly.

Huge and fat, the madam got up. Her bosom struggled frantically to escape over the edge of the heavy brassière she was harnessed in. Her pale blue eyes flashed deep in the rolls of fat in her face. Three or four single bristling hairs on her chin quivered ominously like the whiskers of a mad cat.

"Out of my house, you damn swine, or I'll call the MPs! Head Officer Radajschak will smash your drunken face and make you cough blood. You'll curse the day you got to know me!"

In the course of her mad·torrent of words she spat at all five of us. From a hiding place under the counter she pulled out a long police truncheon and struck Tiny straight across the face.

Tiny gave out a roar, and the next thing we knew, all that was left of Madam was her shoes. The rest was floating around strangely at random in the reception room, where a flock of half-dressed and naked girls huddled in the corners. They seemed to think a V-2 bomb had gone off its course for London and had crashed into the middle of the Hamburg brothel.

Beaming ·with joy, Tiny stepped over the unconscious lady and greeted the girls. "Hello, girls, here I am again. Hot as hell. My balls are boiling. I love you. My friends love you. We're completely gone on you. Let's get something to drink in a hurry, and then we'll go to the bunks according to good custom when decent people meet."

"We can't get anything to drink," Elfriede answered. "Madam has the keys."

"She does?" Tiny said and bent over the mountain of fat on the floor. He found the bunch of keys between her huge breasts.

Elfriede shrieked ecstatically and rushed out for drinks.

We drank for a long time. The Legionnaire then wanted to

teach the girls to do a Moroccan belly dance. The girls, too, were drunk. At the start they had tried to pour out the juice, but we were too smart for them. Tiny held them, one after the other, while we poured the drink down their throats straight from the bottle.

Tiny also tried to pour it in other places. The protests were clearly visible in the long nail marks across his face.

Stein daubed "For our mutual joy" in ink on the behind of one of the girls.

Bauer was lying on top of the grand piano playing with fat Trude. She never tired of telling us that her father had owned an estate in Lithuania. By her description this estate was the size of Pomerania with half of Mecklenburg. We understood that Lithuania must have had a land mass roughly corresponding to that of China.

"Did you have pigs, too, on your estate?" Tiny asked.

Trude gave a mournful nod. She was lying with one leg across Bauer's shoulder.

"And chickens and ducks?" Tiny asked.

Trude nodded. She was on the verge of tears at the thought of all the chickens, ducks and geese they'd lost.

"But the only whore in your castle was you." Tiny smiled blissfully and smacked her bottom.

As time went on we became quite drunk. Several girls were hunched up over the small tables, which were floating with glasses, bottles and vomit. Tiny had gone to work on Ilse. They were too tired to go upstairs. A little later he was playing blackjack with a couple of others, with nothing but his shirt on. "Because," he said to Birte, one of the girls, "we'll soon be at it again."

As time went on a good many new guests poured in, both soldiers and civilians.

For the sake of propriety rather than anything else, we'd placed Madam on a chair in the corner. She muttered something about the MPs, which made Tiny shout "pig," quickly corrected to "bitch."

The lady, gone completely soft and with slobbering mouth, lay flopped over the broad arm rests of the chair. As Tiny passed her on his way to another girl he gave her three smacks in the face with a pink swansdown slipper.

As we turned the corner on leaving the brothel the MPs came rushing along. They had long sticks and drawn pistols and looked very energetic.

"There'll be some walloping in there now," Stein said, looking back over his shoulder. At the corner of Davidstrasse and Taubenstrasse we could hear screams and shouts mingled with high-pitched hysterical shrieks from the women.

"Now the whores are getting a shellacking," Tiny slobbered. He had gotten quite drunk. For no reason whatever
he stopped, put his hands to his mouth and called: *"Stoy!*
Halt!"

The city seemed to die for a few seconds, and then woke
up to even livelier activity.

The three MPs on guard by the car probed the street
with their searchlight and caught us in their cone of light.
Tiny was standing in the middle of the roadway, waving his
arms. He was eager for a fight, no matter with whom.

Boots stamped, weapons rattled. A big engine started and
the differential squealed happily. The MPs had given the
personnel and the guests of the brothel a thorough thrashing.
Now, thanks to Tiny's *"Stoy!"* they sniffed bigger game.

"Come on, you lice, and I'll slaughter you," he yelled to
the bloodthirsty head-hunters, whose job was to manhandle
their own country's soldiers.

No military establishment in the world, however wretched,
has a field or military police which can match the sadists of
the German Wehrmacht, with their head-hunter crescents on
the breasts of their uniforms. They just loved to break the
arm of some little insignificant infantryman. They were adepts
at doing it at different speeds. They could flog away at a
soldier for hours without causing the soldier to lose consciousness. He would lose his mind first. They were professionals. Many soldiers had gone from the steel cells of the
MPs to the rubber cells of the loony-bin, which they left
only in a coffin.

"Allah is wise," the Legionnaire whispered. He felt for his
brass knuckles and pushed them forward on his fingers. They
were Spanish ones with steel points.

Tiny stood splay-legged on the trolley track. Nice bait
for the head-hunters, hungry for torture.

Stein cursed savagely and muttered something about
"smashed skulls." Bauer laughed hoarsely while twisting one
end of his belt about his wrist, making the bayonet sheath
hang at the other end by the steel belt-plate. A murderous
weapon for someone who could and dared use it. And Bauer
did.

Sergeant Major Braun, of the MP, was a human bull who
loved hitting in the groin till the whole thing was a lump of
bloody meat. He was now slowly coming down Davidstrasse
at the head of his bandits. His steel helmet looked small on his
large head. Sergeant Major Braun in the Military Police of

the 3rd Army Corps was tops among the bandits who up to then had worn police uniform. He was a brown-nose to any superior and a dirty bastard to all his subordinates.

He served his apprenticeship on the emergency detail of the Hamburg Police Force. He had beaten a good many sailors to jelly. When there were strikes in the '20's a sizeable number of workers received permanent injuries from Braun's treatment. After being subjected to special treatment in the 7th Police Precinct at the corner of Davidstrasse and Reeperbahn, many of the girls on Sankt Pauli had sworn to take revenge on Hans Braun, who was then First Sergeant of Police. Eventually the asphalt in the streets of Hamburg got too hot for him so he had to agree to being transferred to Berlin.

At the outbreak of the war he entered, the Military Police and again ended up in Hamburg, this time as the leader of a special detail. For a short period he was active in Paris, but became scared of the French *maquis* and got himself transferred to Hamburg again.

Now, coming toward Tiny at the head of his head-hunters, he looked like the Devil incarnate. His face was set in a lustful, evil grin. He tapped his boots with his long black truncheon. It was said that he'd twice killed soldiers with this truncheon, with one stroke. Among the soldiers he was called "Monkey Face," a name he hated. The sound of it could throw him into a savage fury.

Tiny now bawled out the detested name right in front of him. It boomed like thunder through the hushed night and street, only faintly illuminated from the blue emergency lighting.

"Monkey Face, you fat slob, come over here and I'll give you an overhauling."

The command of Sergeant Major Braun sounded like the crack of a whip: "Get him! But catch him alive!"

Seven MPs rushed toward the huge Tiny, towering like a rock in the middle of the roadway. Truncheons whistled, and hollow thumps resounded in the night. An MP let out a rattle and Tiny bellowed like an elk at mating time. The thunder of Braun's commands rumbled through the streets.

After no more than five minutes, Tiny was lying in their car, which slowly had come driving up behind the MPs.

"*Allah el akbar!*" the Legionnaire yelled and stormed forward, hacking his murderous brass knuckles into the nape of a close-cropped MP. Belts whizzed through the air, a knife-blade gleamed, a shot rang out. There were hints of shadows along the houses, but no one came to the

aid of the detested head-hunters. The Legionnaire jumped
on the back of a six foot-seven inch MP and clamped his
steel fingers around his throat till he collapsed with a gurgling
sound. Breaking into insane laughter, with a sidestroke of his
hand Stein nearly broke the neck of an MP who'd drawn his
pistol.

Police whistles shrieked. Loud cries for help bounded back
and forth between the dark walls. A woman called a warning: "The raiding squad is coming! Clear out, boys!"

From Reeperbahn came the piercing horns of the alarm.
Green lanterns glared around the corner. Iron-studded boots
tramped down the street in a heavy trot.

We cleared out, dragging unconscious Tiny with us. A
sub-machine gun barked viciously.

A night watchman from the Sankt Pauli Brewery pulled us
into a gateway, where darkness swallowed us up.

We were washed. Tiny was most damaged. The two big
gashes across his face were bleeding badly. A medic was
brought from the army hospital and with very little fuss
Tiny was sewed up. Each time MC Corporal Peters drove the
needle through his flesh he threatened and howled with pain,
but his handcuffs prevented him from resisting.

By a strange, circuitous route Peters was able to pilot us
into the hospital.

They picked up Tiny three days later. There were ten of
them, equipped with steel helmets and head-hunter badges.
Sergeant Major Braun was in command. He clapped his gloved
hands in an eloquent gesture when he recognized Tiny.
They never found the rest of us.

After two days Tiny was released again. But only because the Battleship managed to swing into action a general
she knew.

On the day she took the field she amazed everybody by
leaving the hospital at 11:15, right at the busiest time, a
completely unheard-of thing. She was dressed in a yellow coat
and red hat and had a green umbrella under her arm. She
resembled the Brazilian flag flying from a battle cruiser, ready
to engage the enemy.

People were hanging out of the windows and following the
battle cruiser with their eyes as she shaped her course up
Zirkusweg with all engines ahead full. She disappeared down
the stairs to the Sankt Pauli subway station. At 5:08 she returned, leading Tiny by the hand. Naturally we could only
guess at what actually happened. But an MP who was on
our side had a fantastic story to tell us.

The Battleship had rumbled into the Precinct like a Stalin

tank at peak performance, followed by an artillery general, three staff officers and an SA *Gruppenführer*. The *Gruppenführer's* answer to anything he was asked was simply, "Well, yes."

Immediately on entering the somewhat surprised MP Precinct, the General trumpeted: "Attention, you scoundrels! The discipline is a bit lax here! The Eastern Front is dying for you, you bulls!"

He repeated this twice, at exactly thirty-second intervals.

Herbert Freiherr von Senne, Lieutenant-Colonel from the General Staff and an artilleryman like the General, expressed the wish to see Sergeant Major Braun, Hans.

He prolonged the Christian name "Hans" like a judge pronouncing a death sentence who corrects "firing squad" to "beheading" because he has become tired of saying "firing squad." The two remaining staff officers, both majors, tapped their holsters in pleased expectancy. Against regulations they shifted their holsters to center. One of them, in rimless glasses, hissed between his teeth: "Pack of rats!" while with cold gray eyes he fixed the perplexed MPs, who had come to attention in grand Prussian style.

The other major was sucking his lips like a monkey eating an overripe banana.

The General adjusted his monocle and kicked at a Bible lying forlorn on the floor.

The Battleship rapped the counter with her green umbrella, sending dust and a pile of documents flying about their ears.

A police sergeant squeaked: "Precinct 7, nothing particular to report!"

"Bastard," the Battleship answered, poking his beer-filled belly with her umbrella.

"Certainly, Madam," the sergeant agreed. He clicked his heels once more for good measure. It was the first time he'd been within such close range of a real general, an artillery general into the bargain. It completely confused him.

Sergeant Major Braun came rumbling from his cage behind the cell corridor, puffed himself up in Prussian manner, and rattled off a meaningless report which he didn't have a chance to finish before the Major hissed: "Lie down, Sergeant Major!"

Braun, unable to understand, shook his bull's head. That order couldn't possibly have anything to do with him. It was at least ten years since he had drilled "lie down" and "advance by rushes."

The Major crinkled his nose, adjusted his artillery cap

with the fiery red braids, and rapped his riding whip against
the legs of his shiny black boots.

"Really, this fellow refuses to obey orders!"

The General nodded and stared hard at Braun through his
monocle. What else could be expected from a lousy infantryman? His artilleryman's soul was filled with contempt.

The Battleship nodded, narrowed her eyes to a slit, ominously thrust out her double chins, and yelled through the
whole Precinct: "Lie down, you pig's ear!"

Braun threw himself on the floor like a mountain caving
in after a dynamite explosion.

"Forward crawl!" the Major commanded.

Edging along on his elbows, Sergeant Major Braun crawled
around on the floor. He had to run through the entire drill-
book before the Major was satisfied.

Squatting, he bumped into a swivel chair. He rolled in
week-old filth. He whined like a cat with its back bitten
by a bulldog. He hopped like a magpie and made absurd
attempts to do handstands. In the process he smashed
three chairs, knocked down a typewriter, kicked his sergeant's knees, and hit his own nose till it bled.

"Exercise is what this bunch needs," the artillery general
boomed and spat at a photograph of the famous commander
of infantry, General Ludendorff. With unflagging energy
he chased the entire personnel of the Precinct round the
room till their lungs were close to bursting. He threatened
the whole pack with court-martial, the Eastern Front and the
inescapable hero's death.

The last words he shouted before he demanded Tiny's release were perfectly chosen for instilling terror into a member of the SS: "This mess will be brought to the Führer!
I'll immediately dispatch your imminent transfer to a battle
unit!"

A feeble "Certainly, Herr General" came from the deeply
shocked MPs.

To Tiny he thundered: "We'll talk with you later!"

Noticing the penal regiment band, he blushed and piped
down. He adjusted his broad belt with the little Mauser,
brushed some motes of dust from his blood-red lapel and
drew a deep breath. "You'll be taking a trip by sled, just
wait and see! The Eastern Front is waiting!" He winked at
the Battleship and hit out at Tiny standing there looking
stupid. "In case of an attempt to escape, this lady will not
hesitate to use her weapon!"

Then they took off.

But not before the Lieutenant-Colonel had received Tiny's

papers. He slapped the police sergeant on the shoulder with
them and assured him: "You'll never forget this, Sergeant!"
Tiny blinked his bruised eyes. Growling sounds emerged
from his swollen mouth. The Lieutenant-Colonel eyed him
critically, smacked him in the side with the documents and
said, "I won't forget you, soldier. I'll keep an eye on you.
Do your duty and you'll fall happily for the Fatherland!"

Tiny had sort of come to attention and was staring stupidly
at the Lieutenant-Colonel, who skipped after the others in peculiar waltz time.

Tiny spat on the floor and said, "Come, Emma, we're
clearing out!"

She took his hand and pulled him along like a little boy
who has had a fall in the street and now is going home to
be soothed by mother.

Tiny was put to bed on milk and rusks. Later he had
home-made cookies with cocoa.

The Battleship and sister Annelise tucked him up in bed
with blankets to keep him from being cold. Late in the night,
after things were quiet, he and the Legionnaire got drunk.
They whispered together for hours. Now and then we caught
words like "head-hunters" and "monkey face."

It was quite late on Saturday when they decided to look
up "Monkey-Face" to discuss his conduct with him in private. They were in a very exalted mood when they set out,
and thanks to a bottle of vodka which the Legionnaire had
brought with him, the mood improved as they approached
their goal.

They found Braun in his underpants. He appeared extremely bewildered, possibly because of the late, unannounced
visit. Naturally it took some time for him to recognize
Tiny, and when he did, the joy of reunion was decidedly
on Tiny's side. Tiny was fabulously sociable. He tickled un-
armed Braun under the chin with his battle knife, pinched
his cheek coquettishly and promised to slash his throat.

Sergeant Major Braun managed only to utter a half-
smothered scream before the steel fingers of the Legionnaire
closed about his throat and squeezed the air out of him.

"I want to send him off myself," Tiny protested as Braun
started turning lilac.

Mrs. Braun was a zealous member of the Nazi Women's
Organization and looked it. She appeared in the door to the
conjugal bedroom, and before she realized what actually was
happening she commanded in a shrill voice: "I demand quiet
immediately!"

Despite the subdued blackout illumination, there was light

enough to show that her wispy hair was studded with paper
curlers. To ward off a beginning cold, she had twined a
pair of blue woollen ladies' panties about her neck. Her flan-
nel nightgown was almost new and faintly pink. On her feet
she had Wehrmacht-socks. Like everything else, the nightgown had belonged to the former owner of the apartment,
a Jewish widow who had died in Neuengamme.

Mrs. Braun's taking possession of that apartment was the
fulfillment of a wish she had entertained for a long time.
Three years had passed since the widow and her three children
were picked up by the SS. The arrest went so rapidly that
mother and children were unable to take anything with them
except what they had on, and that wasn't much, since they
were picked up at 3 o'clock in the morning.

Mrs. Braun took part in the action, dressed in high boots
and a leather jacket. On the stairs, the youngest child, a boy
of three, lost a shoe. When he got into the street, wet with
rain, he cried and said he was cold. An SS *Unterscharführer*
gave him a smack in the face and said:

"Here's heat for you, you miserable Jew brat!"

Mrs. Braun spat in the mother's face and kicked her in the
shins. "Don't worry, we'll see to you and your kids when
we get to the camp."

Then she walked in and started moving around the furniture of the Jewish family. She wanted to have it arranged to
her own taste before the Sergeant Major returned from the
Precinct.

The Jewish mother and the two youngest children were
sent to the gas chamber. The oldest child, a girl of 15, ended up in a camp brothel.

Tiny had discovered all of this through many strange
channels, known only to those who are at odds with society.

Tiny squinted at Mrs. Braun. His throat made some gurgling animal noises. He stretched out a hairy hand and
grabbed the scrawny, vicious human snake by her hair.

She screamed, but only briefly. He slammed her head
against the door panel. Then he dropped the lifeless body
to the ground with a hollow thud.

"She's a devil," he said to the Legionnaire and stamped on
the woman's face with his heavy boots.

He strangled Braun with a piece of steel wire. When he
was sure he was dead, he mumbled piously: *"Et cum spiritu
tuo,"* the only thing he remembered from his childhood Cath-
olic reform school in Minden.

When they left they checked scrupulously if the door
was properly latched.

"Thieves might come," Tiny said. "All kinds of trash are hanging around, you know." Then he hitched up his trousers and followed the Legionnaire.

When they returned to Aunt Dora she put up two glasses for them and said: "How about another glass, fellows?" She said it as if they had just taken off for a dance a moment ago.

"Well, here's to the big rat," the Legionnaire said as they lifted their glasses.

Aunt Dora took an akvavit with bitters for herself and gave out a long and heart-felt sigh.

"Did you get them?" she asked, puffing away at her white cheroot.

The Legionnaire looked at her and winked, clicked his tongue and raised the refilled glass: "Here's to you, Aunt Dora!"

She grinned: "And to the death of all those you're going to settle with!"

They tossed off their glasses.

"I'll be damned," the Legionnaire burped, "but there's nothing as good as this. For all the things that trouble you."

Should anyone be naive enough to ask Aunt Dora if they had been with her all night, she would swear on her soul's salvation that they had never left the room.

But no one asked. The darkness of oblivion had fallen on Monkey-Face.

Next morning the Canadians attacked Hamburg and the part of town where he had lived was a sea of flames.

Tiny looked at the Legionnaire and said, "Thank Heavens we decided to go over there yesterday! Or we'd have come too late. And then we'd never get to Allah's garden where the eternal flowers grow, Desert Rambler!"

"You shouldn't scoff at serious things," the Legionnaire gently reproved him.

"You have to make contacts," said Aunt Dora. "It's essential, like vitamins."

"Pretty Paul" was a good contact. He sent people to the gallows or exempted them from compulsory conscription just as it suited his book. Unless it paid, he did nothing for anybody. It wouldn't pay to neglect doing something for Aunt Dora. When she called, he came.

"Pretty Paul" was one of the most pernicious vipers in the Third Reich, but Aunt Dora possessed serum against his bite.

She laughed and scratched her fat thighs with a corkscrew as she followed the retreat of the Security men with her eyes.

She poured the gin that "Pretty Paul" had sniffed at into the sink as if it were a corrosive acid.

Tiny was sorry for the gin. Stein and the infantry sergeant felt the same way.

chapter viii

Wind Force 11

WE WERE discharged from the army hospital on a Wednesday. The boss, *Oberstabsarzt* Dr. Mahler, kept muttering as he moved about flapping his arms. While shaking hands, he looked us straight in the eye and said something nice to each of us.

It took us three days to say good-bye. Tiny surpassed himself in piggish excesses at the whorehouse. The girls would never forget him as long as they lived.

The Legionnaire and I got stone blind at Aunt Dora's in Wind Force 11. Aunt Dora drank with us. Once in a while she would mumble something under her breath and look at the Legionnaire. She was chain-smoking cheroots. The ashtray was filled to the brim.

We sat in a narrow niche protected by a subdued red light.

123

"Your absinthe tastes like putrid licorice," the Legionnaire said.

"And you're a Moroccan pimp," Aunt Dora answered caustically.

"What are you going to do when the war's over?" I asked, just for the sake of saying something. I couldn't think of anything else just at that moment.

The little Legionnaire finished off his glass and snapped his fingers at Trude, the girl from Berlin, who brought him a refill. She was about to take the bottle away, but Aunt Dora caught her wrist and snarled: "Leave the pot!"

Trude winced at the rough grip and almost said something, but a sharp "Scram, you cow!" caused her to vanish behind the bar counter as quickly as she could.

"What am I going to do when the war's over?" muttered the little Legionnaire, as if addressing himself.

You could see he was thinking intensely. He drank a little and rolled the liquid on his tongue.

"First, I'll give you a few smacks for asking such a stupid question." He drank a bit more, turned his glass in his hand and intently scrutinized the colored reflections. "The first two weeks I'm going to be dead drunk from morning till night. Then I'll have to cut the throats of a couple of acquaintances of mine. If I can bring myself to do it," he added in a moment. "Maybe I'll do some fast business."

"In women, I suppose?" Aunt Dora cut in.

"Well, why not?" the Legionnaire asked and raised his eyebrows. "One thing's like another. In certain places there's a shortage of women, and scarce goods bring high prices. If we'd met twenty years ago, you'd have fetched a handsome sum, you fat-assed bitch. I'd have gotten stinking drunk on the money I made on you, and you'd have had fun with a whole battalion in an Algiers whorehouse."

"Swine," came Aunt Dora's only comment.

"Let's have another beer," I proposed.

We had another beer and mixed a double absinthe in each glass.

"It cleanses the kidneys," Aunt Dora said.

"After boozing and selling sluts," the Legionnaire went on, "and after cutting the throats of a couple of guys whose ties I don't like, I'll retire just as quietly and live like a rich man on the other side of the ocean. In some place where there are no stinking police."

He laughed at the thought.

"You won't even get yourself to believe that," Aunt Dora said. She lit a fresh cheroot with the one just finished.

"*Merde*, what do you know about that? Why shouldn't I believe it?" The Legionnaire was working himself up. "*Sacre nom de Dieu*, why shouldn't I be able to sell the bitches? I could even sell you, though you'd fetch only a sou."

"You're nuts," Aunt Dora said. But she didn't take offense. "Do you want me to tell you what you'll do when you're through with Hitler's war? You'll dive into the first French recruiting office you come to and put your scrawl to a twenty-four year contract!"

The Legionnaire looked at her. He looked at her a good while. The long knife scar running from his forehead straight across his nose flamed red—it seemed as if the blood would burst through the thin skin. He ground out his half-smoked cigarette in a saucer filled with salt sticks.

There was a rustle at the revolving door. It came from the curtain in front of the cloakroom, a beaded curtain with threaded shells like those seen in southern Spain and in the Philippines. A boatswain had given it as a present to Aunt Dora a very long time ago. He later went down with the battleship *Bismarck* in the North Atlantic.

One night, that boatswain had bellowed into a Gestapo's face:

"I don't give a damn about you or Adolf either!"

With that he had flung a glass into the face of the head-hunter, who drew his pistol. Aunt Dora, who'd been standing somewhat in the background, swung a stocking filled with rocks. A hollow thud. Two days later the Gestapo was found in a ditch at the far end of Harburg.

Next day the boatswain sailed off on his tramp. When he returned home again, he brought Aunt Dora the string of pearls with the shells. It was hung like a curtain before the cloakroom door. While the two of them were putting it up Aunt Dora stepped through a cane-bottomed chair. They had quite a laugh over it. Then each of them put away a quart.

The boatswain went to Kiel. He'd just been drafted. This was in 1939. Aunt Dora saw him once more before he set out to sea in the battleship named for the statesman.

The boatswain died cursing and screaming in the ice-cold water. A sea gull ate his eyes, some mackerel a bit of his burnt leg.

"Damned crowd!" were the last words he yelled (in English) before he died.

The Legionnaire took another small draft of beer.

"So that's what you think?" He said this in a strangely low voice.

"Alfred," Aunt Dora said in a remarkably gentle voice hard to associate with her. "Stay with me. You may snooze in bed all day and get drunk as often as you like. In fact, once you've chucked your uniform, you won't have to be sober for a moment more in all the rest of your life."

Did tears glitter in the eyes of that brutal woman—or was it merely an optical illusion? Those eyes, clear as water and hard as a cobra's just before it sinks its teeth into a rabbit. Yes, Aunt Dora wept. She grasped Alfred Kalb's hand. He returned her grasp.

The two resembled each other. The saloon-keeper and the veteran who could boast of fifteen years in the African desert.

A petty officer came over to the table. "How mysterious you are," he grinned drunkenly and nudged Aunt Dora.

The Legionnaire jumped up and hit him to the floor with one stroke. He kicked him in the face and sat down again.

"Dora, old girl," he whispered intimately. "Let's be grown up and not start anything silly. You and I, we know. No rose-colored nonsense for us. You belong here among sluts, tramps and booze and I in the desert with a tommy gun across my shoulder. But once we've grown real old and tired, we'll send each other a postcard and meet. Then we'll find a little place where we can buy a bar with only seven stools."

Aunt Dora took a deep breath and looked lovingly at him.

"Alfred, the two of us are never going to get a bar with seven stools. One day you'll suffocate in red sand while all of your filthy blood is being drained off, and I'll die from the D.T.'s."

Trude, the Berlin girl, came up to them and whispered something to Aunt Dora.

"Go to hell," she snarled. "Can't you see I'm busy!"

"Yes, but it's red Bernard," Trude justified herself.

"I don't care a damn," Aunt Dora cried and hurled her glass after Trude, who hurriedly withdrew.

The Legionnaire got up, brought over a couple of bottles and mixed something. He poured out a beer glass of it for Aunt Dora.

"Drink, girl. All of us have the war tantrums. Why should you go scot-free?"

An air-raid siren started hooting. Others tuned into chorus.

"Alert," some guest said. As if we didn't know.

Several left Wind Force 11. An office clerk looking like a petty embezzler said he wanted to get home before they came. Most of us didn't make a move and went on drinking. Soldiers as well as civilians. Girls and ladies.

A dark-blonde lady inquired about shelters. She looked good, wore high-heeled shoes and a close-fitting knee-length skirt. Her stockings were slightly grayish. Very sheer. She wasn't a common barfly.

The first bombs hit. A whole series of explosions shook the house. Flak began booming away. We could easily make out the sound of the high-altitude shells exploding.

"Can you hear the Tommies?" someone asked.

We listened. Yes, we could hear them. Singing treble, the heavy bombers were circling over Hamburg.

"Oh, shove the Tommies up your ass!" bawled a corporal with the Order of the Frozen Flesh on his breast. "You should have a look at Ivan's combat pilots. Then you might learn something, you hick-town heroes!"

"Who're you calling a hick-town hero?" an NCO shouted and got up menacingly. His entire breast was plastered with jingling combat medals. His nose was missing. The hole was covered up with a black flap.

"Where can we take shelter?" the dark-blonde lady called.

"Here," someone laughed, knocking an empty bar stool.

A new series of bombs hit the houses and streets. A sailor with a U-boat campaign ribbon set up a grin.

"I bet they're shitting in their pants now!" He stuck his hand under a girl's dress.

The girl put her arm around his neck and whispered: "Sailor, you mustn't!" But she let him do it anyway.

The lady who wished to take shelter walked out, followed by a nervous, somewhat corpulent gentleman.

A thundering crash rocked the house, which groaned like a wounded animal. The electric light blinked ominously.

"That was quite a raindrop," the U-boat sailor laughed. He bent the girl back over the counter. She squealed loudly.

The lady and the corpulent gentleman came back out of breath. They seemed to apologize as they wiped their feet on the mat.

"It's terrible. They're dropping bombs," she panted excitedly.

She looked sweet. Her hair was disheveled and red spots of fear were on her cheeks. She obviously wasn't on familiar terms with death yet.

"Oh, bombs, really?" Aunt Dora jeered. "Damned if I didn't think they were dropping flowers on us."

The lady sat down on an empty bar stool. A strip of naked flesh was exposed above her gray stocking. She glanced around bewildered. The corpulent man sat on a chair in the middle of the room, puffing anxiously.

The sailor pushed his girl aside and swaggered up to the lady. The long band around his cap had disappeared. The girl had probably torn it off.

Without saying a word he slipped a big hand up her legs. Offended, she cried out and pulled her skirt over her knees. But it immediately slipped back again because of the tall bar stool. The sailor swayed. His brown eyes smiled.

"Leave my wife alone!" the corpulent gentleman threatened, getting up.

The rest of us watched. His wife! Imagine taking your wife to this place. He must be an imbecile.

The sailor didn't see him. He bent over the lady once more and whispered something about "bed."

"Leave my wife alone, sailor," the corpulent man shouted indignantly.

"Why?" the sailor asked curiously.

"Because she's my wife!"

"Is that your husband?" the sailor asked skeptically, again leaning over the lady.

"Yes, it's my husband. And now, leave me alone. I'm not at all interested in you."

"The interest will come after we know each other a little better. I'm crazy about married pieces!"

The corpulent man seized the sailor's arm. "Haven't I told you she's my wife!"

"Well, so what?" grinned the sailor, who was quite drunk. "I've made up my mind to go to bed with your wife. Can't you grasp that, brother?" He put his hand up higher under the lady's dress. She hit out at him furiously. He guffawed, took a long swig of beer and shouted: "You're just my number. There's nothing as interesting as a little resistance, and tomorrow I glide out to sea on U-189!" He made a gesture of embrace and whispered intimately, "It's my last trip!"

Another crash caused the ceiling plaster to sift down upon us like fine snow.

The U-boat sailor looked up. He had hunched up his shoulders. He smiled contentedly.

"That piece of candy wasn't far away. But it won't hit me. I'll shortly be going on my last voyage. A fortune-teller told me I'm going to be suffocated in the front torpedo room. U-189 is a rotten heap. And the commander, Lieutenant von Grawitz, is a pile of shit!" He looked across at the Legionnaire. "Hey, you panzer coolie with the smashed face, do you know that pile of shit von Grawitz? A man who wears the Knight's Cross about his ostrich neck as a token of gratitude for all those he has sloshed down in the North Atlantic."

"Shut up," the Legionnaire said and continued his mumbled conversation with Aunt Dora. He was in the middle of a lengthy description of shark-fin soup as served in Damascus.

When the bomb exploded, the corpulent gentleman had flopped onto a chair. Now he got up and skipped in short steps up to his wife and the sailor. He puffed himself up before him, trying to appear awe-inspiring. The sailor, who was standing with a full glass of beer in his hand, looked curiously at the pasty-faced manikin.

"I order you to leave my wife alone," he cackled. "And to offer an apology immediately." His fists were clenched.

"*Merde, est-ce-que c'est possible?* The imbecile wants to take on the merman," the Legionnaire laughed.

"What's that to us?" Aunt Dora said and blew away a thick cloud of smoke. "Trude, another keg!"

The sailor flung his beer at the corpulent man's head, bent down over the woman and kissed her violently. The man staggered. Then he aimed a blow at the sailor and hit him on the jaw, while reeling off a string of abuse that no one could understand.

His wife screamed. He swung his arm and hit the sailor again, knocking over his new beer, a double ginger-beer, which was hard to get. This made the sailor mad. He cried "sabotage" and sent the corpulent gentleman to the floor with a kick in the belly.

He received another glass of beer, but not ginger-beer. Then he roughly embraced the lady, bent her back and kissed her noisily. She kicked, and her skirt slipped up.

"Magnificent legs," cried an infantry sergeant and clapped his hands. "Chuck her onto the counter, sailor, and take what you want! You'll see, she'll clap her paws about your hips like the girls in Tripolis."

The husband was again on his feet. He was raving. He grabbed a chair and tried to smash it against the U-boat man's head, but instead he hit his wife, who collapsed without a sound and slid to the floor like a rubber doll.

The sailor stepped over her and pulled down the edges of his tight-fitting dark blue blouse. He stoked up and shot toward the corpulent man like a torpedo boat.

"Damn it, man, now you're going to get a spanking," the

sailor said and gave the corpulent fellow a searing blow behind the ear. He hit the floor face down.

The Belgian threw him into the street.

"Really, what a stupid pig," the U-boat man said. He lifted the lady onto the counter. "Hitting a lady!"

One leg dangled over the edge.

"Now you can take her!" the infantry sergeant cried.
"Let's see what you've got in you!"

"Oh, shut up, you swine," Aunt Dora fumed.

"Can't he take her?" the sergeant asked, looking into our
niche from the adjacent one where he was sitting. He was in
his shirtsleeves. Everything was sagging on him. About his
forehead he had a big bandage, very white. He smelled of an
army hospital and beer.

A Schupo came stumbling through the door.

The Belgian glanced across at Aunt Dora, but as she
didn't give any danger signal, he sat on, pretending he was
asleep. Under his chair lay a stocking filled with sand.

"All Kirchenallee is on fire," the policeman said. "There
won't be a bean left."

He removed his helmet. He was very pale and had black
stripes across his face. His uniform smelled of smoke.

"Good Lord, how it's burning!" he said and ordered a
double, which he finished in one gulp. He wiped his mouth
with the back of his hand: "A fat fellow is lying blubbering
in the street outside. Is it someone you threw out?"

He didn't wait for an answer, but pointed at the lady
lying on the counter, moaning and tossing her head.

"Did she get hit over the head?"

"So you're curious, huh?" the sergeant cried, tottering to
his feet. "Would you like to fight me, cop?"

"Goodness, no," the policeman answered and again wiped
himself with the back of his hand. Soot was now daubed all
over his face, and he looked very grimy.

"You're a little rat," the sergeant said. He aimed a blow
at him, but missed.

"Go and sit down now, infantryman, will you," came pa-
tiently from the policeman. "Christ, how it's burning," he
went on and turned around. "Give me another beer, Trude.
You get so thirsty from all that smoke."

A girl spat on the floor in front of him. "You turd," she
said and spat again.

The Schupo ignored it.

"She says you're a turd," the infantry sergeant grinned.
"And do you know what I say?" he jeered, itching for a
fight. "You're a stupid ox. No, you're something far worse

than that." He flung his arms around and nodded with conviction. "You're a real ass-kisser, sweetening up those Nazi
piles of shit. Will you fight me now?"

"Go away, infantryman. I don't strike a wounded man."

The sergeant swayed and hit out at the policeman. He lost
his balance and fell against the bar. Trude gave him a push
and he fell to the floor.

He managed to get up, though with great difficulty,
grabbed a bottle and slammed it over the policeman's head.
The policeman jumped back with a roar, pulled out his pistol and cried frantically: "What the hell, are you crazy?"

"Yes," the sergeant guffawed. "I'm raving mad!"

He rummaged about in his pockets and pulled out a piece
of paper which he thrust under the nose of the Schupo.
The latter exclaimed in wonder: "What the . . ." He smeared
the blood over his whole head. "A game license! An honest-
to-goodness game license! That's your luck. If you hadn't
had that game license, you'd have been dead now. Through!
I'd have plugged you straight between the eyes."

"You're a pig," the sergeant babbled and staggered into a
nook where he was received by a couple of girls.

Trude handed the policeman a towel. He rubbed his whole
head with it.

"What a monkey! You know he really took a rap at me!"

The seaman again put his hand under the lady's close-
fitting skirt. "I'll just tickle her a bit, then you'll see how she
revives," he grinned.

"How do her bloomers look?" cried the sergeant with the
game license.

With a twitch the sailor pulled off her skirt. "They're
pink," he shouted with joy, displaying the lady's backside in
tight panties. He gave her a smack. "Wake up, now. Tomorrow I pull out to sea, it'll be my last trip. Heinz won't come
to Hamburg any more!"

Another crashing bomb row. Glass clattered down from
the shelves. The lights went out. A girl screamed. The sergeant started singing:

> *Denn wir fahren*
> *seit vielen Jahren*
> *mit grauen Haaren*
> *gegen Engel-land. . . .*

"Let's have some light," called a man way down at the
other end.

"And some beer," another called.

"I'll sock you one," the sergeant shouted.

The policeman's helmet had rolled into a corner when the bombs were coming down.

The sailor kissed the lady. He grinned happily.

"Take her now," the sergeant cried. "Damn it all, man, show us what you can do!"

"You're right, pal. It's about time," the sailor muttered. "It's my last journey." He cursed. Something wasn't going right. "You pig, now you'll get to know the Navy!"

"Bravo, sailor. Go ahead and torpedo her, then throw her out to the beggar."

The lady let out a scream. A scream and a moan.

The Legionnaire laughed. Aunt Dora laughed.

"A round of beers for the wedding party," someone called.

All of us laughed and drank to the sailor and the lady.

"Can't you behave yourself, you bitch," the sailor's voice came from the darkness. "It's my last passage out. By tomorrow night U-189 will have gone down."

Trude brought a candle. By its flickering light we could see something dark lying on the floor.

Someone started playing the piano. The woman broke out in a long and ringing scream. The policeman yelled: "You son of a bitch! Leave the lady alone!"

"Shove it, you beat-pounder," the sailor answered. "This is my last chance."

Aunt Dora got up. Noiselessly and confidently she felt her way through the darkness.

The music struck up a tune:

> This will soon be over,
> There's an end to everything.
> Adolf and his Party
> Will together sink.

"Quiet," roared the policeman, who by now was frantic. A beam of light swept the floor and moved in on the sailor and the woman. Cursing, the policeman bent grimly over the sailor and separated them. The sailor laid about him savagely, broke loose and roared insanely. He stormed towards the door. The Belgian was swept aside.

"Halt!" the policeman called after him. "Halt or I'll shoot!" He cocked his weapon.

The sailor staggered up the basement stairs. There was a smacking of fire picks. Liquid spread out on the asphalt. Fire kindled. Blinding flames shot up. There was a glare as from a blast furnace. Calls for sand were heard. The shadows lengthened. There was nothing except a glaring, bright pale yellow. The street was on fire. All Bremerreihe was on fire.

Aunt Dora lit a white cheroot, the twentieth since the air attack. The Legionnaire hummed: *Come now, death, come!*

The sailor, the U-boat man, was on fire. Slowly he melted down to a tiny mummy. A scorched, singed doll.

The woman he had raped before his last journey sat on the floor staring blindly ahead of her. She rocked from side to side. A long muffled scream escaped her. She began pounding her head against the wall. Faster and faster, like an accelerating train.

The sergeant with the game license laughed.

Aunt Dora slapped the woman with the back of her hand. Four times she did it, and very hard. The woman quieted down.

"Carl is dead," she whispered. Then she screamed again. She hopped around the floor like a chicken that has had its head chopped off. She began singing a chorale, which rose to a shrieking treble. She seemed to want to outsing the howl of the bombs.

"She's gone batty," said an engineer NCO with a missing arm. A flame-thrower had burnt it off in the retreat from Kharkov.

Aunt Dora spat on the floor and glanced briefly at the singing woman. "Get her out the back way," she ordered, and nodded to the Belgian and Ewald, the pimp.

A new wave of bombs shattered the houses. The screams were drowned in the torrent of fire, which swept everything before it on the other side of Hansaplatz. An enormous vacuum cleaner devoured everything, good and bad.

Aunt Dora brought grilled chestnuts. We dipped them in the common salt standing in the middle of the table.

The Schupo picked up his helmet, put in on and walked toward the door. He was furious over the affair with the sailor.

In the same moment a Security patrol stepped in. There were four SS men and an SS *Oberscharführer*. They looked at the Schupo in gay amazement. One of them played with the magazine of his sub-machine gun. He was smiling, but not with a real smile. It was rather the contented purring of a cat when confronting a mouse that has forgotten where its hole is.

The SS *Oberscharführer* blew a long whistle.

"Well, look what we found! A dirty copper. Warming himself in the chimney-corner, eh? I dare say our coming here was quite a surprise to you. But that's life, you see.

Chock full of good and unpleasant surprises. It might really be nice, you know, if you delivered a report."

The policeman got up and spluttered out a report: "Police Sergeant Krüll, Precinct 15, Hauptbahnhof, carrying out ordered patrol. Nothing special to report."

The SD patrol laughed. The *Oberscharführer* scratched his ear with his little finger.

"Imagination certainly isn't your problem, gramps. Half of Bremerreihe is gone, and yet you say you have nothing special to report. Right above the stairs are two small lumps of cinders that were people not so long ago. Still nothing special to report?"

The SD patrol laughed again.

The Legionnaire was spitting out chestnut shucks. Aunt Dora lit another cheroot. The sergeant with the game license shouted: "Hang him!"

With a grin the SS *Oberscharführer* held out his hand to the Schupo. The policeman gave him his service order and his muster roll without saying a word. The SS *Oberscharführer* indifferently leafed through the gray booklet. He didn't read the service order. Then he put them both in his breast-pocket.

"You seem to be very eager to get a bullet through your brain, eh, grandpa?"

The policeman blinked and muttered something under his breath.

"The court-martial are smacking their lips for you," the *Oberscharführer* grinned, tipping the policeman's nose with his finger.

"And we are the court-martial," smiled the SS man who resembled a cat. The *Oberscharführer* nodded.

"He can allow himself to sit in a whorehouse making himself comfortable, while the rest of us carry out the Führer's order about defense and duty!" He walked full circle round the policeman and examined him carefully, pulling out his Mauser pistol from its holster and sticking it in his own pocket. "You're just the one we have been waiting for. We're going to make a fine example of you. And now, get your snoot to the wall, and be quick about it!"

The man who looked like a cat seemed to be in a glorious mood. He nudged the policeman with his sub-machine gun and dangled the barrel before his nose. He looked hungrily at him.

"You're going to swing, you lazy flat-foot. And you'll have a little tag on your breast with only one word on it: DESERTER."

His four pals broke into a roar of laughter.

"And then we'll twine the pilfered sausages around your neck, you kleptomaniac," the *Oberscharführer* bawled. He walked over to Trude at the counter.

"Five doubles, and make it snappy."

Aunt Dora put away her cheroot and got up. She winked at Trude, who disappeared into the back room where the telephone was. Aunt Dora took Trude's place behind the counter. She pulled fiercely at the long cheroot.

The SS *Oberscharführer* gave her a searching glance. He seemed to become uncertain of himself at the sight of the short plump woman with the brutal eyes indifferently looking at him, as if he were a fly on the wall.

"Five doubles." His voice was shrill.

Aunt Dora slowly removed the cheroot from her mouth and blew the smoke in his face.

"Why're you making so much noise? We aren't deaf."

"Then let's have the five doubles."

"No."

It rang like a shot from a 9 mm. storm rifle.

We looked up. The Legionnaire smiled ominously. Lazily he got up and slid over to the bar stool beside the *Oberscharführer.*

"Smart chap?" he asked Aunt Dora and nodded toward the man. She shook her head.

"No, he's not smart. Stupid."

"Who's stupid, you pimping broad?" the *Oberscharführer* cried.

Aunt Dora again blew smoke in his eyes.

"You, my boy. If you'd been smart, you and your house-carls over there would've been far away from here by now."

Trude appeared. She nodded imperceptibly to Aunt Dora. She glared at the SS men with malicious pleasure.

The SS *Oberscharführer* was getting worked up.

"Are you threatening us, you screwed up whore? It seems to be about time for you to take a trip up to Headquarters. Then I'll personally beat you to mincemeat."

His men laughed boisterously. The one who resembled a cat placed his sub-machine gun on the counter. The Legionnaire gave it a push with his finger. It crashed to the floor.

"What the hell are you doing, you louse?" the cat cried.

The Legionnaire bared his teeth in a vicious grin.

Aunt Dora once more glanced at Trude, who again nodded reassuringly.

"Pick up that sprayer," the SS *Oberscharführer* ordered his

housecarl. He turned to Aunt Dora. "And now, look sharp
about those doubles I ordered, or we'll help ourselves."

"You can't have anything," Aunt Dora said, placing a
bottle on the second shelf from the top.

"What the hell is the meaning of this? Aren't we good
enough?"

"You can't have anything from me, though. I'm sure you
are doing a brilliant job of what you're hired for."

The *Oberscharführer* bent all the way over the bar counter
and whispered with suppressed rage: "Five doubles, you disgusting pig, and right NOW!"

The cat sneaked noiselessly behind the counter. "Do as the
'Oberschar' tells you, or your wig will go up in smoke."

The sergeant with the game license got up and staggered
drunkenly up to the bar counter.

"Does someone want to fight!" he hiccuped in a drunken
drawl.

The *Oberscharführer* looked at him indifferently and contented himself with spitting and hissing: "Clear out, you foot-
slogger!"

The sergeant swayed like a tree in storm. We all expected
he'd fall over, but he kept his balance. He brought his
face close up to the *Oberscharführer*. "I can see you're badly
in need of some massage."

The SS *Oberscharführer* hit only once—with the handle
of his .38. The sergeant came down, blood streaming from
his nose. He fell like a post.

"That'll do!" Aunt Dora cried, putting down her white
cheroot. "If you five won't clear out of here awful fast, you'll
have a bigger row than you bargained for!"

She picked up the cat's sub-machine gun and placed it
in his lap with an expression which brooked no contradic-
tion. "This counter is not an armory. It's a bar counter, meant
for different things." She began feverishly dusting off the
counter with a napkin and glanced toward the revolving
door out of the corner of her eye.

The Legionnaire was about to say something. He managed to bring out only a *"Merde."*

Aunt Dora hissed at him venomously: "Shut up and mind
your own business!"

"What the hell," the *Oberscharführer* exclaimed. "You
filthy whore, we'll know how to make eyes at you when you
come up to us. We're going to wreck this piss-box so thoroughly that the devil himself will envy us."

In his fury he kicked the unconscious sergeant in the
face, so that his big head bandage fell off and a long fresh

operation wound appeared. It had burst in several places and water oozed out. Red flesh could be seen. A drain fell out.

A girl bent over the unconscious man. "Oh, Hans, poor Hans!"

She had some trouble lugging him into the niche. The SS men laughed. The *Oberscharführer* shrugged his shoulders.

"Bring that baby along when we leave. He's in for a shellacking. And now, those five doubles!"

The Belgian coughed a warning by the door. Aunt Dora looked up and smiled brightly.

In the revolving door stood a little man with striking features, dressed in a tight-waisted coat. A white scarf was wrapped about his neck several times. He wore white gloves and a light gray homburg. His eyes were another matter. Cadaverous and watery.

Aunt Dora lit another cheroot, snapped her fingers, and said, "Good evening, Paul."

The little man nodded and said, *"Heil Hitler!"*

As he walked forward a couple of steps, his pointed black shoes creaked. He put a cigarette into an extremely long silver cigarette-holder with an ivory mouthpiece.

The SS men and all the guests looked at him in fascination.

With his cigarette-holder he pointed at the SS *Oberscharführer*, who was now sitting on a tall bar stool, swinging one of his booted legs.

"What are you doing here?"

The *Oberscharführer* became confused. He didn't quite know what to do. Jump up and reel off a report or just shout: "Shut up, you filthy swine, who do you think you are?" He would have preferred the latter, but the barking voice sounded too familiar. It reminded him of the barracks and of the dark corridors at Police Headquarters. Something paralyzed him. Experience had taught him that behind ridiculous civilian rags the most unbelievable things could be concealed.

He slid down from his stool, even though he didn't much feel like it. He brought his heels together only partially, without a click. And the report was very unmilitary. He reported that he was making a routine razzia and had caught a shady-looking Schupo he suspected of desertion.

The little man cast an indifferent glance at the policeman by the wall.

"Your razzia order," he requested.

The SS *Oberscharführer* shifted his feet. He blinked, as he always did when he couldn't quite manage something.

A hand in white kid glove, with long fingers resembling snakes, was held out insistently: "The order for the razzia, *Oberschar!*"

"I don't have any, *Herr . . .*"

A surprised eye looked at him, a left eye in a pale gaunt face. The right eye, empty and watery, stared into nothingness. It was of porcelain. It wasn't a very good imitation, but the little man was pleased with it. His victims always got so confused when they saw it and noticed its icy chill. It was quite as unfeeling and cold as the little man's brain and soul.

"What do you mean by that? Am I to understand that you don't have any order for razzia, *Oberschar?*" The question came out with an air of simulated surprise.

"N—no, *Herr. . . .*" He seemed to be searching for a service rank. He still didn't quite know whom he was dealing with.

Only one person knew—Aunt Dora.

He continued in a slight stammer. "We thought there was someone in this pigsty who needed an overhauling."

The little man pulled up the corner of his mouth for a smile, which looked more like a sickening grimace.

"Who're 'we'? And what do you mean by 'pigsty'? Because the only swine here is you, *Oberschar,* and you came here only a short time ago."

A long pause. Everybody was waiting for the answer of the *Oberscharführer.* Far away a couple of bombs were falling.

"Well, have you lost your voice? I asked, Who're 'we'?"

"The patrol, *Herr. . . .*"

Again the crooked smile.

"Are you in command, *Oberschar?*"

"Certainly, *Herr. . . .*"

"Indeed! That means you're the one responsible for the misbehavior, which is both unlawful and incomprehensible. Self-appointed razzias and actions are punished with court-martial! Or, maybe you are of a different opinion, *Oberschar?*"

"No, sir."

"H'm. Indeed! You haven't yet answered my question whether or not you have the responsibility."

The *Oberscharführer* swallowed and again shifted his feet. He had now brought his heels completely together and extended his fingers along the seams of his trousers. He had long ago realized that this little civilian was more important than he looked.

Aunt Dora, who was cleaning glasses at the counter, was obviously delighted with the situation. The Legionnaire was muttering to himself.

"SS *Oberscharführer* Brenner reports that the responsibility for the operations of the patrol is mine."

The little man raised his eyebrow. The living eye darkened slightly. The dead eye stared on coldly.

"We'll discuss this later at Headquarters, *Oberschar!* Now clear out and take your men with you."

"I would like to ask where I am to report, Sir."

The little man was walking around the premises and didn't answer. After peering into the many small half-darkened niches where candles were fluttering, he pointed at the policeman, who was standing by the wall with his hands folded behind his neck.

"Take that fellow with you, *Oberschar!*"

The *Oberscharführer* turned on his heels at attention so that he always faced the little man in the black tight-waisted coat.

"Where are we to report, *Herr. . . . ?*"

No answer. Seemingly, the little man hadn't even heard the question. He stood by the bar looking at the bottles, which stood in serried ranks like a battalion on parade on the two low shelves under the mirror.

Aunt Dora pretended she didn't see him. He was rubbing stains off the counter. Trude, the girl from Berlin, poured out a large glass of gin for him. He sniffed at it.

"From Holland," he said, as if talking to himself.

He played with the glass and looked pensively at the liquid as if expecting something strange to emerge. He hummed: " 'Jewish blood shall flow.' "

He put the full glass on the counter, turned it a couple of times, sniffed at it again and mumbled: "From Amsterdam. Keizersgracht."

He sniffed at the glass once more, nodded curtly and got up without tasting the gin. He walked rapidly toward the door. In passing, he laid his hand on Ewald's shoulder.

"Drop in to see me tomorrow at 12:10. You can get the address from your boss."

The pimp went deathly pale. He smelled trouble. The little man's invitation was too cordial.

In the door he turned to the *Oberscharführer*. "My name is *Kriminalrat* Paul Bielert, Central Security Officer, Department 4, II A."

Then he disappeared.

"That's our damn luck," the *Oberscharführer* mumbled,

taken aback. " 'Pretty Paul' himself." He looked at his house-
carls. "That means 'Good night, my dear!' Next stop: The
central sector of the Eastern Front."

They kicked the policeman and struck him with their rifle
butts as if it were his fault. They threatened the Belgian and
spat after Ewald, but didn't say a word to Aunt Dora. There
was something they didn't understand.

They yelled at the policeman: "In case of escape we use
our weapons." This was the last we heard of them.

Aunt Dora gave a round of drinks to us all. Everybody
could have what he liked. Most of us wanted doubles. We
finished another dish of grilled chestnuts.

The all-clear was sounded. The long shrieking sound of
the sirens was heard all over the city. The streets rang with
hooting and clanking from the turnout of the fire brigade.
Blazing fires raged everywhere.

A whiff of scorched flesh forced its way down into Wind
Force 11. It could have been from burning cattle, but it was
from people.

The sergeant with the game license didn't come to. He died
in the arms of a girl who sold herself to get butter and
coffee, at the moment of greater value than bars of gold.

"Sacre nom de Dieu," the Legionnaire exclaimed. "What a
riotous evening." He glanced at Aunt Dora, who sat beside
us again drinking gin and bitters. "Who's Bielert, and how
did you make his acquaintance?"

"Curious?" Aunt Dora smiled. "Paul Bielert is a big wheel
at the Central Security Office here in Hamburg. *Kriminalrat.*
His signature can retire a person for eternity without any
legal forms, without asking either court or judge. Eventually
they also made him an SS big shot. *Sturmbannführer,* or
something."

"And you associate with someone like that?" the Legionnaire exclaimed. "Phew!"

Aunt Dora went on without heeding the interruption. "A
long time ago when Paul didn't yet amount to much—he was
a petty villain in Investigation—I gave him a hand." She
started picking her teeth with a long toothpick and continued.
"Otherwise 'Pretty Paul' would've lost his head, and he'd never
have become a big shit who took care that others lost theirs."
She was still busy picking her teeth. The chestnuts bothered
her. "But of course I took my precautions." She laughed
noiselessly. "When you have to deal with vipers, you make
sure you have a good serum."

The Legionnaire stuck a pencil in his ear and scratched

away fiercely. *"Sacrebleu,* you have something on the little shit?"

"You bet your life I do," Aunt Dora said, weighting every word.

"H'm," came thoughtfully from the Legionnaire. "I only hope it isn't unhealthy. What if Pretty Paul should take it into his head to knock you cold, my lamb, so you wouldn't know a thing any more? In his position I certainly wouldn't think twice about it."

Aunt Dora blew away the smoke and again laughed. "Tell me, Alfred, do you think I'm a tender little thing from the sticks?"

"Merde, of course I don't. I'm not a dimwit. If you'd been a ninny you'd have been laid out a long time ago. But, Dora, that guy Bielert or whatever his name is looked like someone who wouldn't stop at anything. For my part I'd hate like hell to know anything damaging about him."

Aunt Dora laughed heartily. I've never heard anyone laugh as heartily as that. "If someone should be stupid enough to step on my toes, all I know would rise from the grave. The executioner would get busy—he'd have to work over-time. Business would take quite an upswing. I'm dead sure I'll survive this war. When Adolf has crapped out I'll prob-ably be standing all alone on the tower of St. Michael's Church with a couple of miserable little whores looking for customers."

She downed a glass of gin in one gulp, then ran her hands through her black wig.

"What the hell do you really know about him?" the Legionnaire asked.

"It wouldn't do you any good to know." She casually scratched one of her breasts.

"Is it political?" the Legionnaire pumped.

"Naturally," Dora laughed softly. "Do you think murder and that sort of thing cuts any ice with the likes of them? But anything political is a good squeeze. When you whisper some-thing political, Adolf loses his sense of humor completely."

We drank in silence.

The policeman who had stepped down to rinse the smoke out of his throat was brought before a special court, where the whole matter was settled in twenty minutes. The judge, an old man, had pronounced thousands of sentences. He had been relieved of his work shortly after the assumption of power because he had displayed a little too much tenacity of purpose under the Weimar Republic. But he liked being a judge. You feel so wonderfully great when you sit lording it up there behind the tall desk. He pestered the new rulers in Berlin until eventually they gave him a post. When the war came, however, he had more work on his hands than he had bargained for. His wife read out most cases for him while he ate. Many of them he signed without having read even a single line.

After the war he was pensioned and cultivated tulips and carnations in his little house in Aumühle. On the door-plate is written: Heinrich Weslar, ret. judge. "Ret." is tiny and almost unreadable, but "judge" screams at you. The plate is of brass and is polished twice a day.

He lives five minutes from the railroad station, close by the Bismarck Monument—in case someone would like to pay him a visit.

The day he pronounced sentence on the poor Schupo he was extremely busy. Beside his carnations and tulips he had carnivorous plants as a hobby, and he just remembered that they ought to have had their flies an hour ago. Death could be the result if he didn't get home in time.

"In the name of the Führer the accused shall forfeit his life for cowardice and attempt at desertion, but in view of his long period of service in the civilian police, the Court will bar beheading and sentence him to be shot on the Army's stand."

His *"Heil Hitler"* came only half from within the courtroom.

The fifty-year-old Schupo, with thirty years of service behind him, was led out by two prison guards. He sobbed and collapsed in the little corridor behind the court and so they had to carry him down to his cell. He was given a tranquilizing injection before they drove him by truck to Fuhlsbüttel.

They tried to prop him up when they stood him before a butt in Putlos, but he kept on falling down. One of them thought he had already died from fright before the twelve carbine bullets went through his body.

One of the police riflemen hit his face. It didn't look pretty. It was too obviously suggestive of violence, something which didn't belong on a court-martial stand.

The police lieutenant who commanded the firing squad was fuming. He said it was a dirty trick to shoot in the face, especially since the man they had shot was a comrade.

He went on giving them hell all the way to Hamburg.

The detail was penalized with a regular turn of rifle duty, and two weeks later the men were sent by convoy to Poland to be thrown into the battle against the partisans. One dark night their company was sent out into the forests north of Lvov. Two of the trucks got stuck. As they were busy digging them out of the sucking mire, flames suddenly shot up from the dark forest with the violence of an earthquake, countless small blue vicious flames. First they came from the left, then slantwise from the right. And later from directly in front.

The whole thing lasted exactly fourteen minutes. Then it became quiet, apart from the crackling of fire in the burning trucks and the moaning of some wounded.

Figures in peasant dress emerged. They kicked the killed and the wounded. Here and there a rifle or pistol shot popped.

First Lieutenant Vassily Poloneff's partisans vanished into the immense forests as quietly as they had emerged.

All of the 175 MP soldiers annihilated were older men who for many years had plodded the streets of Hamburg, Lübeck and Bremen as obscure policemen. They hadn't had the slightest suspicion that somewhere in the east there lived a young fanatic killer, Vassily Poloneff, First Lieutenant in Unit X 103 B of the Red Army and an expert in partisan warfare.

The encounter had been brief and violent. Shortly afterward, the postman would bring a nice card to the bereaved: "First Sergeant Schulze or Meyer has been killed in action fighting for the Führer and for Greater Germany. The Führer thanks you."

Many would have liked to write in the newspaper, "With profound sorrow," but that was prohibited by the Party. A German woman must be proud when her husband is killed for the Führer. Likewise, the children have to be proud when their fathers are killed. A German isn't merely husband, father, son, or brother, but first of all a soldier and a hero. That's what he was born for. That's what he lived for.

Heil Hitler!

To show sorrow was un-German. It could easily be interpreted as sabotage of the will for defense. Reading the death notice of one of the fallen, you couldn't help blinking your eyes:

"With pride we have received notice
that our son, Lieutenant in the Reserves
Heinz Müller,
born on May 3, 1925,
of 44th Regiment of the Panzer Grenadiers,
was killed in action on June 10, 1944,

fighting bravely for the Führer.
Gudrun and Hans Müller."

Evening after evening the lights were not turned on at the Müllers'. They were proud in the dark.

Three weeks later arrived an oblong letter. Personnel Office, Army High Command, Berlin. It was a money order for 147 marks and 25 pfennigs. The Army's thanks for the sacrifice.

Müller got furious and said a whole lot about blood-money. Forgot to be proud. An air-raid warden picked up a little of it. On the following evening two well-dressed gentlemen appeared.

They came from Central Security.

People's Court followed. Indictment for making hostile statements. Sabotage of the will for defense. Un-German conduct. Insulting the Führer and instigation to revolt.

Next, transfer to Plötzensee. On a November morning with drizzling rain, the top assistant to the executioner of the Reich cut off proud Müller's head.

Mrs. Müller, who had lived with anti-social Hans Müller, was sent to Ravensbrück for re-education.

A pandemonium of shouts and screams from thousands of throats choking with terror.

Bombs dropped like hail. People swarming along the street were burnt to crisps.

They called upon God, but God was silent.

St. Nicholas' Church was a roaring sea of flames. The parish priest wanted to save the altar relics. A big stone crucifix fell down and broke his back.

Everything was ablaze.

Hamburg was going under.

We sat drinking in the basement of the army hospital.

Tiny let the dog eat an inflamed appendix.

In an underground restaurant by Baumwall, the upper class and the Party bosses of Hamburg were celebrating.

Paul Bielert was looking for a murderer.

It was a good night for corpse robbers, and the crop was abundant.

chapter ix

Bombs in the Night

A FEW stray bombs had come down by the army hospital. Blockbusters. The youth hostel facing Landungsbrücke had been blown away. A screech, a deafening crash, followed by a sky-high dust cloud—the hostel had vanished. With its eagles, its Hitler Youth decorations and all the boys in the basement. The nine twelve-year-old boys who worked the two cm. flak guns shared the same fate.

All of it had vanished, as if a skillful sorcerer had turned his wand: Hey presto, turn to dust and dung! Only, no one applauded.

One wing of the army hospital, the one facing Bernhard Nocht-Strasse, had been destroyed. Scraps from iron bedsteads were lying around. They looked like twisted pipes. There was a naked leg. It had been torn off at the knee, cut clean.

145

A swarm of buzzing and hissing blue-black flies were feeding on it. The flies were fat, well-fed.

A hand was lying in the roadway, a coarse worker's hand with black nails. On one of the crooked fingers there was a worn plain ring.

"Some fellow has lost his paw," Tiny said and gave the hand a kick. Two lean dogs set off after it.

"Merde, mon camarade," the Legionnaire said. "A war's going on. The end is approaching. The Reich has become the front."

A woman sat crying in the gutter outside the Sankt Pauli brewery. She was sprinkled all over with chalk dust. She was in a slip, bare-legged, and with half a blanket wrapped about her shoulders. Once it had been a beautiful red blanket. Tiny was telling a joke as we walked past. We laughed noisily.

The woman doubled up and burst into frantic sobbing. She cried. She cried alone. There were many who cried alone. We laughed at Tiny's juicy story and remained indifferent to her.

Out of Hamburg a huge mass procession was moving north. Foreign contract workers. No one attempted to stop them. The police force had collapsed. Under their arms they carried parcels tied up with string, on their shoulders bundled-up blankets. They trudged through Neumünster, across the bridge at Rendsburg and approached the border. They'd had enough of Germany's war.

They crossed the border without control. They just walked on. An endless terror-stricken snake.

The SS sentries stood as if drugged, just staring.

Germany was on fire. Hamburg trembled. Hosts of rats were streaming north, thousands of them. Away from it all, away. From a hell of flames.

For some mysterious reason or other our departure from the army hospital was postponed.

Tiny threw himself flat on the landing where the rest of us were sitting.

"It looks to me pretty much like some sort of life insurance. I wouldn't be surprised if the Eastern Front ends up by coming to us instead of we to it. What a great day for Ivan. The girls will begin learning Russian and making love in Russian." He lifted a leg and blew one of his special trumpet calls. It sounded like the Day of Judgment.

He grabbed lustfully after a nurse's aide who came running up the stairs.

"How about the two of us fornicating tonight, carbolic auntie?"

"Stupid pig," she hissed, trying to kick his face. "I'm engaged to be married."

"So much the better," Tiny grinned. "Once you've tasted blood you're more bloodthirsty."

She kicked again. Tiny roared with laughter.

"I'll give you the whole works, you hypodermic whore. Tiny is always ready for turn-out. Just you come along! Ask Emma and you'll find out what Tiny can do."

He let her go. She dashed off.

We were ordered to help clearing away debris, but the person in charge had no experience handling veteran soldiers. She was a recently arrived head nurse with a big bun on her head the color of an old Parker pen. A lean smug Teuton. The golden Party emblem on her gray dress glared scornfully down at the less gaudy, but more genuine nurse's pin. She spoke like a camel with a cold.

"Get started, you four lazy bums! Get a shovel and clear away the rubble on Station 3!"

"Just one shovel?" Tiny asked.

"Snotty fellow!" the thin woman barked, rapping the floor with the black tip of her toe.

The Legionnaire nonchalantly got up and strolled down the corridor.

"*Voilà,* come along, fellows!"

"We speak German here!" she yelled after him.

"Up yours," Tiny grinned shamelessly, getting up to follow the rest of us.

Cursing and swearing, she disappeared up the stairs.

A little nurse who had witnessed the incident whispered a warning: "Look out for Mathilde! She has a brother in the Gestapo. Her father was killed in '23. A word from her and you're in for it!"

The Legionnaire turned to Tiny, bulging big and imposing behind him.

"Remind me to put Mathilde's name down on Porta's list."

"You said it," Tiny grinned.

"Why're you doing that?" the little nurse asked, surprised.

The Legionnaire put his hand under her chin and looked into her eyes: "*Merde.* The day the accounts are going to be settled there won't be time to make too many investigations. So, every time we meet them, we put them down."

"Heavens," the little nurse exclaimed. "Are you anti-social revolutionaries?"

Willy Bauer, the big truck driver, burst into a peal of

laughter. Tiny neighed and pawed the ground with his foot.

She shook her head and stared after us. Shortly afterward she said to a friend, "Watch out what you say, Grethe, the revolutionaries are collecting names. It's about time to jump off the bus. We're getting close to the end station."

Sister Grethe laughed loudly. "I've never been on that bus, my dear. My old man has been in a concentration camp for more than four years. The sucker belonged to the German National People's Party and couldn't keep his trap shut. SS Heinrich looks upon them as upper-class socialists. So you see, I'll be all right—thanks to the stupidity of the esteemed head of my family."

"If only I could say the same. But unfortunately my old man is a major in the SA division 'Feldherrenhalle', and two of my dear brothers are with the SS division 'Das Reich.' "

They went on cleaning hypodermic needles and syringes in silence.

Then the little nurse said thoughtfully: "Maybe I'd better report to my boss. That's one's duty, you know, when coming in contact with anti-social elements or overhearing subversive remarks."

Buxom sister Grethe gave her a long look before she answered: "Don't do it, Margaret. That would mean certain death for you the day Adolf retires to Hell. That sort of duty it's best to forget about. Don't look, don't listen, don't talk." She turned on her heels and left. Parting, she remarked casually, "If you remember this, you'll always have a chance of landing on your feet. Eat, sleep, fornicate, and keep your mouth shut. The last is the most important."

Sister Grethe is still in the army hospital. For four years she nursed wounded Wehrmacht soldiers. Closed their glazed eyes, filled them with morphine when insanity hit them and caused them to howl savagely, slept with them when she felt like it, drank when her nerves rebelled. For a time she even used morphine. It gave relief.

For two years she nursed English soldiers. She shot hypodermic needles into them, bawled them out and otherwise carried on with them as she'd previously done with German soldiers.

Dr. Mahler, the head surgeon, traveled for a while. Reportedly, at least. The truth was the rulers wanted to crush him because he was a brave physician. He returned and is still flapping his arms along those long corridors.

The soldiers were followed by civilians. Strange and unheard-of illnesses got to this hospital.

Red Cross sister Grethe became *Krankenschwester*. She

wasn't interested in getting a ward. She gave her shots, emptied bedpans and changed sheets as usual. Once in a while
she would meet an old patient—German, Norwegian, Danish, English; a Negro from the Congo, an Arab from Algiers;
a Legionnaire from Indo-China shaking with fever. She would
laugh on meeting them again. Drink with them in small
cosy dives. More than once she had also hospitably shared
her bed with them.

"We're human, after all," she said. "And it's later than
you think."

Sister Grethe was a great nurse. Many looked down on
her and jeered: "Immoral." But there were more who said:
"A splendid girl."

If some day you go to the city on the Elbe, walk down
to Landungsbrücke. Looking up toward Reeperbahn, you'll
notice a well-hidden hospital to the left of Hafenkrankenhaus.
It's a special hospital. There you can find sister Grethe. If
you're of the right sort, have a drink with her and greet her
from the thousands of unknown men in green and khaki.

Little Margaret hanged herself on a mild May day in 1945.
She died as stupid as ever. She was very moral. She reported
to her superior far too often and forgot Grethe's words:
Don't look, don't listen, don't talk. But where could she
have learned to know the East's symbol of. wisdom, the
three sacred monkeys?

May she rest in peace! She has many fellow-sufferers.

Instead of cleaning up we went down to the basement,
to MC Corporal Peters, and played blackjack. We played
for several hours, while that shrew Mathilde led the clearing
operations. As the Legionnaire said, if we helped cleaning
up we would help those we didn't like.

Laughing, Peters raked in the winnings for the fourth time.
He picked up a big sausage from a wastebasket and cut it
into five equal parts. With the sausage we drank 90 per cent
ethyl alcohol diluted with water. We were content. We
were alive, and that was the main thing in Hamburg in 1944.

"They'll be coming back tonight," Peters said and swallowed a hunk of sausage.

"You think so?" Tiny asked. He looked out of the window
toward the Elbe, where the smashed Stülckenwerft rose tortuously in the air.

Peters nodded with conviction. "They'll be coming. They've
too much gasoline, too many bombs and far too many young
men who like flying."

"But we also have plenty of idiots who like flying," Tiny
said, "so that they can get some silly magnet stuck on their

collar. The old women are simply nuts about wings."

"You're right," Peters said. "The difference is that we have no planes for those who go ape for flying. The others do."

"Soon there won't be a city any more," the Legionnaire said.

"That's right," Peters said. "Then they'll start bombing the ruins, and when they're gone, they'll bomb all that isn't there any more, till every lousy cat and rat is burnt up. And first then the paratroopers will come."

"To hell with that," the Legionnaire said, playing a king.

Bauer laughed, slammed an ace on the table and called: "Twenty-one."

Tiny pointed at a bowl in which a nondescript object was floating around. "What's in there?" he asked, craning his neck.

Peters cocked his head. "An appendix. An inflamed appendix."

Tiny got up and gazed with deep interest at the little bit of gut. He whistled for the dog lying under the X-ray apparatus with only the tip of his yellow nose sticking out.

"You pig," the Legionnaire said, seeing the dog swallow the appendix.

"That will be too much for him," Peters said. "He'll throw it up."

"Why?" Tiny asked.

"Would you care to bet he won't make it? A quart of your schnapps against three of my sausages," Peters challenged.

"Gladly," Tiny answered, confident of victory. "Since you're so keen on getting rid of your sausages."

They bet, and when at the end of five minutes the dog hadn't yet delivered the gut, Tiny demanded his sausages. He got them.

He immediately rammed his teeth into them and swallowed big hunks of each one as if afraid he wouldn't be allowed to keep them.

"Damn dog," Peters cursed and made threatening gestures at the yellow mongrel in the corner which followed Tiny's guzzling with greedy eyes.

Suddenly the dog stood up. Its body was shaken by a violent spasm—there was the appendix.

"Hand over the sausages," Peters yelled joyfully and lunged at what was still left of them. "He couldn't stand looking at you stuffing yourself."

Tiny's face flushed deep red. He spat after the dog.

"You yellow bastard! You son of a bitch! I'm going to stuff it down your throat again."

Before Peters had succeeded in snatching the last sausage away from him, Tiny had taken a big bite from it. He grabbed the dog by the scruff of the neck and ground its nose in the vomit. The dog put up a fierce struggle, scratching the floor with its claws.

The Legionnaire cursed and asked him to stop it right away.

In a fit of magnanimity, Peters let Tiny have one of the sausages. He told us in confidence that in Ward Number 7 there was an artilleryman who could eat all sorts of vermin.

"Phew! I'd like to see him," Bauer said.

"Let's go up there and take a closer look at that worm of an artilleryman," Tiny proposed.

"Can he eat frogs?" I asked. "I once saw a Russian doing that for schnapps."

"As if that was anything," the Legionnaire cut in. He never let himself be impressed by anything. "I saw someone swallowing glass and tubes till his throat was on fire."

"Good it wasn't his ass," Tiny said. "But let's take a look at that gunner and put him to the test. He's going to eat two frogs and a razor blade, and if he doesn't we'll give him a beating."

"I just hope you won't meet a fellow some day who'll give you a beating," the little Legionnaire warned.

"Such a fellow doesn't exist," Tiny decided confidently.

On our way through the garden to Ward 7, Tiny found a frog. Much to his annoyance he could find only one. He found an earthworm also.

"You pig," the Legionnaire said.

The artilleryman turned out to be a short, stocky, muscular miner with shovels for fists. His thick eyebrows were grown together on his stupid low forehead. His small black eyes stared dumbly at us. He grinned proudly when Peters asked him if he could eat a frog.

"I can eat anything, but not for nothing."

"I'll give you one on the jaw if you don't do it," Tiny said, shaking one of his large fists at him.

"You'd better shut up," the artilleryman answered. "I can lick anyone, you too, you big hulk."

Tiny brought his fists together with a resounding smack.

"Did you hear that? Did you hear what that crud said? By everything that's good and sacred, I'll kill him! I'll grind him to sausage meat and let that yellow dog lap him up."

"You're free to try," the artilleryman grinned, quite untouched by Tiny's excitement.

Tiny was going to rush him, but the Legionnaire held him back.

"*Merde*, leave him alone. No ruckus here!"

Tiny looked around, eager for a fight.

"I won't stand for that! I must kill him, or I'll bust! Holy Virgin, I swear I have to strangle him."

"Shut up, Tiny," the Legionnaire ruled. "You can take care of him when you meet him in town."

The artilleryman guffawed and turned to his comrades. "Tell them about me, fellows, and bring that lame ox back to earth."

A mountain chasseur got up and came over to us. In almost unintelligible dialect, he said: "Emil over there can break a table leg with his bare fists. He can knock down a cow." He swung his arm and felled an imaginary cow. "He goes like this—and next, the cow groans in her sleep. He can lift an artillery horse off the ground with saddle and all."

Snorting contemptuously, Tiny walked over to the large three-light window. He took hold of the frame and gave a couple of tentative tugs at it. Then he pulled with all his strength. The room rang with loud creaking and cracking noises and Tiny was showered by plaster and bricks. Then he stood there with the large window frame in his hands. He looked around triumphantly, then dropped it. It crashed against the flagstones in the garden, where shouts and curses could be heard.

The inmates of the ward protested loudly.

The artilleryman nodded and heaved himself to his feet. He grabbed hold of the large table in the middle of the floor, tore off a leg and broke it on the edge of a bed.

Tiny shrugged his shoulders. He seized a bed occupied by a patient and lifted it above his head, making the occupant scream with terror. Then he hurled the bed and everything in it straight through the room. It ended up in the artilleryman's bed, which got totally crushed. Then he walked over to the only washbowl in the room, broke it loose with such force that bolts went flying around his ears, and pitched it at the still grinning artilleryman.

"We want quiet in the ward!" a sergeant major yelled from his bed.

Tiny looked at him. "You shall have it, my boy!" He hit him twice over the head so that he passed out.

"Now that you've untidied my bed I suggest you straighten it out," the artilleryman said, pointing at the big mess.

"You snotty bum," Tiny yelled. "I'm going to mess your guts up so bad that even your mother will be ashamed of you!" Growling, he walked over to the artilleryman who was standing in the middle of the room as if the whole matter didn't concern him.

Tiny hit him only three times. The artilleryman went down, his mouth gaping in vacant surprise. Before he managed to get up, Tiny gave him a kick in the face.

The Legionnaire nodded to the rest of us. We seized Tiny and dragged him away from the room.

"You'll get caged for this," Peters prophesied. "They'll rat on you. I'm pretty sure they'll rat on you. The worst part is the window and the washbowl."

"Yeah, why? A whole lot of washbowls and windows go up in smoke these days, you know," Tiny said. "I had to show those fellows who I am." He took the frog out of his pocket and dropped it on the writing desk of one of the nurses.

She flew into a rage.

"Shut up, you officers' bedwarmer," Tiny shouted modestly, "or I'll give your ass such a shellacking you'll think the whole military academy has been banging you."

As Peters had prophesied, they did return. After being fed with fresh phosphorus from the air, the still smoldering fires blazed up again.

More victims. Barefoot children toddled down flights of stairs to die like rats in humid cellars.

Somewhere close to the harbor, diagonally across from Admiralstrasse, a group of prisoners were trudging off to find shelter in a warehouse. The SS guards were making an awful racket and smacking them with rifle butts and whips to make them hurry up.

They didn't even hear the screech from the direct hit that got them. All that was left of them was a pool of bloody, writhing mash, beside the usual pervasive stench of blood, saltpeter, and scorched flesh.

A legless SS man dragged himself blubbering over to a prisoner whose abdomen had been ripped up. They died in each other's arms. And together they were burned to cinders by the engineers' flame-throwers.

Around Mönckebergstrasse a figure was prowling about, bending down when he came across a corpse. A knife flashed, a finger dropped to the ground, and a ring vanished into a capacious pocket. The dark spectral figure flitted on to the next corpse. The fourth one he got to moved and cried out.

A stroke with a charred board, a groan. Nimble fingers
rapidly searched a quivering body. A billfold, a passport, two
rings, and a purse was the booty.

Then on to the next. He must make the most of the panic
and the terror. On Hansaplatz, in Kaiser Wilhelm-Strasse,
around the Alster—the same sight everywhere.

At the corner of Alter Wall and Rödingsmarkt a woman
let out a piercing shriek of insane horror. A small catlike
figure pounced upon her. Steel claws closed tight about her
neck and caused the scream to die down. He kicked her in
the hollows of her knees till she fell over. With feverish fingers he grabbed her under the close-fitting skirt and ripped
the sheer underwear to pieces. The woman kicked frantically, but her legs were powerless against his agile strong
body.

Hot soothing words rang in her ear, while a flickering
tongue fluttered across her face.

"Please, let me do it, please! What's the harm? Nothing
will happen to you. Why don't you let me!" His voice was
almost tender. "When it's over I'll let you run!"

The woman chanced it. Better this than death. She sobbed,
she moaned and whimpered in fright. Far above them a
Christmas tree flared up. From the Alster Canal came the
sound of gurgling water. High up in the air target indicators
stood out in luminous and blinding white. Dust and flames
surged to the sky. The earth trembled like the woman under
the rapist.

The young woman had been on her way to a shelter when
she met the sick jackal lurking in the night.

Don't cry, she thought. Let him do everything, or he'll
kill me.

A bomb dropped. They didn't notice, didn't feel the earth
showering them. Carefully, tenderly, he pulled off one long
stocking, ran his lips along it, kissed it, hid his face in it.
His breath came fast and short. In the glow from the surrounding blaze his eyes shone with a glazed stare. He bit
her face, grabbed her hair with one hand, with the other
quickly twisted the stocking about her neck, and pulled tight.
She gurgled, kicked and hit out savagely.

The man laughed.

Her lips went blue. Her eyes popped out from their sockets. Her mouth opened. She went limp, stiffened—she was
dead. Strangled with her own stocking.

He stuck her panties in his pocket.

He raped the corpse once more and kissed her dead lips.

Once again he was quiet. He looked at the desecrated

corpse and smiled. Fell on his knees and folded his hands.

"O Lord, my God, holy ruler. I'm your scourge. A she-devil has been punished as you commanded me!"

Then he got up, bent over the corpse and cut a cross on her forehead. He laughed loudly and vanished over charred beams and rubble.

A little later the murdered person was found by two women. They burst out screaming. Seized with panic, they rushed off as fast as their legs could carry them.

This was the fifth woman murdered in a short time.

The case went from the Criminal Investigation Department to the Gestapo.

Kriminalrat Paul Bielert took over the inquiry, "Pretty Paul," Aunt Dora's protector.

In black overcoat and white gloves he stood silently looking at the corpse. The long silver cigarette holder dangled from the corner of his mouth. A bit of ash got stuck on his sleeve. Reverently he brushed it clean, then held a scented handkerchief to his nose.

His men rushed around barking like terriers. Commanded, measured, and took photographs.

A doctor rose to his feet. An old shabby figure. A typical police doctor.

"Before he strangled her she was raped. The cuts were inflicted after death."

"Rather than giving me all that rubbish, tell me who did it! I'll have to consider whether you wouldn't benefit from a trip to the Eastern Front!"

He turned his back on the doctor and slowly walked down the street toward Neuer Wall, where his Mercedes was waiting.

He saw nothing, heard nothing. His brain worked at high pressure. In the service of the Security Police this same brain had devised the most diabolic methods of torture. At long last the brain that had helped to bring Edgar André to the gallows several years before the war was being used for something sensible.

On the fourth floor of Police Headquarters on Karl Muck Platz the casualties were being added up. It could never be determined quite accurately how many were dead and missing, but a couple of hundreds more or less didn't really matter. An old frowsy typist assembled the lists. After a lot of jabbering back and forth they had arrived at 3,418 dead and as many wounded. In addition came the large number of missing. Many had been completely incinerated by the flame-

throwers which the pioneer soldiers used in their clean-up operations.

Cards were crossed off and filed. A pile of stamped death
certificates with facsimiles, and then everything was ready
for the next attack.

A civilized society must maintain order.

"Pretty Paul" was sitting with a couple of colleagues in
room 367 on the third floor. They were studying five photos
of murdered women. The youngest was 16, the oldest 32. All
of them had a bloodstained cross on their forehead. Every
one had been strangled with a stocking, and in every single
case the murderer had taken the panties with him.

"The man is a soldier," Paul Bielert said suddenly,
standing up.

His three colleagues looked at him in surprise. An SS man
helped him on with his coat. He primly slipped his hands into his white gloves. With the long silver cigarette holder stuck
in his mouth he left Police Headquarters.

For hours he walked through smoking streets, holding the
scented handkerchief to his mouth. Now and then a passer-by
would glance warily at him. Others greeted the great man
from Karl Muck Platz humbly and ingratiatingly.

He visited Aunt Dora, chatted with her girls and yelled at
the pimp, Ewald, till the poor man felt groggy. He strolled
down Neuer Wall, dropping in several places.

Toward evening he entered a de luxe restaurant at Baumwall, situated a couple of floors underground. From the outside it resembled more than anything an old, dilapidated
basement junk shop, but after the visitor had walked down
two flights of steep concrete stairs, he was in for a surprise.
Here a new world opened up. Subterranean halls with automatic ventilation and an air conditioning plant. Tables dressed
with white cloths and the finest china and silverware stood
in cosy little rooms and intimate niches. Colored table lamps
enhanced the charm. There were upholstered club chairs and
heavy carpets on the floors and in the corridors. Waiters in
full evening dress, followed by assistants in shining white jackets with red lapels, served the laughing, elegant guests.

In these underground luxury restaurants there was no menu
or wine list. All one had to do was to make a wish. And the
price was determined accordingly.

A scantily dressed lady took Pretty Paul's coat and hat.
Nonchalantly he threw himself into a chair in the middle of
the room. He didn't even bother to glance at the bowing
waiter as he ordered partridge with mushrooms and *pommes
frites*. For wine he ordered a bottle of Oppenheimer. The

waiter took down his order without moving a muscle in his face.

Paul Bielert leaned back in his chair to study the many guests. Elegant army officers in gray and green uniforms. Navy officers in dark blue with sparkling gold trimmings. Airmen in gray-blue dress uniforms and gleaming white shirt fronts. Black-clad SS officers with dazzling silver on collars and shoulders. Party officials in showy golden uniforms plastered with so much gold and silver that a field marshal under Emperor Franz Josef would have envied them. Ladies in costly silks and furs, looking completely unconcerned and laughing merrily with their partners.

An admiral sat with two very gay ladies. The Iron Cross, with sword and oak leaves, dangled from his neck, and beside it the *Pour le Mérite* from World War I.

Paul Bielert snorted scornfully as the admiral gave him a condescending look. The admiral would have shivered to the very marrow of his bones if he could have read the thoughts of SS *Standartenführer* Paul Bielert. *Just wait, you fop! When victory is won at last, the tin about your neck will blow up in smoke the moment your stupid head tumbles into the basket.*

Pretty Paul hated the upper classes, the officers and the Junkers. This he showed clearly after the attempted assassination of July 20, when as SS *Gruppenführer* he came directly under the command of Gestapo boss Kaltenbrunner in Prinz Albrechts-Strasse.

He ate his partridge in silence. He gnawed ferociously at the carcass without bothering about the fact that the other guests were looking at him with condescending smiles. Bird bones crunched between his strong teeth. Now and then he would spit out a splinter, open his mouth and pick his teeth with his fork. A slight belch escaped him, too.

A civilian gentleman followed by a lady greeted him politely, almost humbly, as he passed by. Paul Bielert nodded carelessly without taking the partridge leg he was holding with both hands out of his mouth. When they were some distance away, the gentleman whispered discreetly to his lady: "High-ranking Gestapo officer! Heaven only knows what brings him to this place!"

A Party official in a uniform of excremental yellow entered, followed by three ladies and their escorts. Swaggeringly he ordered a cognac and smacked one of the ladies on her wiggling posterior. Her partner angrily raised his eyebrow, but when he realized where the smack had come from he smiled and nodded.

The Party man undertook the same maneuver with a lady who was dancing with an Air Force major. The major protested and made lame threats. The Party man grinned and glanced at the major's service cross, shining lone on his gray-blue breast. "You seem to be looking for a hero's death," he said. The round face of the Air Force officer flushed deeply. His lady smiled and looked at the Party man.

"Is there anything else?" he asked provocatively.

The Air Force officer turned purple and his mouth opened and closed like that of a stranded fish. He drew himself up and said faintly to the Party man: "You shall hear from me, Sir."

"And you from me," the Party man said. He led some ladies to the bar, where he sat like a king on a high stool looking out across the room.

Pretty Paul wiped his mouth with a white napkin and ordered a mocha.

The falling and rising blasts of the air-raid sirens sounded from far away. The heavy steel doors with their gas air locks were shut. The world on fire was locked out. The crashing of the bombs was felt only as a faint tremor.

The waiters went about serving as before, without haste and without fear. Quietly and deliberately. There was no pity for the people up there in the streets. People dancing through blazing asphalt with shrieks of terror. People rolling in their own intestines. Children melting in the glaring light of phosphorus.

A select orchestra was playing sentimental dance music. Here you could dance with the blessing of the Party. The guests were the cream of Hamburg's upper class. Jewels sparkled around women's bare necks. Rings worth sums written with a string of O's flashed on well-kept fingers.

In the surrounding streets far above lurked the specters haunting the city during air attacks at night, in the hope that the elegant restaurant would get a direct hit. In the ensuing panic, the corpse robbers would have an easy time of it. There were those among them who wore the swastika on their lapels.

A lady pointed at the people who were laughing, drinking and dancing and whispered to her partner: "Don't they have any heart at all? Don't they know that a whole world is going to ruin, burnt to cinders by incendiary bombs?"

Her partner, an elderly SS officer, put a piece of juicy red meat into his mouth and took a sip of red wine. "Today the brain is more important than the heart, my dear. People without a heart have a bigger chance to survive."

A beautiful lady in a light blue dress and high-heeled, low-cut shoes strolled slowly down the central passage. She stopped at Paul Bielert's table and gave him a smile of recognition.

"Hello, Paul. You here?"

With eyes asquint and the long silver cigarette holder teetering between his lips, he nodded to her and pointed at the chair across from him. "Have a seat, Elsebeth. Sit down and let us have a little chat."

Elsebeth sat down. She crossed her legs and pulled up her dress, revealing a pair of fine, shapely legs in sheer stockings.

"Is it to be private or official?"

Pretty Paul took a sip from his glass and pursed his lips. The living eye flashed ominously.

"I'm always official. There's a war going on, Elsebeth."

She laughed sarcastically. "I realize that, Paul. Even if I only have lost a husband and three brothers." She lit a cigarette. "And a son," she added thoughtfully. "Just one son. Do you understand what that means, Paul?"

"It means nothing, Elsebeth, absolutely nothing. The only thing that matters is that the victory will be Germany's at the end. To die for the Führer should be the ultimate wish of every German man and woman. It's a beautiful death, Elsebeth, and you are to be envied. Not everyone can boast five fallen heroes!"

She stared for a long while at his dead eye. "Did you say heroes?"

"Yes, heroes fallen in battle for the Führer!" He drew himself up as he said "Führer."

She uttered a forced laugh. "My little boy, Fritz, was seven. A falling beam broke his back. My son, my little Fritz. You should've heard him cry!"

"No victory without tears, Elsebeth. That's a law of life. In order to live we have to suffer. The Führer too has harsh moments."

She played with a napkin ring. The waiter brought a glass of wine. She sipped at it.

When the waiter brought the mocha he bent familiarly over Paul Bielert. "There has been a good deal of noise over Barmbeck and Rothenburg for the last twenty minutes. It's said that a heavy blanket of bombs has fallen this time."

Paul Bielert raised the brow of his dead eye. "Why do you tell me, waiter? Did you see it yourself?"

The waiter started. "No, Sir. I heard it. Everybody's talking about it."

Paul Bielert took a sip of his mocha. "Rumors, that is," he noted menacingly. "Rumor-mongering is a crime prosecuted before the People's Court. Do you realize that? Why, incidentally, aren't you in uniform? You certainly look as if you could run an obstacle race with an MG 42 on your shoulder!"

The waiter changed color. He ran a well-kept finger between his neck and collar. It looked as if he was about to choke. Finally he managed to stammer out: "I was rejected because of heart disease, Sir."

"Heart disease!" Paul Bielert jeered and laughed loudly. "What's heart disease? Today that means absolutely nothing. You shoot with your hand and take aim with your eye. Isn't that so, my friend? It has nothing to do with the heart, and you won't have to look for the target at all. It will come of its own accord, and right at you. We are going to transport you and your sick heart straight to the trenches, and when we stack you up there, you'll only have one thing to do: blaze away! We're a great power and do a great deal for our infantry. In most other places the infantry has to trot on their flat feet, but with us they're carried straight to their position. And yet a malingering Fritz like you dares to talk about a weak heart!" Paul stuck the long cigarette holder in his mouth and hissed viciously: "As long as you aren't dragging your heart on a plate, cut in four pieces, I won't recognize such a thing as a weak heart. Do you know what you are? You're a saboteur of your country's defense, my dear man. A disgusting defeatist, an anti-social element!"

The waiter sent a pleading look across to a Party man standing at the bar. Their eyes met.

The Party man stood up, adjusted his uniform jacket and rolled high and mighty toward Paul Bielert's table. The waiter was standing there in a cold sweat.

"What's going on here?" the Party man asked, giving the waiter a friendly slap on the shoulder and grinning condescendingly at Paul Bielert. Pretty Paul, who was leaning back in the commodious club chair, crossed his legs, taking care not to disarrange his trouser creases.

"This gentleman is threatening me with the People's Court and the front," the waiter whispered, with terror still in his voice.

"Now, now," the Party man growled, thrusting a round face with a lustful mouth toward Paul Bielert, who was indifferently puffing at the long cigarette holder. "Don't you realize this man is my friend?" Like a schoolmaster he raised his finger in an admonishing gesture. "If anyone is going East, I'm afraid it's you. Show your papers!"

Paul Bielert gave a venomous smile. The watery-blue healthy eye flashed ominously. He resembled a reptile hypnotizing its victim before it devours it. Slowly, extremely slowly, he put his hand into his pocket, pulled out an identification card, and with two fingers held it up under the nose of the Party man, who reacted with astonishment. He clicked his heels when he saw the red Gestapo card and read the service rank: SS *Standartenführer* and *Kriminalrat* Central Security.

For a moment Paul Bielert's glance shifted from the Party man to the waiter. "Gentlemen, we'll discuss your eastern itineraries in greater detail tomorrow morning at 10:15 in room 338 at Headquarters on Karl Muck Platz." He dismissed them condescendingly and continued his conversation with Elsebeth.

The waiter and the Party man heard him say to Elsebeth: "I pounce ruthlessly on these wretched skulks wherever I find them."

"Have you been to the front yourself?" she asked softly.

"No, not the front you're thinking of, but another one," came in harsh staccato from Bielert. "Adolf Hitler ... "—he perceptibly drew himself up saying the name—"can use some people right here, people who take care the whole thing runs like well-oiled machinery. People who mercilessly seek out traitors and anti-social elements and watch out that the plague bacillus of defeatism won't destroy the heroic German people. Don't imagine our work is a bed of roses, my dear. We must harden our hearts. We must be hard as Krupp steel! Know nothing of foolish pity or childish softness. Believe me, I don't even know what a heart is!"

She looked at him.

"I can well believe that."

The Party man was scolding.

"Theo, you've gotten me into a stinking mess. A fellow like that should be shunned—and what do you do, you stupid pig? Get into a discussion! Even an ass like you should be able to see what he is. You can smell Stapo miles away."

"But, Peter, you started arguing with him yourself," Theo protested mildly.

"Shut up," the Party man flared up. He threatened the unhappy waiter with his clenched fist. "Don't you get any ideas. That's what one gets for picking fellows like you from the gutter. But now you are..." He turned down his thumb in an

eloquent gesture. "Before a week has passed you're going to
be in Putlos or Sennelager for infantry training, and there you
can shove your weak heart up your ass. Don't dare greet me
any more. I don't know you. Never have known you and
will never want to get to know you!" He called the manager.
They whispered together. Both looked across at Theo Huber
standing by the buffet.

The manager nodded eagerly and answered, "Gladly, *Herr
Ortsgruppenleiter*. Of course, *Herr Ortsgruppenleiter*. In this
place we want only nice and respectable employees. Be assured of that, *Herr Ortsgruppenleiter*."

Theo Huber's former friend rubbed his hands with pleasure.
He pointed openly at the waiter, who was feverishly polishing a plate.

The manager nodded and bore down on Huber. He had
put on his "strong" face, as he always did when something
special was up. He would thrust out his lower jaw, push out
his cheekbones and knit his eyebrows to a fierce-looking
wad of hair. He was overjoyed the first time he saw himself
like this in the mirror and discovered how much a brute and
a superman he looked when he put on this mask. He rubbed
his milky white, soft hands and jumped upon Theo Huber
with a shower of abusive language.

Ten minutes later the waiter was putting his things together and leaving the paradise of luxury by the narrow iron
staircase reserved for the staff. The rumbling steel door
slammed tauntingly behind him.

He was struck by a glaring light.

Hamburg was burning.

He lay down behind some rubble. He cried. He sobbed
with self-pity. His heart ached. Tears ran down his cheeks
at the thought of the wonderful world that would be closed to
him from now on.

Six weeks later panzer-jäger Theo Huber was sitting in a
Russian peasant hut smoking a self-rolled makhorka cigarette
while wearily chatting with three Russian peasants and a
couple of buddies.

They were drinking vodka and playing cards. The youngest
of them, a boy of seventeen, was joking with a peasant girl.
They slapped their thighs and laughed deafeningly. None of
the panzer-jägers, who had arrived only the day before as a
substitute crew, had yet been to the front.

A swell of sound, long and growling like the howl of a
wounded wild beast, reverberated through the night.

All in the hut stiffened and looked toward the window. The

dirty little window high up on the wall. Then the report from the firing reached them, a muffled roll.

"*Predsmertny chas!*" whispered the little Russian girl who'd been playing with the seventeen-year-old soldier. *The death song of the artillery.*

"God," exclaimed one of the soldiers, and at the same moment it struck. A 30 cm. shell plowing its way like a hurricane, tearing up the road, knocking down fruit trees, sweeping away the big well, and blowing away the outhouse with the cattle.

But those inside the hut didn't see all that. They heard only the swelling roar, saw the ceiling collapse and the walls tumble down on them. Poisonous fumes paralyzed their breathing.

Then it was over.

The seventeen-year-old soldier was hurled through the air and impaled on a sharply pointed, half-severed tree. He turned round like a propeller a couple of times, waved and kicked with arms and legs, and let out a long, piercing scream. Then he died.

Former waiter Theo Huber lay on his back across a beam, staring into the darkness with dull, almost glazed eyes. The heavy Russian artillery, which was pounding the German supply lines to bits with strict precision, drowned his scream.

He ran both hands over his belly. Where the pelvis had been he felt a deep hole. A mushy, jelly-like hole where a shapeless piece of steel the size of a saucer had wedged itself.

Again he gave a long moaning scream. The blood gushed over his feverish fingers.

He quieted down. The pain seemed to recede for a moment. He pressed the half torn-off leg up against him and rested his head wearily against the crossbeam. He was lying as if asleep.

"I'm bleeding to death," ran through his mind.

In a naive hope of stemming the blood he pressed his hands deep into the gaping wound.

Again he screamed. The house caved in. He struggled desperately to avoid being buried in the rubble.

The leg fell away from him. It floated around in a pool of clotted blood and shreds of flesh.

He sobbed and moaned in a monotone. A violent shiver tore through him. His arms became heavy. Slowly consciousness oozed out of him.

He died almost insane from pain.

In Hamburg the dance went on below Baumwall.

Sometimes a guest would ask the manager: "Tell me, wasn't there a waiter here named Theo?"

The manager would look thoughtful. "Theo? Nah, I can't recall any."

And so Theo Huber was forgotten. Thrown on a dunghill east of the river Memel. A cadaver who had had heart disease.

No one missed Theo Huber.

New Theo's appeared. The "hero-hound" saw to that.

He prowled about in many different guises, trawled through army hospitals, guard battalions, police units, factories, and offices. Invalids, old men and boys were caught in his net.

"Forward, comrades!" In training camp they would sing when marching. Grinning, sadistic NCOs always ordered them to sing: *"Es ist so schön, Soldat zu sein."*

"Long live Greater Germany! Long live Adolf Hitler! And long live a hero's death!"

Pretty Paul was constantly walking around. He could be seen everywhere. One day he was sitting at Police Station 32 drinking cognac with the chief of the station's criminal department and looking out on Reeperbahn. After they'd sat around being bored for a while, they ordered two women to be searched. It took a couple of hours.

When he left the station Paul Bielert was a bit warm and somewhat tired. The "searched" women had been released. Everything has its price.

Three days later a new sex murder was committed, this time in Hein Hoyer-Strasse, a few yards from Reeperbahn. Not very far from the hospital.

Kriminalrat Paul Bielert became frantic. He summoned a dozen experts and let them loose like a pack of bloodhounds with the wildest threats buzzing in their ears.

"Don't show up, you dead ducks," he roared, "till you can show me some results! You have five days, not a second more. Any of you who reports no success by that time will make a long but swift detour to SS *Lehrdivision*, the central sector of the Eastern Front, where he can croak in the swamps according to military regulations."

Two by two they slipped out of the large gray building on Karl Muck Platz.

The sixth victim was a nurse from our hospital. A young girl of twenty-one. She had been violated in exactly the same manner as the others.

His mother, a minister, and Nazi hypocrisy were guilty of his crime.

He murdered to do good. He believed he served the God of the Church.

The thousands of prayers with his selfish mother had become a black curtain shutting out the light.

Everything that imbecile theologian had told him etched itself into his brain and darkened his understanding.

When things went wrong no one wanted to understand him.

Like so many others he was killed by a ruthless police hunting for the sake of hunting.

Tiny killed. The Legionnaire killed. All of us killed. But we did it as the lawful murderers of the State. From the moral angle a small, but nonetheless very great difference—though not for those who were killed.

"I have never killed anybody," a famous man once said, "but many death notices have delighted me."

chapter x

The Sex Killer

IT WAS Heinz Bauer who found the panties.

First we laughed and exchanged coarse jokes. But then Paul Stein pushed the newspaper under our noses. We read in amazement: As in the case of the earlier victims, the murdered woman's panties had been robbed by the brutal unknown murderer.

"I'll be damned!" Bauer exclaimed and stared perplexed at the rucksack where he had found the undies. We counted them feverishly. Six pairs! Again we counted. Right, six!

The little Legionnaire gave a long whistle. *"Saperlotte!* Six pairs of panties! And six corpses! It tallies like hell!"

Tiny craned his neck and peered curiously into the large gray rucksack beside the bed. We could see a couple of packages of rye biscuit and some Air Force underwear, neatly folded with the eagle up as prescribed in the regulations.

"How did you find them?" Tiny asked, poking the ruck-sack with his foot.

Heinz Bauer shook his head. "Why the hell did I have to stick my nose into his rucksack? I was only looking for some-thing to write with and then touched something smooth with a familiar smell."

"Dirty pig," Tiny said, letting on to be annoyed. "Nah, the truth is you could smell those ass-cases. That's why you dived into George's sack."

We five were the only ones in the room. All the others were doing fatigue duty or taking physicals.

"Christ, what should we do?" Bauer asked, looking around despairingly.

"You mean, what should *you* do," Stein answered. "You found the holsters, not us. We don't put our noses into other guys' business."

"You rotten corpse," Bauer burst out angrily. "So you want me to sweat out this one alone, huh? Of course, you never stick your nose into anybody else's traps, right, Judas? I wouldn't be surprised if white wings sprouted from your back!" He bent forward and gave Stein a menacing glance. Stein squinted and hunched his shoulders as if expecting trouble.

Bauer grinned venomously and accusingly pointed a dirty finger at him.

"Who's the guy who doesn't pry into another guy's things, you rat? Maybe it wasn't you who pinched Tiny's schnapps that time we were going chasing broads? What do you have to say now, you bum, huh?"

Tiny was outraged. He flew up and bellowed, "Holy Moses, Abraham and Jacob, if this isn't the most low-down bunch I've ever been with!" He grabbed Stein by the chest and screamed with foaming mouth: "You hog louse, have you committed sacrilege against Tiny?"

Stein gave out some half-smothered inarticulate sounds.

"You deny it?" Tiny cried, giving him a backhand slap. "So you want to make me use force? Me who hates using force?"

Stein shook his head in protest.

Tiny spat at him and said gently, but ominously: "You have abused my confidence. Given me a terrible disappoint-ment. You've hurt my feelings deeply."

Stein looked completely crushed as he hung limp in Tiny's fists, feet off the floor.

"I won't say anything about pimps and guys who murder

whores," Tiny roared in indignation, "but to have to be together with someone who steals from his comrades, ugh!" He shook Stein so his head went flying back and forth. With a curse he let go his hold and spat after him. "As a punishment you have to steal three bottles of schnapps for me as soon as possible—but fast, fast, you crippled hero! My patience is short, and if it gives out, may Jesus Christ and all his saints show-you mercy, because I won't!" He picked up a pair of panties from the floor and sniffed at them. "They still smell of pig!"

"Shut your mouth," the little Legionnaire dismissed him and turned to Bauer, sitting lost-looking on his bed. "What have you figured out? Call the cops?"

"The cops?" Bauer jumped up. "You must be going crazy. What do you think I am? Do you think I'm a fink playing patsy with dirty cops?"

The Legionnaire nodded. "That's what I thought. But something has to be done. Any suggestion?"

Bauer shook his head helplessly.

"In that case, maybe you won't mind me telling you what to do?" the Legionnaire asked, and without waiting for an answer he pulled his long Russian battle knife out of his boot leg and pitched it to Bauer. "Use it right so we can get this over with as soon as possible."

Bauer held the long broad knife in his hand. His eyes wandered from the knife to the Legionnaire, who sat cross-legged on his bed smoking.

"Do you want me to kill George? You can't expect me to do a thing like that."

The Legionnaire looked at him in surprise. "Are you stupid or nuts, *mon camarade*? Do you want me to do it? Or Sven? Or Stein? Or maybe Tiny? You discovered the holsters. It's your business. But because you told us about it, it's partly our business, too. Therefore we insist that something must be done. You're right, you can't go to the cops. That's out of the question. The Police long ago violated their solidarity with us. We have to get along by ourselves. George must be made harmless. He shouldn't be loose. But we can't lock him up because we've no police. He has killed six women. Now, you might give an excuse and say that a lot of people get killed. True, but this is something different, and we knew the little nurse. She was a sort of comrade. When he killed her, George did something that can't be forgiven, because she was also his comrade. I'm sure you see we've got to do something."

Bauer closed his eyes. He had turned deathly pale. "I just

can't kill George! He hasn't harmed me, after all. What you expect me to do to him is murder. I may get caught and executed—by the man with the axe." He shivered at the thought.

The Legionnaire got up and slowly walked up to Bauer's bed, tore the knife out of Bauer's hand and slid it back into his boot. He snarled: "Cowardly bastard! If we did what was right you would be butchered!"

Bauer rocked from side to side. He was miserable. He shrank with shame before the utter contempt of the Legionnaire.

Tiny magnanimously offered to cut George's throat.

The Legionnaire turned his face toward him and looked at him for a long while in silence. Then he sat down on his bed again, looking probingly from Bauer to Tiny.

"*Milles diables!* Do you want to cut him down just for the pleasure of it, or why?"

Tiny simply laughed. "That filthy whore-killer is going to knock off anyway. So I think I might as well pack him off to heaven as someone else. What the hell is the difference?"

"Don't you think there's anything wrong at all in killing him?" the Legionnaire asked, glancing sideways up at Tiny, who stood in the middle of the room. He was assiduously trying to balance a glass of water on his forehead, as he had seen a juggler do it.

Tiny answered, the glass wobbling ominously on his forehead. "Nah, what wrong could there be in it? George is a shit. You said that yourself, Desert Rambler."

The Legionnaire rocked with laughter.

"*Monte la-dessus!* By Allah, you're a fine one!" Roaring with laughter he fell back on the bed again. "Because George is a shit you quite coolly cut his throat." He slowly raised himself. With scarlet face he looked at Tiny. "For the sake of future society I dearly hope you'll die a hero's death before this war is over."

He pulled a bottle of rotgut from under his mattress and guzzled down nearly half of it. He looked around him briefly before handing it to me, and I passed it on further. He said, as if talking to himself: "*Bon,* so you'd like to lay George out?"

"I have as good as told you so twice," Tiny bawled sullenly, hitting his glass. It wasn't responding as it should. He threatened Stein: "When are you going out to pinch some schnapps for Tiny, you rat?" He kicked at a pair of light-blue panties lying on the floor and jumped at Bauer: "How long will those ass holsters be lying around here, egging people on to whoring?"

Bauer began collecting the undies and stuffing them into George's rucksack. Then he meticulously laced it up and pushed it under the bed.

He glanced at the Legionnaire, who sat on his bed playing with three dice. He was continuously tossing them in the air and catching them again in his hand, now with the back of his hand, now with the palm.

"In God's name," Bauer whispered hoarsely, holding out his hand. "Give me that knife and I'll cut up George so bad that not even his own mother will recognize him!"

The Legionnaire looked up. A subtle smile played around the narrow, brutal mouth in the scarred face. Without a word he pulled the Siberian knife, sharp-edged on both sides, out of his boot and handed it to Bauer. Bauer's face was deathly pale as he took it and hid it under his pillow.

Amid uproarious laughter George and the other men entered the ward. In his hand George had a large cake. One of the nurses had given it to him. All the nurses loved the little twenty-one-year-old flak private who looked only sixteen.

"Give me a knife, someone, so I can cut the cake," he called.

An ugly smile spread across Bauer's face as he pulled the Siberian knife from under his pillow and gave it to George.

"Use it, pal. It is good both for cutting cake and for cutting up a whore!"

For a split second George stiffened. Then he laughed in his boyish way, took the knife and started cutting the cake.

"Is anyone going whoring with me?" Erich, a big engineer, called.

He accepted a piece of cake which George handed him. He gobbled it all up in a mouthful. Then he shadowboxed along the floor, knocking out his formidable opponents.

Tiny stood for a short while looking at him. The Legionnaire gave an imperceptible nod, and as Erich came close to Tiny, the latter gave him a crushing blow and commanded in a stentorian voice: "Don't waste your energy, you fake hero! Get your pennies together and buy beer for Tiny, or I'll show you some shadowboxing!"

With a howl Erich landed in the bed of Thomas Jensen from North Schleswig. Thomas got up and moved over to another bed. He never mixed himself up with anything. He was said to be a volunteer from 1939. Thomas himself neither confirmed nor denied it. The most he would say when asked was "Why?" But anyone could see that Thomas

Jensen was homesick. Volunteer or not, he'd had enough war. People even said he'd shot his arm to pieces himself and that he'd had a close shave escaping prosecution before a special court. When you wanted to find out something from him, he clammed up.

The Legionnaire had ordered Tiny to seek information from the Matron, who definitely knew everything about Thomas. But Tiny had managed to ruin this chance in the course of twenty seconds by saying coolly: "Emma, the Desert Rambler told me I should ask you about Thomas Jensen, you know, that ass from North Schleswig. Because, if he's a volunteer, there's a thrashing in store for him, but if he plugged himself with a Nagan, he damn well deserves a bottle of cognac. You should do it quietly, Emma, the Desert Rambler said, you understand, so they can't guess what we have in mind."

The Matron had looked at Tiny, long and thoughtfully. Then she nodded reassuringly. Tiny received his bottle of cognac, and then they went to bed.

Afterwards they came down to the ward together. The Matron walked up to the Legionnaire, who was lying asleep without a care in the world. She seized him by his chest, lifted him out of bed and hurled him to the floor with a crash.

"You Moroccan snake! Tempting Tiny to be a spy! You brute!" In her fury she kicked him. Then she turned around and left, but first she patted Tiny on the cheek. "My little darling, just trust me, Mother's going to look out for you!"

Tiny almost tied himself in knots with pleasure and blew kisses after her. When she had closed the door he trumpeted through the room: "Holy Moses, great God, how hot Tiny's balls are!"

The Legionnaire had got up and stood in front of Tiny, who looked affectionately at him in his big and stupid way.

"You're the biggest ass in the world. What the hell did you tell her?"

Tiny kicked the bed and smiled happily at the Legionnaire.

"I admit, Desert Rambler, it came out rotten. I know it. I got the words topsy-turvy. I get everything wrong when I'm in a hot spot."

The Legionnaire gave up. Shaking his head, he said: "By Allah, how true!"

"Aren't you coming with me to the bird cage, George, to pick up a sweetie?" Bauer turned to George, staring hard at the little flak soldier. "A twenty-year-old bunk athlete should be just the thing for you."

George laughed.

"No, that's not for me. I follow the watchword of Dr. Goebbels for young soldiers, to keep away from alcohol, tobacco and women."

Bauer. picked his teeth with the Siberian knife which George had handed back to him.

"Yes, that watchword is quite right. Women are a nuisance. You can catch syph from them, the whole works. It would be better to liquidate them all, don't you think?" He burst into a roar of laughter and made an eloquent gesture with the knife. "Cutting them up with a knife like this?" Again he broke into a roar of laughter.

George_had stopped eating his cake. He sat with open mouth, staring at the guffawing Bauer, who was swinging the Legionnaire's knife above his head.

"Why do you say all that?" he asked quietly.

"I just think broads are trash.. What do you think?"

"I don't understand you at all," George answered. "You never acted like this before."

He put the half-eaten cake on the table and walked around the room restlessly. He stopped in front of Bauer.

"I've nothing against women. Those I know are all good to me. My mother also was always good. I remember her coming to say good night to me before I went to sleep when I was a boy—how wonderful it was! Now she's dead. They burned her. Phosphorus splashed all over her, but now she's in heaven."

"God only knows where she is," came brutally from Bauer, who had stopped grinning. He squinted at the Legionnaire, who sat on his bed playing with three green dice as if outside it all. "You've never been in a cathouse playing pig?" Bauer asked, leaning slyly across the table.

Stein started whistling. He was nervous. Like the rest of us he felt that Bauer was going too far.

"No," came from George, like a scream. "I hate it. Don't you understand, I hate it. You are animals, repulsive animals, when you think about women, and when women want the same thing you do, they are a devil's trap."

Bauer fell back in horror when he saw how wildly George's eyes stared at him. There was a gleam of insanity in them.

George grabbed his hair and pulled as if wanting to tear it up by the roots. He flopped down on his bed and covered his face with his hands. Every fiber in his slight body was shaken with violent sobbing.

The room became quiet. We looked at the little soldier in amazement. Only five of us knew what was wrong.

Tiny got up, hitched up his trousers and wobbled over to George.

The Legionnaire jumped up like a panther, caught Tiny by the shoulder and said severely: "Come along, Tiny, we're going down to have some beer!"

Tiny smiled cheerily and asked in surprise: "Beer, on you?"

The Legionnaire nodded and pulled Tiny out of the room.

"Shouldn't I finish him up?" asked Tiny naively. He pointed over his shoulder at the sobbing George, who fortunately didn't catch on to anything.

Stein and I went with them.

When we came back a few hours later the excitement in the ward had subsided. George sat with the nurses, helping a student unrolling bandages. They had fun and their laughter could be heard from far away.

Bauer lay on his bed staring emptily at the ceiling. He looked at us out of the corner of his eye and muttered, "I'll do it tonight. It's necessary."

The Legionnaire nodded. "The earlier the better."

We sat down and started drinking. We did it quite openly, not caring that it was forbidden. Tiny walked up to the Matron.

It was very late, and we were quite drunk when the Matron suddenly walked in, out of uniform, wrapped only in a robe of verdigris green. She had never done a thing like that before.

Walking noiselessly, as if on padded paws, she bore straight down on Bauer, stretched out her hand, and whispered hoarsely: "Give it to me!"

Bauer looked at her in a fright. "What do you mean?"

She bent down close to him and whispered, in order not to wake those who were asleep. "You know well enough! Hand it over!"

Bauer got up and looked dumbly at her. "I swear I don't know what you mean!"

"You don't know? You should be glad I'm the one who came and not the head-hunters." She stuck her hand under his pillow, pulled out the battle knife and put it away under her robe. Then she sailed out of the room without looking at anybody.

The Legionnaire flared up. "That silly ass talked!"

"What the hell are we going to do?" Bauer asked, casting a frantic look about him.

"What's up?" someone asked in the darkness.

"What's that to you?" the Legionnaire dismissed him.

It was already late morning when Tiny came down. He was in an exalted mood and was making a lot of noise.

The Legionnaire and he whispered together. They went out to the toilet and continued their conversation there. When they came back, Tiny was almost sober. He was silent and slightly uneasy.

The Legionnaire threw himself on the bed and began smoking. He said nothing and acted as if he didn't hear our inquisitive whispers. We could almost feel his brain working.

Inspection, headed by the boss, *Oberstabsarzt* Dr. Mahler, went off as usual. The Matron looked officially strict. Not with the slightest glance did she reveal what had occurred during the night.

The new patient, an artilleryman with an amputated hand, grinned foolishly when Dr. Mahler asked him how he was.

"Fine, Herr Field-butcher, stinking fine! Been to the cathouse, had cognac. Report I'm damn fine! Dismissed, Field-butcher!"

All at once we came alive, expecting an eruption. But Dr. Mahler just looked at the artilleryman for a moment and patted him on the shoulder.

"It's nice you're so well, Fischer. If only all of us were."

The Legionnaire glanced at me and pointed a finger at his forehead.

As the last one to leave, the Matron turned around in the doorway and looked at the Legionnaire. Their glances sank deep in each other's eyes. Those two understood each other. The hardened soldier and the equally hardened army nurse. One of them lean and wiry, the other big and ample.

The door shut with a resolute bang.

George was rummaging in his rucksack. Looking up, he moved his eyes searchingly around the room. Again glanced into the rucksack. Then he seemed to make a decision. Quickly, he tied it up and shoved it far under the bed. He took a few quick turns between door and window. Suddenly he stopped, let out a loud cry and ran stumbling out of the room.

"What on earth got into him?" the Legionnaire asked Bauer, who lay on his bed sucking on a pickle.

"Haven't the slightest idea. He must've gone crazy."

"They'll turn around and crush you," bawled Leo Fischer, the artilleryman. He burst into an insane fit of laughter and cried: "They'll crush you slowly. They'll squash your bones.

Hurrah, comrades, forward! In battle we are never alone!
We are panzer-jägers, the stupidest swine on earth!" Again
insane laughter.

"Shut up!" roared the East Prussian, who'd had his abdomen riddled by a burst from a Russian tommy gun.

Leo looked archly at him, clicked his heels and whinnied
in treble: "Yes, Herr General, we'll shut up! I believe in the
Holy Trinity and victory! In Adolf's name, amen!"

The East Prussian raised himself on his elbow and looked
in surprise at Leo, who had by now started to whimper.

"He must be stark raving mad," he said.

The Legionnaire got up and nodded to Tiny, who followed
him like a shadow, just in case. They placed themselves in
front of Leo, who was weeping while standing severely at
attention.

"At ease, gunner," the Legionnaire commanded. As if he
were on the drill-ground, Leo put his foot forward and relaxed. He stared at the Legionnaire, yet he seemed to see
nothing.

"Go to sleep," the Legionnaire commanded, and Leo
hopped over to his bed like a crow, came to attention in
front of it, and called:

"Battery in position, fire! Excess crew take cover!" With
an enormous jump he landed in the bed. He rolled over on
his back, lay quiet as a mouse and stared up at the
ceiling.

"That beats everything," the East Prussian exclaimed.
"Christ, he's nuts!"

Shortly after dinner had been brought in, the door opened.
A large red-haired figure with a Tyrolean hat on the back of
his head pushed himself in, followed by a bull-like, dark-
skinned fellow in a filthy gray felt hat pushed over his forehead as if too large for him.

"Heil!" saluted the red-haired fellow.

Fifteen men looked up from the nettle soup with interest.
The East Prussian answered modestly: "Shove it up your
ass!"

The red-haired fellow grinned: "Drop in to see me some
day, you future hero, and I'll stoke up under your balls till
you can boil eggs on them!"

"Are you from the Winter Collection?" Tiny asked, peering
inquisitively at the two civilians.

Red roared with laughter.

"Winter Collection? That's a good one! Nah, small fry. We
do come from a collection, but that isn't it!" Doubled up

with laughter, he slapped the shoulder of the dark-skinned fellow, who maintained an air of uncanny seriousness.

The Legionnaire watched them attentively. Squinting, he asked: "Police?"

Red nodded.

"Righto. You hit the nail on the head. We are Kripo joes. You haven't seen any such before, have you? Which of you tired heroes is George Freytag? Flak gunner George Freytag of the 76th Flak Regiment?"

We looked at George, who was sitting at the table. He was pale as a sheet.

The red-haired policeman puffed himself up in front of him.

"Well, my angel, are you flak gunner George Freytag?"

George opened and shut his mouth without getting out a word.

Red bent forward, smiling. "Lost your voice, you little rabbit? Lost it from fright because Uncle comes to visit you from Kripo? Maybe we have a nice message about a big inheritance from a lady who just conked out. With a good conscience there's no need to be scared of Uncle from Kripo."

Trembling as if seized with a convulsion, George remained speechless.

There was an ominous silence in the ward. Then the basso boomed again: "So you refuse to chat with Uncle? What a shame. Do you mind if we take a look at your baggage to check if you're the heir we're looking for?"

Without waiting for an answer he bent down and pulled out George's rucksack.

"No," George screamed. "You can't touch that. It's mine."

Red laughed, as if he didn't hear the screaming protest.

The dark-skinned fellow stood like a rock behind George, keeping a watchful eye on him.

Red began rummaging in the rucksack. His black leather coat opened, showing a light brown leather belt by which his shoulder holster was held in place under his armpit. You could sense the heavy .38.

George stared hypnotically at Red as he brutally pulled the neatly folded military underwear out of the rucksack. A can of marmalade rolled along the floor, followed by a fluttering picture of a gray-haired lady.

"Mother," George screamed frantically, following the photo with his eyes.

A couple of schoolbooks were thrown to the floor. A Bible

followed. A knife in a sheath appeared. The sort of knife Finnish soldiers always carry in their belt.

Red slowly pulled the knife out of the reindeer sheath and looked briefly at the shining steel with the deep blood track.

"It's yours, isn't it, my little friend?" He slipped it into the pocket of his black leather coat.

Then, between two fingers, the Kripo cop held up a pair of white undies for our inspection. A blue pair followed. Again a white pair. All in all, six pairs.

He stood up, nodded to George. All his friendliness seemed blown away. It was the bloodhound that barked: "The comedy's finished! You're the one who murdered the girls! Denying it will only make it worse for you. So come along!" He nodded towards the door. Both he and the dark fellow caught George by the shoulder.

"Leave me alone! I'm sick. I have fever!" George screamed desperately. He tried to kick the two large men.

"Take it easy," the dark fellow said. These were the first words he had uttered.

Far down the stairs we could hear George cry: "Leave me alone, leave me alone! I have fever!"

When the car halted at the Reeperbahn shortly afterward, George succeeded in tearing himself loose from his guards. He rushed along Glacis Chaussee and jumped over the fence to the sports ground.

The two policemen followed close on his heels.

"Halt!" they roared. Three times they called "Halt!" as demanded by regulations. Then there was a crack of volleys behind George. It was like a fleeting kiss. The bullets from the two machine guns swept him into the air and made him hover there for a moment as if on an air cushion, then flung him brutally to the ground again.

He scratched the black earth with crooked fingers and stammered unintelligibly.

Red turned him over with the toe of his boot. "Our job is done," he decided tersely. "He's kicked off. Let's hurry off to Pretty Paul with the body."

With the dark fellow at the wheel they drove to Police Headquarters.

"Aren't we lucky, the two of us!" Red grinned. "No front command for us!"

"The man I could get to love hasn't been born," Aunt
Dora said.

"Love for the individual is barbarism," the Legionnaire
said.

But they said this before they met each other.

*They had become children, dreaming about a paradise
with seven bar stools and a conch curtain.*

*Aunt Dora wanted the Legionnaire to desert, but he was
too old and foxy to attempt such a naive act of madness.*

*The train drove off. They separated, the same way as so
many others.*

The war went on more savagely than ever.

The war was running out of control.

chapter xi

The Leave Train

THE DEPOT officer, a captain, looked at our papers and said
curtly: "The leave train Berlin-Warsaw-Lemberg on Platform
4."

"It's all up," the Legionnaire sighed.

The captain glanced at him and said with a jeer, "I see you
can say what Caesar said when he crossed the Rubicon!"

The Legionnaire grinned. *"Alea iacta est!"*

The captain looked in surprise at the little scarred panzer
soldier. "Are you a student, Corporal?"

"No, a holy swine, 2nd Foreign Regiment," the Legionnaire
grinned. He enjoyed seeing the captain's amazement.

"Perhaps you don't know what it means?" the captain
asked.

"Oh, yes," the Legionnaire answered caustically. "In soldier's language: Sophie has had it!"

The captain flushed and waved us off.

Further down the platform Tiny asked: "What sort of
foreign stuff did you serve up to that silver pheasant?"

177

"Just what you heard. Sophie has had it!"

Tiny stopped and burst into a roar of laughter: "You'll have to teach me that! I'll use it on First Sergeant Edel when we're back with the gang. Christ, that'll make him gape, the stupid pig!" He shoved back his cap, uttered another howl and stormed forward on the platform.

He had caught sight of the Battleship, who surprised everybody by coming to say good-bye to him. They clashed like a pair of army elephants.

A crowd of soldiers milled around beside the train, which was standing by the platform like an insatiable serpent.

I glanced at the large depot clock. The second hand was rushing across the dial. Black and menacing. Round and round. Minute after minute. Soon it would be over.

The East Prussian and Thomas Jensen slouched slowly through the platform control, dragging heavy infantry packs.

Stein and Bauer hung out of a compartment window shouting they had five seats. They received our equipment through the window.

A Red Cross sister asked if we'd like some coffee.

Drinking from a common metal cup, we finished off the hot liquid which was supposed to be coffee, but which tasted more like soup boiled on a jute sack.

"Everybody on board!" the transport officer roared for the fourth time. But no one reacted.

A couple of soldiers were brutally shoved into the train.

Tiny hit out at an MP noncom. "Scram, head-hunter!" he shouted.

The NCO grumbled and uttered all sorts of threats, but beat it quickly. He didn't want a row on a leave train. He knew from bitter experience that the most fantastic trouble might arise. At such train departures nerves were on edge.

A woman's voice called: "Alfred!"

The Legionnaire whirled around and walked rapidly up to one of the kiosks, where Aunt Dora stood half hidden with her collar turned up around her ears.

Putting her hand on the little Legionnaire's shoulder, she said gently: "I have brought civvies with me. Hurry to a toilet and change. Get away from them!"

The Legionnaire squinted at her.

"Dora, old bitch, let's not do anything foolish! You know the head-hunters as well as I do. Not one in a thousand gets away safely, and if they catch me with you, you'll go straight to jail."

"I'm not afraid of their jails."

"Nah, but of their bullets." He pulled a newspaper clipping

out of his pocket. The latest news from *Völkischer Beob-achter.*

She moved her lips while she read:

WARNING AGAINST DESERTERS AND COWARDS

I called upon the German people and German women in particular to be on the lookout for cowards trying to escape from east to west by hiding in refugee columns. Show no misplaced pity for these dirty dogs. Men who run away from their detachments in the Army, Air Force and Navy do not even deserve a piece of dry bread.

On you more than anybody else, proud National-Socialist German women, rests the sacred duty of being on guard against these elements.

Do your duty. Do not let yourselves be persuaded or affected by anti-social elements. Denounce ruthlessly, and on the slightest suspicion. Have no pity, whether they are strangers or your own husbands, brothers, or sons.

Show them the contempt they deserve. Make them once more recognize their duty. If words fail to bring them around, have them picked up by the Military Police, which knows how to punish these miserable rats who do not know what honor is and for whom there is no room in our National-Socialist Greater Germany.

> *Heinrich Himmler*
> SS *Reichsführer*
> Chief of Police
> Minister of the Interior
> Commander-in-Chief of the Replacement Army

Aunt Dora nodded.

"A rotten bastard, but just wait. The balls of that black shit will boil some day, believe me!"

"So will ours probably," the Legionnaire answered dryly. "If we lose our heads. Our only chance of surviving this madness is to fall into line. Quietly, without any fuss. Hold back wherever you can get away with it." He passed his hand under her chin and went on. "And take care to have valid papers in your pocket, or they won't be proof against the meticulous scrutiny of the head-hunters!" He pointed at an MP sergeant who looked like a hippopotamus. "Look at that fellow with his crescent-shaped badge! He's dying to nab deserters and string 'em up with a piece of cardboard on their chests. Listen, old girl—but you're crying! What's this? Aunt Dora doesn't cry!" Clumsily he wiped away the tears from her heavily made-up cheeks.

"You're a stupid pig," she sobbed and hid her face on his shoulder. "I'm going to write to you, Alfred, every week." She stroked his cheek with its long knife scar.

She looked at the train, which was hissing out steam in white clouds, thinking: It's like an insatiable grinding machine asking to be fed with flesh, blood and bones.

She looked up at him: "Where are you heading for, you think?"

He looked toward the bridge at a couple of rattling trolleys before he answered.

"The Old Man wrote in his last letter that the Regiment is now standing in the vicinity of Orsha in the central sector. Orsha is a junction of the highway Minsk-Tula-Moscow. Well, actually it leads all the way to Siberia," he added, "ending in Kolyma, where our comrades from Stalingrad are now slaving in the mines."

Orsha, she thought. A name. An unknown name. A dot on the large maps. A filthy and infinitely sad spot in the immensity of Russia. A place through which thousands of soldiers are marching. Men dressed in green and brown, most of whom never return. She stroked his hand, destined by evil fate to press the trigger of a machine gun and cause death and destruction to other soldiers. She could teach those hands to shake a mixer.

"Alfred," she whispered, looking into his ugly, scarred face. Her unfeeling eyes were blinded by tears. "But don't you understand, you stupid pig, that I love you, you stinking desert jackal. I swear to God, I love you! Why, I don't know myself. I was raped by some man when I was twelve. When I was fifteen I liked it. Now it doesn't interest me any more. We'll love each other as two people who know enough to see our fellow men as swine till the opposite is proven. We know that life is one long rotten carnival night and the only requirement is that you have on a good mask. Alfred, I'll wait for you even if it takes thirty years! One of these days we'll wake up from this bad dream. Then we'll sell the saloon and slip off where we can run a decent place with girls, schnapps and beer!"

The Legionnaire laughed. "And where would that be? In Tibet, perhaps?"

She shook her head. "No, in Brazil. I have a sister there

who runs a regular brothel. There's the right soil for us two. No head-hunters. No Stapo. You have the right to breathe as you like."

Sister Lotte, a little nurse who'd been to the Führer school of the League of German Maidens, came dancing along the platform and fastened a spruce branch to the door of one of the cars. She had seen this done in a war movie. She wiped her eyes with the corner of her handkerchief. She had also seen this in a war movie. Then she kissed the nearest soldier on the cheek. Flinging her head back like a Valkyrie, she cried in near ecstasy: "My hero, my unknown hero! I thank you for fighting for us German women and for making us feel safe from those Soviet monsters!"

The soldier, an infantryman with a foxy face, glanced at her, farted loudly and yelled: "Go to hell, you officer's bed-warmer!"

Lotte's cheeks flushed. "You swine!" she hissed. "I'll see you get a trip east."

The retort was a loud roar of laughter from the soldiers nearby. The infantryman smacked her behind.

"Hurry home and make yourself ready for the victors. They're on the way!"

Gnashing her teeth Lotte retreated. She tore the spruce branch from the car door and placed it three cars further down where she thought they were more worthy of receiving her branch. She said something to an MP sergeant, who just shrugged his shoulders and pushed her aside.

A whole family had showed up to take leave of a seventeen-year-old boy who'd been drafted and was going to a training battalion in Poland.

"Be proud and brave," cried his father, who turned out to be a *Regierungsrat*. "You have to be a credit to your family!"

"We'll be looking forward to a letter from you soon, nephew," whinnied an old white-haired man wearing the phantom uniform of a colonel from the time before World War I, "in which you'll inform us that the Führer has awarded you the Iron Cross."

"Send us a picture of yourself in uniform as soon as possible," his mother squeaked, whisking away a traitorous tear.

The father looked reprovingly at her through his monocle. "German women don't cry, Louise! We Germans are proud."

A minister with a stiff white collar and a ridiculous derby hat on his head put his arms around the mother's shoulders and said unctuously: "How wonderful it must be to be able to send a son to the battlefield to fight our barbarous enemies who threaten to overrun our Fatherland!"

A member of the family in a brown uniform looked at him. "What do you mean by saying that our enemies are about to overrun our Fatherland? Hasn't the Führer explained that the strongly winding front lines have to be straightened out?"

Making sure the Party man didn't overhear, an NCO in the compartment window beside them muttered: "We'll be straightening out the front lines till we stand with our backs against the Chancellery of the Reich in Berlin."

The minister nervously blinked his eyes. He passed a finger along his starched collar. His Adam's apple bobbed up and down. He looked ingratiatingly at the Party man.

"The District Leader probably misunderstood me. I mean that our enemies are overrunning the Ukraine, which according to the Führer's words also is our Fatherland."

"Where and when did the Führer say that?"

The minister looked at him. "The Führer has said many times and also the Minister of Propaganda has often written in *Völkischer Beobachter* that the Greater German Reich is going to extend to the mountains of the Caucasus, and that's where our enemies are at the moment."

The District Leader glanced passingly at the minister, who had put his head to one side and folded his hands on his stomach.

"In that case it might be a good idea if you, Herr Vicar, were to take a trip east. Then you could help our heroes chase our enemies clear out of the Greater German Reich." The Party man beamed with joy as he saw the minister collapse in fear.

A gray figure moved along the train in an almost stealthy manner.

Bauer neighed with enthusiasm when he saw who it was. Ewald, Aunt Dora's pimp, in fatigues. Two days ago, as so many times before, he had again stepped through the little gray door leading up to Gestapo Headquarters on Karl Muck Platz. After a long wait, he was taken to Bielert's office by an SS man in black uniform.

Bielert received him sitting on the edge of a table and accepted the closely written pages Ewald, as usual, delivered to him.

Bielert tapped the papers. "How much of all this is lies and fabrications?"

"Nothing, *Herr Brigadenführer*, everything is true!"

"*Herr*, you may skip. Here with us it's only *Brigadenführer*. Remember that, you rat," Bielert snarled.

Bielert scolded, threatened, roared, and still Ewald didn't understand a word.

Finally Bielert pulled out a piece of white paper. A red line had been drawn straight across it. He thrust the paper under Ewald's nose.

"Here I have your induction papers to a penal field regiment. You were once a soldier for six whole weeks, weren't you?"

"Certainly, *Brigadenführer*," Ewald trumpeted and clicked his heels as he'd once been taught to on the drill-ground at Grafenwöhr. Just the thought sent shivers up and down his spine. Better jail than the infantry barracks, he'd said then. How happy he'd been when it came out that he'd served jail sentences for "gainful crimes." During the Ragnarok of mobilization he'd been inducted through clerical error, an error "which the Wehrmacht deeply deplored." He was speedily dispatched from the Army and lived in a whirl of pleasures in Hamburg's underworld. But now they weren't so fastidious any longer.

Now, anything could be used at the front, even guys like Ewald. There was a whole army of penal regiments to receive paltry bandits like him.

Bending toward him, Bielert whispered: "But, my little friend, there is another possibility!"

Ewald's face lit up with hope. He already felt safe from the most terrible thing that could happen to him. He had bought exemption from jail by becoming a stool pigeon. A respectable number of people had found themselves squirming in Gestapo's net thanks to Ewald's reports. Actually, Paul Bielert could thank Ewald that he'd become *Brigadenführer*, because quite unawares Ewald had gotten on the track of something really big.

"I'll do anything you request, *Brigadenführer*," Ewald stammered, giving Bielert a fawning look.

Bielert put up a gloating grin. "I'm not requesting anything from you. You've the choice between two alternatives: induction in a penal battalion or being hauled before a court-martial as an anti-social element!"

Ewald caught his breath. "Court-martial!" he groaned. "But how can I be brought up before a court-martial? I haven't done anything. I never got mixed up with politics."

"Really?" Bielert answered, pointing at the papers lying on his writing desk. "Maybe all that has only to do with butter and coffee coupons? Nah, my fine friend, you're stuck to your neck in political filth." He turned to the door and roared: "Geige, Potz!"

Two big men in the black uniform of the SS edged into the room.

"Get that thing court-martialed," Bielert hissed and pointed

at Ewald, who stood chattering his teeth in the middle of the
floor, swaying as if about to fall.

The two big SS men went over to Ewald, caught his arm
and said with chilly joviality: "Come along then, little one."

"No, no," Ewald cried, "you can't do that to me, *Brigadenführer*. I've always been good and done exactly what you
asked. I'll do anything you want!"

Bielert laughed.

"I don't want you to do anything at all, you skunk. I just
never again want to have the pleasure of seeing your bastard
face."

Ewald screamed like one possessed. He who had never had
pity for others now had dropped into the fire himself. He had
been foolish enough to mention Aunt Dora's name in the
previous report, and Bielert was Aunt Dora's bodyguard.

"Well, get a uniform for him, and off he goes with the next
transport."

That's why Ewald was now sneaking alongside the train in
a uniform without shoulder straps and collar insignia.
Bielert hadn't been content only with sending him to a penal
regiment; he had sent him to Penal Field Training Battalion
No. 919, Brest-Litovsk.

If Ewald had suspected what he was in for he would
probably have slipped away right there and gone under cover
in Hamburg as a deserter. He would have better chances of
escaping unhurt as a deserter than as a member of the most
notorious unit in the German Armed Forces. In this battalion
the new arrivals were always welcomed by Staff Sergeant
Neuring, who would say:

"You probably think you have a chance of saving your
skin here in No. 919, but you're mistaken. At 11:55 you
are all going to be shot in the nape of the neck according to
regulations."

The MPs were running alongside the train with their tin
badges flashing on their breasts. They were shouting at and
threatening the many soldiers who just couldn't be driven into
the train.

The little Legionnaire put his arms around Aunt Dora
and pressed her to him. "*Bon*, I have to board the train now,
Dora. This war will never end happily unless Corporal Alfred
Kalb of the 2nd Foreign Regiment is there. What if Hitler
should win! That would be no good for the two of us."

Aunt Dora pressed up against him. Her big bosom covered
his narrow chest. Her lips found his. She held him caught in
her grip as if she would never let him go.

"Alfred," she whispered. "You will come back!" It wasn't

a question. It was a prayer. A cry, almost a command to God.
The Legionnaire mustn't die, fall for a foolish cause.

He nodded and forced a faint smile. "I'll come, Dora. By
Allah, I'll come back! The lousy Ivans won't be able to bring
down a French corporal from *La Légion Etrangère*. Kabyles
are wanted for that."

"Alfred, you must write to me! Every free minute you must
write! I'll go nuts if I don't hear from you!" She flung her
arms about his neck and kissed him so savagely that she
even got frightened herself. She felt as if an era was about
to be annihilated.

She cried. Tears flowed down her cheeks and made deep
furrows in the heavy layer of powder.

"All aboard!" the MPs roared. "The train is leaving. The
doors will be locked. Marching orders and leave papers are to
be held in readiness on boarding the train! On the double!
On the double!"

The Legionnaire slowly stepped on the train. In the door
he stopped.

Aunt Dora passed her hand over his scarred, haggard face.
"Good-bye, girl," he said hoarsely.

She curled up her lips to a forced smile. "No, my Moroccan, not good-bye. *Au revoir!*"

He laughed. "True, *au revoir*. I'll see you soon!"

Tiny hurled his pack through an open window. Then
followed his cardboard box with three black puddings, one
loaf of rye bread and a couple of bottles of schnapps.

"Watch out, you soft macaroni sticks," he called. "Here
comes strong ammunition for the crapper."

Then he rushed again into the arms of the Battleship, who
lifted him off the ground and kissed him.

"Take care of yourself, you big bear, so I can get back the
stumps of you," she growled in a deep basso. "Then we can
get married and have twenty-three kids just as ugly as you."

"Hell," Tiny laughed, "that's going to be the best job of
my life! Christ, how I look forward to losing the war!
Twenty-three snot-nosed kids, holy Jesus! We'll make the
first one in a haystack," he shouted cheerfully. "I always
wanted to sprawl in a haystack. Do you like the smell of hay?"

"Pig," she said in her mannish voice. "Can you imagine
begetting our children in cow-feed? A thing like that is
done in a bed with clean white sheets and not in a cow barn
or out in the field." She gave him a ringing smack on the
cheek. "Believe me, I'll grind off your rough edges for you,
you gutterpup!"

"I think I'll be getting the blind staggers pretty soon. I'm steaming hot," Tiny grinned happily. "I'm hot as hell for you. You're just as good as the best one of those sex machines you can take a crack at in Wienert Neustadt. And that, you know, is quite an efficient machine, with her whole chassis running on self-lubricating ball bearings!" He brightened up as if a great idea had occurred to him. "Emma, when the war's over we'll go to a whorehouse together—then you can see for yourself you're just as good as the pigs there."

"You swine," the Battleship snarled, hitting him in the stomach to make him gasp for breath. "You shouldn't even think of comparing me, your fiancée, with whores and such trash. I'm a decent woman and no whorehouse bitch, remember that! Or I'll settle your hash for you!"

Tiny put his head to one side. He looked like a little boy. "You'll have to forgive me for that one. I'm no fine gentleman, you know."

"All right, all right, you bear. Now, please, don't make me blubber!"

An MP sergeant major came rushing toward them. He yelled at Tiny: "Get into the train, you lazy ox-gut!"

Tiny didn't bother looking at him but kissed the Battleship with a loud smack.

The sergeant rushed on. Tiny took no notice of him and remained standing by the Battleship.

"Listen, keep a sharp lookout when Tommy unloads his dung-cart," Tiny admonished. "Don't get curious now and stick out your big mug!"

She smiled. Her eyes vanished completely in folds of fat.

"The same goes for you!" She stroked him fondly on the cheek, which was blackened with soot. "My lovely bear," she whispered, "you're stupid as an ox, God knows, but how wonderful! Don't you get any misplaced ideas of comradeship out there. I want you back. A leg blown off wouldn't matter so much as long as you're alive." She thought for a moment and went on: "In fact, it might not be a bad idea at all if you lost a leg. I could manage you better."

"Emma, are you crazy? Then I couldn't run when Ivan gets up steam. Porta himself says that he who can run the fastest has the best chance of getting through this war alive."

The MP came back. He stood splay-legged before Tiny, both fists on his hips.

"Just tell me this, you Corporal Nil. Do we have to give you a written invitation before you board that train?"

Tiny didn't turn around but answered coolly: "Please, do that, brother, but write slowly and slip the letter into one of those mailboxes that get emptied only once a week!"

"Shut up, you ... you ..." the sergeant screamed, "or I'll take care of you! Into the train, you filthy bastard, and right this minute!" He seized Tiny and pushed him into the train.

"In two weeks I'll be back with you," Tiny yelled out of the window to the Battleship. "Engagement leave, wedding leave—I'll apply for all the leaves there are!"

When the train took off, he was on the point of falling out of the window. At the last moment his buddies in the compartment managed to pull him in.

"Make way," he bellowed, rushed to the window and leaned far out. His head hit against an iron pillar as the train passed. Blood poured down his face from the big gash. "Hurrah! I have a skull fracture! Behave yourself now, Emma, till I'll be home with you again! I'll be coming soon," he added, pointing at his head.

"Naturally!" She was running alongside the train on her heavy legs, which were moving like drumsticks. With one hand she held her skirts above her massive knees. With the other she waved her red nurse's cape. Her bosom sloshed over. Her face glowed. "Come back, Teddy Bear, do you hear? Come back to me!"

Aunt Dora stood by the kiosk some distance back on the platform. She was waving to the little Legionnaire who hung out through an open door.

A woman of about fifty had a three-year-old child on her arm. She fell and the tiny tot rolled screaming along the asphalt.

A soldier in the light gray uniform of the Marines let out a terrified scream.

The long train rolled faster and faster between the many ruins of Hamburg, carrying three thousand eight hundred pieces of uniformed beef cattle in the direction of Berlin.

An MP making his way through the corridors roared: "Shut the windows! Fire will open up on anyone who stays by an open window!"

"Dungbeetle," snorted an artillery NCO lying on a luggage rack drinking.

In another compartment they started singing:

> Come back, I am waiting for you.
> I am waiting for you.
> For you are to me
> All my comfort.

Behind on the platform stood hundreds of sweethearts, parents, wives, and children. They were looking at the spot

where the train had vanished from sight' and where the
clouds of smoke from the locomotive merged with the rain
clouds.

Most of them were never to see each other again.

Aunt Dora stood alone by the kiosk, face chalk-white, eyes
staring. Her lips moved.

"Come back, Alfred. For God's sake come back to me!
It doesn't matter in what shape, even on crutches, but do
come!"

The Battleship stood all the way at the end of the platform. She was still waving mechanically with her large red
shawl. Her lungs worked like a pair of bellows. She wheezily
gasped for breath after the violent and unaccustomed exertion.

"Big stupid Teddy Bear," she whispered. "Don't you get
stuck out there!"

Then the hardened woman did something you'd never have
believed her capable of. She prayed. Folded her hands and
prayed. Right in the middle of a dusty railroad platform,
under the broken glass roofs.

"Dear God. You don't often hear anything from Emma
Kloters, but now I'm here, you see. Let my big, stupid cub
come back home to me. I don't mind if you make a ham-
burger out of him as long as he is alive! I pray you, God,
with all my heart, let my big, stupid, ugly cub come home
alive!"

It had started raining. A dense drizzle. The platform slowly
emptied. Sirens began wailing. People started running. Far
away the first bombs were falling.

At the entrance to the platform a young girl was standing,
as if petrified. She was biting her handkerchief, tearing the
material to pieces with her teeth.

"Otto," she whispered hoarsely. "Oh, no, Otto!" Suddenly
she set up a piercing scream: "Otto, don't let them murder
you!" She pulled her hair frantically. "Hitler, you murderer,"
she shrieked, loud enough to echo along the platform.
"You're a murderer, Hitler!"

As if conjured up, a couple of young civilians in black
leather coats stood beside her. A silver badge glittered in the
hand of one of them. Those who were closest heard him hiss:
"Stapo!"

She resisted frantically and continued screaming as she was
hauled away. She vanished into the mysterious darkness of
the Police Station.

Otto, an infantry Pfc, sat in the departed leave train, whis-

pering: "My own Lotte, we'll soon see each other again!" To
a buddy he said: "My wife's going to have a child."

But his Lotte was never to give birth. She had spoken the
truth in a country where truth was dead.

The train rumbled through Germany. It halted shortly at
an overcrowded depot. New droves of tired soldiers boarded
the train. They clambered over suitcases, rucksacks, haver-
sacks, knapsacks, gas masks, rifles, tommy guns, steel helmets, rolled-up coats, and cursing soldiers in gray, green,
blue, black and brown. All services. Sixteen- to twenty-
year-old seamen in dark blue with U-boat badges on their
sleeves. Fanatic SS men in field gray with vacant, glassy-
eyed Teutonic expressions—they were educated in the so-
called Order Castles, to the abysmal intellectual impoverish-
ment of the dictatorship. Oldish policemen in uniforms of
poisonous green on their way to an MP division. They were
to be slaughtered by the enemy's savage partisan units lying
in wait for them like hungry beasts of prey.

There were black tank gunners, their filthy uniforms giving
off a stench of gasoline and diesel oil. Broad peasant-like
cavalrymen with loud yellow shoulder straps. Sedate mountain
chasseurs with a tin edelweiss on their sleeves. Artillerymen
with sparse decorations on the grayish-green breasts of their
uniforms. Engineers with faces as sad as their black shoulder
straps, dead tired from endless toil. Stout and contented naval
gunners happy to belong to the guard units on a stretch of
coast far behind the front. Intelligence soldiers with bright
faces who generously sprinkled their speech with foreign
words to show they were proficient in languages. But the
majority were infantrymen in tattered uniforms, a living
loud protest against the designation "the queen of all the
services."

In every nook there was card-playing or drinking. One
group of men was having a whispered confab as they huddled around an MC noncom.

"Jaundice is crap," he told the listening soldiers, "with
that, it won't last long till you're out of the rest-home again.
Syph or the clap isn't any good, either. Holy Mother, they
practically cut off your tail if you turn up with something
like that." He cautiously looked about him, but seeing no
dangerous-looking persons nosing around he ducked into the
group again. The conversation became a muttered whisper.

"No, fellows, typhoid, real first-class typhoid, that's the
stuff. A temperature that almost splits your asshole. When
you're about half dead, they just can't resist any more. They
stroke your hair and pat you like a little boy. They're so

kind to you you think it's all a dream, because they're certain you're going to pop off. And it's a long sickness."

"How do you get typhoid?" a short thin infantryman wanted to know.

"In the dairy, you baby ass," an engineer Pfc grinned.

The little infantryman looked offended.

A number of small packages changed owners. The MC noncom put away big bundles of bills in his pockets. He smiled mysteriously and again looked around.

"You just take the stuff in those packages and dissolve it in coffee, and on top of it you take a nice swig of vodka. After two weeks the latest you'll be farting in a lovely bed, and the war will be over for half a year at least."

"Can you die from it?" a cavalryman asked suspiciously.

"Have you ever gotten something without taking a risk, you horse's ass?" asked an airman in an elegant gray-blue uniform with his breast studded with decorations. He was at most twenty years old, but the war in the clouds had aged him ten years. It looked as if Herman Göring's aerial Teutons had had enough of heroic battle.

We passed through Berlin in the dark of night. An air-raid alarm was on.

On the overcrowded train there was a fight to get to the toilets. Cursing remarks flew back and forth in the heavy fetid air.

In a compartment in the middle of the car the little Legionnaire sat squeezed between Tiny and me. On the opposite seat Ewald, pale as a sheet, was reduced to invisibility between Bauer and Stein.

The East Prussian hung on a rack telling jokes.

"What's the news from the Führer?" Bauer called to the little East Prussian, who was an expert at imitating voices.

"Yes, let's hear what the Führer has to say about the momentary situation," Stein expectantly grinned.

The East Prussian put his gas mask up to his mouth for a microphone, pulled the hair down over his forehead, and thrust out his lower lip. He looked like a horrible caricature of Hitler, but his voice was an amazingly skillful imitation.

"German women, German men, German children, my dear racial brothers! We have never been closer to final victory than we are right now. I have given my Army commanders orders to straighten out our strongly winding front lines, which made our operations difficult and demanded too great sacrifices, so that now our operations can proceed everywhere as planned! Many enemies of the people and pernicious elements have claimed that these adjustments of the front are a kind of retreat. But I tell you, my dear racial brothers, that my heroic soldiers will remain where they have taken their stand. The Soviet masses are bleeding to death. Stalin, that arch-criminal"—here the voice of the East Prussian rose to a roar of rage that would have made Hitler turn pale with envy—"has lost all chances for winning this war which he forced upon us. My German engineers are working at high pressure to design new weapons, miraculous and epoch-making, for crushing our barbarous enemies. German men, German women, my brave Army, my heroic Air Force, my proficient Navy—one more tiny exertion and final victory will be ours! Rest assured that a hero's death will be yours!"

As he wanted to raise his arm for *"Heil,"* he rolled out of the rack and landed on top of those who were sitting underneath. Then he rolled onto the floor.

"The Führer has fallen!" Bauer called.

Tiny rolled a cigarette for himself. He did it very painstakingly, taking extreme care not to lose the minutest speck of tobacco. He wetted it, closed it and handed it to the Legionnaire. He rolled another which he handed to me. Only then did he start rolling one for himself. Before he'd finished he discovered that mine didn't quite stick together in the gluing. He cautiously put away his own half-finished cigarette, picked up mine, licked it and pinched it firmly together.

"Now it's better," he said, handing it to me again.

During the four months' stay in the army hospital Tiny had collected every single butt, not only his own but also others'. He had cleaned the tobacco conscientiously and was now the owner of a large bag of it. He would go on preserving the butts from the cigarettes he was now smoking and so on, forever, so that every grain of tobacco would be utilized. His poverty in the past had taught him never to waste anything. Everything can be used. Everything can become new.

"Do you think they'll give me leave if I get spliced with Emma?" he asked, passing his tongue along the adhesive edge of the cigarette paper.

The Legionnaire laughed. "Decidedly, no! When you ask, First Sergeant Edel will answer: 'Tiny, you're a notorious fool. Fools shouldn't get married, and why should you turn the sweet girl into a war widow?' "

"Oh, shut up," Tiny said. "Emma isn't a sweet girl. She's an armored car in the shape of a woman and could give Edel such a slap on his snout that he wouldn't wake up."

The Legionnaire went on: "And Edel will tell you this besides when you apply for leave: 'Tiny, hurry up and get yourself shot. A hero's death is your only hope. Because, after the war you're going to be sent to a liquidation camp anyway, as a danger to the national health.'"

We grimaced at the thought of the familiar tone we would have to put up with soon again.

"First Sergeant Edel can kiss my ass," Tiny muttered peevishly.

"He definitely won't do that," the Legionnaire laughed.

Soon after, in the middle of a conversation about politics, Tiny said: "Actually, I don't understand very much about it."

"We can believe that quite easily," Bauer laughed.

With a meditative expression in his face Tiny went on. "After all I'm only a swine from a reform school. My mother didn't care a damn about us nine children. And I only remember my old man when he was drunk. I never saw him sober. In reform school they thrashed us, and if they didn't, we thrashed each other. Does anyone of you know what a holy reform school is like?"

When no one answered, he went on, all the while sketching imaginary patterns with his rifle butt.

"Nah, that's just what I thought. Look, these mission people are real devils when they get power. We really had no school. You won't have any use for that anyway, the principal said. Many years ago he'd been a pastor in Thüringen. He was said to have run around with the organ-pounder's wife. Because of that he was thrown out of his Thüringen church. And it's true, we didn't really need to know how to read and write to haul iron girders or dig ditches. So that when I became a member of our club, I said to myself"—he looked about him—"Don't forget you're in active service, you're not a reservist. Those who hold the stick must be right."

"And so I marched off, clean to the horizon. A good many tried to checkmate Tiny. But even a hundred push-ups didn't put Tiny out of breath—before I got tired, the shits who commanded lost their voices. They told me to shoot well. An order is an order: I shot well and got a rifle ribbon. Then we went to war and they told me: Tiny, everything that moves in front of your muzzle is an enemy and you should shoot at it. Fine! I blazed away with my rod. They told me: Your bayonet, Tiny, is to stab with. And, believe me, I've cut and stabbed on every side. They told me: You go to war to defend the Fatherland. ..

"For twenty seconds I asked myself why I really should de-

fend the Fatherland, because it has never done anything for
me. But, then, they weren't fighting the war for my sake.
So I began defending the Fatherland. You're fighting against
a ruthless enemy, against subhumans, they told us. All right,
I said to myself, you're fighting against a ruthless enemy,
against subhumans. Those up there ought to know. They've
more on the ball than you, Tiny. Not a single one of them
has been to reform school, not one has dug ditches. They've
gone to a fine school and have learned to eat nicely with a
knife and fork. They've scars on their cheeks as proof that
they're learned. Therefore, Tiny, you should listen to what
they tell you. You're only a piece of beef cattle.

"I've thrown myself in the mud when I was told to. Fired
at everything they ordered me to fire at. When they said 'Attention!' I stood stiff. When they said 'Beat it!' I took off.
For six years this has been going on, with me running around
gingerly, afraid of doing something wrong."

He looked about him slyly.

"But now something has happened. Things are beginning
to hum in my top. You see, I've gotten engaged and I'm
going to have twenty-three kids. I'm going to be hitched up
with the loveliest whopper of a wench in the whole world!"

He looked up again, wiping his head clumsily with a cal-
loused hand.

"Something doesn't mesh," he went on. "I'm thinking of
the fellow from the other club, the muzhik from Kharkov,
Kiev, Elbruz, Sebastopol and all the other places where we
have been defending the Fatherland. If you say to him: Listen, Ivan Ivanovich, why do you really shoot at me? he'll
blink his eyes once and say: Tovarich Fritz, I've no idea, but
Papa Stalin tells me to. Bang, and there's a hole in your
head!" Tiny spread out his hands. "Crazy, isn't it?"

The Legionnaire looked around nervously, hastily slammed
the door to the corridor and said brutally: "Shut up, you
stupid pig! Or else they're going to throw you out and string
you up, regardless whether you or Ivan understands it or not."

"But that's just what I'm saying!" Tiny cried, throwing his
head from side to side. "All other places in the world you get
things explained to you when something is to be done, but
here they just tell you: 'Shut up, you brute, and do as I say,
'or we'll string you up!' I don't understand it."

"It doesn't matter a damn whether you do or not," the
Legionnaire answered rudely. "Just do as you're told. That's
healthiest for you and us both. You'll only get sick from
pondering. You didn't get your noodle for that. It was made

only to carry a steel helmet, and you'll have to be satisfied with that."

Tiny shrugged his shoulders and answered, "Well, I guess I must!"

"I know what this means," the Legionnaire said. *We stood looking at the hanged soldiers swaying like pendulums in the wind.*

The head-hunters were busy at the moment. The new order of the Führer was forcefully executed. Up to now it had been called drumhead court-martial. Now the big word was drumhead warrant decree, which was applied to the following offenses:

> Defeatist utterances
> Desertion
> Sabotage
> Insult to the Führer's name
> Looting
> Corpse robbery
> Treason

"I know what this means," the Legionnaire said, *"the Army's beginning to break up. Most wars end this way."*

chapter xii

The Roller Conveyor

WE SAT in the train for twelve days and twelve nights, and now we were standing on the roller conveyor Pinsk-Gomel a little to the southwest of David Gorodok. Judging from the announcement of the front Army post-office, the regiment was lying in Piotrków or Skrigalów.

A person who has been on a roller conveyor will never forget it. This particular one extended in a dead-straight line from east to west, from south to north. From 130 to 200 feet wide. A road that is no road, pressed and trampled to firmness by thousands of wheels and millions of feet. And nevertheless this roller conveyor is an important life nerve for the existence of the armies, in the same way as the main artery

is essential to the heart: if an organism is to live, this artery
has to throb uninterruptedly. Day and night thousands of
engines rumble on the roller conveyor. A continuous wave. If
it were to be broken, the front would collapse.

In one direction rolled long columns of munitions, provi-
sioning, guns, armored cars, reserves with fresh troops, the
field mail with bags of fateful letters. All of this was a necessity if the war was to proceed according to plan. In the opposite direction went destroyed artillery, smashed motor
vehicles, gutted wrecks of tanks, twisted tin affairs that up to
quite recently had been silvery airplanes, and endless columns
of Red Cross ambulances with mutilated human wrecks. Also
a necessity of war.

This roller conveyor was always a path of suffering for the
soldiers. In the winter a roller-coaster; in the summer an
indescribable sand waste; in periods of rain and thaw a bot-
tomless, sucking swamp reminiscent of flypaper on which
everything got stuck.

We sat coughing and spitting on the river slope, waiting for
a truck to take us along.

With this communications paradise along the front, Tiny
had rambled off as usual.

"Here my achievement begins," he'd said and vanished
among some bushes. His motto was that a soldier who doesn't
"organize" hasn't finished his education.

He stayed away for three hours. Then he came back, hauling a big bag stuffed with canteen goods.

"Have you gone insane?" the East Prussian asked. "Don't
you know this is looting?"

"Hell it is," Tiny answered blithely and took a bite of
onion.

"What do you call it then?" Bauer asked.

"Self-preservation," Tiny answered coolly. He stuffed a
sausage in his mouth.

"If they nab you they'll make you swing for it," Bauer
warned.

"Chickenheart!" Tiny dismissed him. "What d'you think
happens when we retreat? And, you know, once we've gotten
used to straightening out the front we'll go on retreating.
Those jackasses will blow up the whole sausage supply!" He
looked at Bauer and the East Prussian. "You probably think
some QMC colonel will drop over and invite you in so you
can get stuffed first?" He held a banana above his head and
shouted with conviction. "Naw, they put up guards, oh, yes,
so you can't get hold of as much as a dry cracker or a rotten
egg. The order says that the whole caboodle should be blown

up. That's that. The whole works are blown sky-high. Do
you recall what they did in Kuban, how they dispatched two
thousand tons of provisions? An engineer charge. Boom,
they were gone!" He patted his bag and smiled slyly. "Look,
here I have extra rations for two weeks. Vitamins for
victory!" He laughed rapturously and stuffed two bananas in
his mouth, both at once. He tossed the peels on the roller
conveyor.

"You shouldn't do that," the Legionnaire said. "Someone
might come along and slip on them."

"That's the reason I do it," Tiny answered. "Maybe Adolf
will come walking past and break his neck on my banana
peel. Then I'll become history and children will learn about
me in school."

"Every time I see the roller conveyor again," Bauer said,
flicking a cigarette butt into the river in a long arc, "my
bottom itches as if tapeworms were bustling around in it."

"They probably are," Tiny grumbled, looking defiantly at
him.

Tiny had started getting bored and was out to pick a fight.
His notion of entertainment.

Anything could have happened if a big gasoline truck
hadn't stopped.

A sergeant leaned out of the driver's cab and yelled:
"Where are you going, you lazy bums?"

"Twenty-seventh Panzer Regiment," I answered. Since I
was the one with the longest service I stood at attention.

"You'll never get there at this rate," he barked harshly.
Communications was written all over him. A tailor-made
uniform. An elegant cap with high crown. A belt with an
officer's pistol, against regulations. Although he belonged to
the supply troops, he had taken the liberty of decking himself out with yellow cavalry ribbons instead of the blue ones
worn by the commissariat troops and universally despised by
fighting men.

I was the only one to get up. The others kept lying nonchalantly in the grass, staring at the bawling sergeant, who in
the meantime had jumped out of the truck. Splay-legged,
fists on hips, he cried: "Get up, you duds, will you, and
march, march, with your noses turned eastward, where a
hero's death is waiting for you."

They were infuriatingly slow getting up. Tiny slung his
bag over his shoulder like a peddler and trudged off without
bothering even to look at the sergeant.

"I say, you, Corporal," he neighed after Tiny, "what
kind of bag is that?"

"A jute bag."

The Sergeant gasped with rage: "Don't get fresh. The make-up of the bag doesn't interest me. What's in it?"

"Mail and grub for our commander, Lieutenant Colonel Hinka," Tiny answered carelessly.

"Let me see!" the elegant sergeant requested.

"Out of the question," Tiny answered, locking the mouth of the bag with his clenched fists.

"What do you mean?" the Sergeant yapped.

"*Gekados*," Tiny breathed, winking.

"*Bon*," the Legionnaire burst out in admiration.

"What does *Gekados* mean?" the Sergeant roared.

Tiny leaned his head sideways. "Lieutenant Colonel Hinka told me: 'Tiny, don't let anybody get at that bag! It's strictly *Gekados*. Top secret. This is what the Commander said, Herr Sergeant, and he gave me these knuckles"—he hit out with his hand—"to guard the bag."

Squinting at us in bewilderment, the Sergeant observed us forming a narrower circle around Tiny. He jumped on the truck and cried: "Off with you, march, march! I'll call you to the attention of the Military Police!"

The truck vanished in a cloud of dust.

Tiny pulled a couple of boxes of chocolate out of his bag and divided the contents among us like a brother.

Like a band of vagabonds who have all the time in the world we started moving along the roller conveyor. After tramping about six miles we were tired, flopped down and went to sleep.

In the middle of the night we were awakened by engine noise. The whole roller conveyor was crammed with vehicles: trucks, passenger cars, artillery, trench mortar batteries, rocket batteries, troop transport trucks, long engineers' trucks, armored cars, storming guns and a host of other things an army treks around with.

"It looks like the whole army is on the move," Bauer exclaimed.

"Yes, and it's moving west, away from the front," Stein said.

"Mac, is the war over?" Tiny shouted at an old staff corporal behind the wheel of a munitions truck.

"Guess again, you lunkhead," the staff corporal shouted back. He stuck out his tongue at Tiny, who would have rushed straight at him if a mechanized artillery unit hadn't come in between us and the munitions truck.

"I wonder what the hell is going on," Bauer said, looking around.

"We're straightening out the battle lines," Stein laughed. "But we'd better get away before Ivan starts blazing away at the roller conveyor!"

A major walking at the head of a long column leapt into the middle of the road and started brandishing a pistol above his head. "Make room for my regiment," he yelled. "Make room! I command, or I'll shoot you like dogs!"

But no one bothered to notice him.

The never-ending line of vehicles crawled onward as before. The major's regiment had to stay where it was.

A large gray Horch with a square tin plate on its fender was slowly winding ahead. Inside we had a glimpse of some disguised staff officers.

An MP lieutenant colonel appeared with a unit of head-hunters. He cried: "Make room for the Army Commander!"

But the long line didn't move an inch. The cavalry general in the Horch had to be good enough to wait.

The MPs ordered that the vehicles standing in the way of the General should be tipped down the bank. The vehicles rolled over one after another.

"That's a bit thick!" Bauer growled. "Wrecking a whole lot of vehicles for a fellow like that. I don't get it!"

The little Legionnaire laughed. "*Voilà*, you have been in our club only four years. Wait till you have been a member for as long as we have, then even you will understand."

Bauer shook his head in puzzlement. "I've always been told the generals are taking the lead in this war. Why is this one in such a hurry to clear out?"

The Legionnaire merely shrugged his shoulders.

A colonel riding at the head of a horse-drawn artillery regiment got very excited and started raving when the MPs made ready to tip his vehicles down the steep slope. When an MP lieutenant colonel grabbed the reins of the colonel's horse, the colonel struck him in the face several times with his riding whip, shouting:

"Hands off my horse!" He wrenched the horse back. The horse reared, neighed and beat the air with his forelegs. The colonel galloped beside the road to where the General was halting, jumped off his horse and confronted the little man.

Before he even could say a word the cavalry general yelped: "Who do you think you are, Herr Colonel? How dare you keep my orders from being executed by my military police? Do you think I have time to stay in this gutter longer than necessary?"

"Herr General," the Colonel answered icily, "I can't get

off the road with my batteries. My horses are worn out and won't be able to pull a single one of my vehicles on to the road again."

"What's that to me?" the General snorted. "I have to get on, and this minute!"

"I refuse to carry out your orders! My vehicles will stay on the road!"

The General measured him up with cold, appraising eyes. "If you don't immediately clear the road of all the vehicles belonging to your regiment, I'll . . ."

The Colonel drew himself up a little. He was a whole head taller than the General. The Iron Cross hung from his neck. "What will you do, Herr General?"

The General's eyes were like slits in his face. "I'll make use of my authority and have you court-martialed for insubordination. The German Army has no use for officers like you."

The Colonel turned deathly pale. "Is that your final word, Herr General?"

The General didn't answer, but turned to the MP officer standing a little behind him.

"Lieutenant Colonel Scholl!"

The Colonel shot his hand to his belt, pulled out his pistol and cocked it in a split second.

The General jumped a step back. His face turned completely white.

The MP officer stood paralyzed. For a few seconds everything seemed to come to a standstill on the roller conveyor.

The Colonel's pale lips formed a thin smile.

"Don't be afraid, Herr General. You're too small and vile for an honest officer to want to shoot at. But I won't serve in an army like Greater Germany's today."

"Seize him!" the General yapped.

But even before the lieutenant colonel and his head-hunters were able to move, the Colonel put the pistol in his mouth and pressed the trigger.

A sharp brief bang. The pistol fell to the ground.

For a brief moment the Colonel stood stiffly at attention. Then he swayed a little back and forth, doubled up like a jackknife and lay flat before the General's feet.

The General about-faced and took a seat in his car, where an adjutant wrapped his thin, booted legs in a red woollen blanket.

Those who were nearby heard him say to his First Officer, a colonel: "What ridiculous fools one runs into in one's time!"

They began tipping the dead colonel's vehicles down the slope. Screeching horses whirled round with the vehicles.

The dead colonel was thrown on a truck, and soon after the Horch with the cavalry general disappeared down the roller conveyor.

"My God," the East Prussian exclaimed. "That colonel sure knew how to resign!"

Tiny sprang up and roared: "There's a truck from our division!"

Quite right. A large truck with a fly sheet and with our emblem painted on the backboard and the front mudguard —two crosses on a blue ground.

"Hi, Mac," Bauer cried, "where are you heading? Could you take us along with you?"

"I'm heading for Cologne, you stupid pig."

"What did you say?" the Legionnaire cried, astonished.

"Are your ear flaps dirty? I said Cologne." He spelled: C-O-L-O-G-N-E.

On all sides soldiers started craning their necks. The name Cologne had the effect of a bomb of laughing gas.

"Did you hear that? This ass wants to go to Cologne."

"Make sure you don't forget to transfer, because this train doesn't go further than Breslau!"

Ringing laughter. They crowed with malicious glee.

"Did you remember to buy a ticket at the gate?" an NCO whinnied, slapping his thighs.

"If you want to go to Cologne you'd be better off using a shoemaker's crate, because you'll never reach Cologne in that box!"

An artilleryman jumped on the footboard of the truck and squealed, "I'd better give you a pass so you can take a short cut!" He handed him one of the dropped leaflets every German soldier on the Eastern Front had in his pockets, despite the heavy penalties involved. The leaflets were printed like a kind of pass. Crates of them were dropped by Russian pilots.

"Will you take us to Berlin?" the Legionnaire asked dryly. "Just let us off close to a subway station and we'll be satisfied."

The Corporal, who didn't allow his serenity to be disturbed, answered: "Gladly as far as I'm concerned, just climb aboard!"

We tossed in our equipment and climbed up.

Through the smashed rear window the East Prussian asked the driver: "Mac, are you really serious about going to Cologne?"

"Damn it, yes. I'm going to pick up some important stuff for our commander."

He handed us his marching papers, and in amazement we read that as a special assignment he had been dispatched with truck WH 381 556 through Lemberg, Warsaw and Breslau to Berlin, Dortmund, and Cologne.

"Holy Mary, Mother of God, I must have gone crazy," Bauer cried. "If this isn't the most idiotic thing I've yet seen in this war. Sending an old truck thousands of miles to pick up something!"

"Is it something important?" Tiny asked. "Are you going to pick up some laundry for the gang?"

"Yes, my commander wants to have his love socks brought out to his position."

More soldiers clambered on the truck.

"The war will soon be over," a dirty NCO remarked and squirted a stream of tobacco juice over the side.

"How do you know?" asked a staff corporal in panzer uniform.

"Talked to Adolf over the 'phone yesterday," the NCO answered. He looked around cautiously as if to make sure that no outsider was listening.

"Adolf said it was *'Gekados'* that the war was over!"

"So that's why we go on with it?" asked a little pale infantry Pfc.

"By the way, do you know why Adolf never shows up at the front any more?" asked the staff corporal.

"Naw?"

"He's afraid we'll shout: Führer, we'll follow you!"

"But we always shouted that," Bauer said.

The staff corporal looked closely at him. "You must be from the country?"

"Shut up, you turd," Bauer growled.

But the staff corporal didn't let himself be frightened by Bauer's threatening voice and went on.

"Adolf is afraid we'll take him up on it and follow him to Berlin!"

An eighteen-year-old infantryman in a brand-new uniform and a Hitler Youth badge on his breast stood up. His face was completely white.

"I forbid you to talk like this! It is defeatism, favoring the enemy. I demand that all present in this vehicle give me their names and service ranks. As a National-Socialist I am duty bound to report this treacherous talk."

Stein caught the boy by his chest and hurled him against the bottom of the truck.

"Won't you please shut up, you puppet! What a dud! Don't worry, we'll settle your hash for you!"

The boy cried for help from the bottom of the truck. To drown out the noise we started singing:

Ja, das Temperament,
Ja, das Temperament,
Das lieght mir
so im Blut!

"God, we're lost," the staff corporal shouted. "Before us the Russians, behind us the Party. Help! We're surrounded."

Tiny let out a howl, jumped over the side of the truck, scooted some distance into the plain and dived down for cover.

"Mille diables!" the Legionnaire exclaimed, and was off.

All over the roller conveyor soldiers were running away from the vehicles.

"Rattas," the East Prussian yelled, plunging head over heels out of the truck.

Three Russian fighters zoomed down on us. They swept the road clean with their quick-firing guns. We hunched our shoulders in terror and pressed tight to the ground.

We felt the cold air hit us as the low-flying planes boomed across the plain. The red stars twinkled on their wings. They seemed to be laughing derisively at us.

"Jesus Christ!" a corporal cursed beside us. "I've 1600 gallons of gas in my truck. If our colleagues hit it, good night, my dear! We'll have a funeral with fireworks and Bengal light!"

The three planes turned around and came crashing back over the roller conveyor. Bodies were blown into the air by the exploding shells.

Some young infantrymen naively started to shoot at the shrieking Rattas with rifles and light MGs.

"This is getting precarious," the East Prussian mumbled and pressed still closer to the ground.

The little Legionnaire started getting to his feet. He raised himself to a half-kneeling position and stared toward the road, where a host of vehicles were burning.

From all sides there were cries of "Medics!" But they hardly got through to our brains. We had become deaf to that cry.

The East Prussian pulled the Legionnaire into the hole. He just had time to shout "Butcher!" before six fighter planes crashed out of the sky, one after another. They made a nose-dive, which made their wings look like straight lines.

"They have us in their sights!" As I slid down to the bottom of the hole, this thought flashed through my mind.

One group of soldiers on the roller conveyor had failed to notice the danger popping out of the blue sky. An engineer lieutenant was giving them hell. He wanted them to fall in.

Malignant blue flames flashed from the wings of the fighter planes—the muzzle flare from their guns. At the same moment the dirt on the road was whipped up as if a couple of sacks of rocks had been dropped from a high altitude.

Loud screams. Savage curses.

With both hands the Lieutenant made menacing gestures at the low-flying planes as they roared over us. They swerved some distance into the plain and then came zooming back.

The Lieutenant doubled up. A stream of blood spurted from his neck. His head rolled down the road like a melon. His eyes were wide open. His cap lay forlorn a little way off.

An eighteen-year-old infantryman shrieked as he ran on his leg stumps. Both his legs had been cut just above the ankles. The blood formed a steaming streak after him.

General panic broke out among the soldiers, who got up and did the worst thing possible under the circumstances: They started running on the roller conveyor.

The fighters made a regular slaughter, driving volley after volley into quivering bodies.

A lieutenant in the black uniform of the armored troops came flying into our hole in one long leap.

"Ohlsen," he puffed. He was a typical field officer, with a sub-machine gun over his shoulder and his breast covered with decorations.

The Legionnaire raised his head and fixed his eyes. "Bon, Kalb."

The earth was being lashed up around us. Everything was ablaze. It was raining fire.

Once more the planes came to the attack.

We pressed up against each other and flattened our bodies to the ground.

An ear-splitting explosion lifted us out of the hole. Waves of burning hot air rolled against us. A sea of fire welled from the road as from a volcano.

"My 1600 gallons of gas," the Corporal groaned.

To top off the fireworks the planes dropped a series of bombs. Parts of vehicles flew through the air. Then it was over. The planes disappeared eastward.

The sunlight was reflected on their silvery fuselages.

We slowly stood up and walked toward the road, where

a profusion of charred corpses were scattered.

An Air Force colonel took command. We were ordered to clear the road of corpses and wrecked matériel.

The corporal bound for Cologne stood looking dejectedly at his burnt-up truck.

"This is mad," he said. "And my papers burnt up with the truck."

Those soldiers who didn't belong to any definite unit were put together in a "pick-up" battalion.

Tiny still dragged his bag with him. He gave each of us a banana. A flak artillery Pfc asked if he could have one too. He said "comrade" to Tiny.

"I'm no comrade to an oaf from the Air Force, and when you talk to me you should address me as *Herr* Corporal! You bet I'll make you see eye to eye with me on that."

The company comprised all kinds of services, from seamen to front-line fliers. All of the Axis nations were represented in it: Rumanians, Hungarians, Bulgarians, a Finnish corporal, Yugoslavs, and an Italian Bersagliere corporal with a cock's feather in his cap.

Tiny was unable to hold himself. He hit a Polish MP over the head with his helmet and yelled provocatively: "Get out of rank, traitor!"

This caused a big uproar in the company, twenty-five per cent of which were volunteers from occupied countries like the Ukraine, Poland, Czechoslovakia and Yugoslavia.

Lieutenant Ohlsen tried to soothe the roused tempers and quiet the loud voices of those who had been offended by Tiny's clamor about "traitors." A Cossack from Tiflis swung his knife at Tiny and set up a cry in broken German. Tiny guffawed and called to the Legionnaire, who walked beside Lieutenant Ohlsen at the head of the company.

"Desert Rambler, they want to cut me to bits because I tell them the truth. Should I kill them?"

"You should behave yourself," the Legionnaire crowed back.

Lieutenant Ohlsen laughed. He tried to put awe into Tiny, who towered above all others as he walked with his bag across his shoulder in the middle of the rank.

The Cossack made ready to move behind Tiny, but Tiny grabbed him by his wide stiff cravat and pulled him in front of him.

"Better come to the front, you muzzle cover. Then I can see you and help you in case you should slip in your own snot!"

A Pole in the uniform of the Polish auxiliary police protested on behalf of the Cossack.

"Leave him alone. He's a volunteer and is fighting for National Socialism just like you and me!"

Tiny gaped, bent down and peered into the face of the Polish policeman. He scrutinized it as if he wanted to make sure whether he was walking beside a real person or not.

"You must have crab-louse on the liver! I'm not fighting for anything like what you're talking about, oh no! I'm fighting to save my neck and nothing else! Haven't you ever heard of Kolyma, you clod? If you haven't, just wait and see and you'll get there. There you'll get rotten fish every day while Tiny sits in Bremen stuffing himself with English beefsteak!"

"Shut your trap, you swine!" the Pole yelled, making a movement with his sub-machine gun.

With the palm of his hand Tiny smacked him on the throat with such force that he toppled over. A rattling noise came from his throat.

"Self-defense, according to Regulations," Tiny grinned.

A menacing mutter rose from the company.

Tiny drew himself up to his full stature. "If someone would like to commit suicide, all he has to do is to come here and Tiny will be glad to help him out."

A rock hit his shoulder. He just managed to see that the culprit was a Czech in the green uniform of the sabotage police.

With a snarling grin Tiny slowly moved down upon the man, who pulled back in terror. But Tiny caught him.

As if it were a state secret he whispered to him: "Are you quite sane? Do you want your ass to be knocked cold? Or what do you mean by throwing rocks at an honorary corporal of the 'Disarmed Forces' of Greater Germany?" Suddenly he set up a staggering roar: "What a crud!"

He caught the terror-stricken, almost paralyzed man by the throat, swung him above his head and hurled him into the plain.

Then he shuffled indifferently to his place in the ranks between the East Prussian and me.

"What a crazy bunch," he said, shaking his head resignedly. "We'd better clear out as soon as it's dark on Joseph's plains. This bunch beats everything. Pure scabs!"

He started singing:

Yesterday on silky cushions,
Today a bullet in the breast,

Tomorrow in the chilling g-r-a-v-e.

He held his voice on the last word interminably. Then he spat and hit the Polish policeman directly in the hollow of his neck.

Three days later we reached Proskurov, where the mixed battalion was dissolved and everybody had to look out for himself.

In Proskurov we saw the first sign of a new and harsher policy. Two old infantrymen had been hanged, from separate telephone poles. On their breasts were signs, with these words written in red letters:

Too cowardly
to defend the Fatherland!

We stopped for a moment to look at the two of them. They were hanging there in the middle of the market-place, swinging like pendulums in the wind.

"For them the war's over," the East Prussian remarked philosophically.

"It's better to stay with the gang," Stein decided. "Then you have at least a slight chance of escaping with your life."

"*Voilà*," the Legionnaire said, scratching his nose. "I know what this means. Good signs. The same thing happened in the Rif Mountains when the Legion was about to give up the game. It is a sure sign of the end."

We roused ourselves and continued through town.

We sought quarter for the night in a building that looked rather like a barn. A stench of rotten potatoes and musty straw welled against us as we stepped in.

"The hell with that," the East Prussian said, "we'll stay here and snooze."

"Everything taken!" a voice growled from the dark.

"That's too bad for *you*," Tiny thundered, "because we must have room, you know. You'll be the first to take off as not wanted."

"Shut up, you rotten swine!" the invisible owner of the voice retorted.

Tiny crashed into the darkness like a locomotive. Shortly the darkness rang with crying and screaming, oaths and curses.

Then the first two came flying through the air. In the course of a few minutes there was room for all seven of us.

Lieutenant Ohlsen laughed softly. "I'd call that being consistent!"

From the inner darkness someone asked: "Tiny, is that you?"

The Legionnaire lit a field lantern, which to his surprise disclosed Ewald, Aunt Dora's Ewald.

Tiny stood up. "Holy Mary, Mother of God, you also in town?" He turned to the Legionnaire, who still held Ewald in the cone of light from the field lantern. "It's not that I'm lazy, Desert Rambler, but I'm a bit tired after trudging around with that traitor bunch. As soon as I've had some sleep I'm going to give Ewald the thrashing that's coming to him."

The Legionnaire nodded and passed the cone of light further over the many sleeping people.

Letting out a roar of rapture, Tiny dashed across the sleeping figures in the musty straw. He chanced to hit the lantern out of the Legionnaire's hand so the light went out.

From the darkness we heard him grunt and shout with joy: "Hell's blazes, what luscious tomatoes!"

We could hear him romping around between cursing soldiers and stepping on them. Then, a piercing shriek from a woman and a moment later Tiny's ecstatic yell:

"I've a roast on my fork. Ah, what sweets!"

Several women started protesting.

"Hurry up and get here, boys. A traveling whorehouse has settled here!"

A lantern was lit. It was a captain, we saw. He gave Tiny a regular dressing-down.

What Tiny had taken for a traveling brothel was a unit of Red Cross nurses and telephone operators from the Air Force. Tiny was inconsolable. We almost had to use force to keep him down. Lieutenant Ohlsen was able to quiet the captain, who swore he would report Tiny for attempted rape.

Shortly after midnight we were waked up by a trampling of officious boots. Field lanterns flashed. Brutal voices called for service records and marching orders.

The heavily armed head-hunters stood before us like rocks. Their crescent badges gleamed ominously in the dark. An enemy machine-gun post wasn't as dangerous as this badge.

Terror spread. An Ivan could be reasoned with, not a German head-hunter. He was the incarnation of all evil and brutality.

After a short while they had their first victim. An artillery NCO. He put up a violent resistance, screaming:

"Leave me alone. Let me go! Comrades, why don't you let me go! You aren't going to kill me, are you?" He was silent for a moment, then moaned softly: "Comrades, you must try to understand me! I've children, I've three children. My wife was killed in an air attack. I have to get home to the children. I'll be sure to come back!"

"Shut up, you swine," barked a head-hunter sergeant. His crescent badge emitted twinkling Morse sparks. The signal for death.

The artillery NCO suddenly went crazy. He ran completely wild.--

"Let me go, you dirty bastards, you filthy comrade-killers!" He kicked and laid about him savagely. "I don't want to die! I've three children. With no mother. I don't want to die!"

But this sort of thing was an everyday occurrence to the head-hunters. Without comment they started beating him. One of them gave the NCO a kick in the groin that made him double up with a hoarse roar. For a moment he was lying on the ground like a bundle of rags. Suddenly he jumped up and rushed at the nearest head-hunter, who was pushed over by the unexpected attack.

Fear of death lent the artillery NCO the strength of a wild beast. He bit the head-hunter in the face and bellowed like an animal.

Other head-hunters rushed to the aid of their comrade in distress. With the butts of their sub-machine guns they pounded away at the artillery NCO. His face was a mushy, bloody mass of tears and groans.

They threw him on a truck which stood outside the barn, then calmly continued their patrol.

A sergeant major examined our papers with painstaking thoroughness. "Panzer Regiment of the Army to be used for special assignments," he muttered. He looked at the Legionnaire and gave Tiny a crushing glance. His eyes roved to me and the East Prussian, then fixed Stein watchfully.

"H'm, so you have made a slight detour, you tired heroes, eh? Looks like illegal departure from a battle unit!"

Cold shivers ran down our spines. We knew that a drumhead court-martial wouldn't listen to excuses. They were very busy at the flying court-martials. After a ten-minute hearing you were dragged before a firing squad or hanged from a tree.

"Last unit, you tramps?" he growled, glaring at us.

"Reserve Army Hospital 19, Hamburg," the Legionnaire rapped out.

"And now you're here, you corpse-robbers! So you've been on a little pleasure trip on the Russian lakes? You

probably assumed that the war was about to end, eh?" He
pointed at the door and called to an NCO standing with his
sub-machine gun at the ready: "Here, look after this pack
of swine. Suspected of desertion! Get out, on the double!"

The thought, *It's all over*, flashed through my mind. From
the corner of my eye I looked at Tiny and the Legionnaire.
They were pale, but seemed indifferent as they trotted out
of the building, prodded by a brutal head-hunter NCO.

They ordered us into a truck. Its tarp had just been daubed
with fresh camouflage paint.

Right behind us stumbled two telephone operators.

"Make room for the ladies," a head-hunter grinned. He
aimed a jet of tobacco juice at the face of one of them.

When she wanted to turn her head, he roared frantically:
"Keep your neck straight, you bitch! There are others who
will turn it for you, take my word for it!"

Four nurses came running out. One of them fell as a
sergeant tripped her. Another MP kicked her in the back. She
screamed loudly.

A murmur rose from the truck.

"Shut up, you deserter swine," yelled a lieutenant with the
head-hunter badge twinkling gaily on his breast.

Aunt Dora's Ewald howled as he was dragged to the
truck by two large MPs.

The Legionnaire whispered: *"Bon.* The whole German
Army seems to have decamped. It can't take long now before it's over and Ivan comes to pick us up. Then I'll immediately join the Russian Army in order to be permitted
to shoot head-hunters."

An NCO with tin badge flashing from his breast peered
into the truck but couldn't see anything. He contented himself with yapping: "Shut your traps, you sons of bitches!"

Three trucks crammed with the catch of the head-hunters were driven to the former GPU prison in the center of
town. Here we were received with blows and kicks.

All cells were filled. Curses and prayers ricocheted from
the gray, damp walls.

A little tank gunner was shouting his hatred of Hitler,
Himmler, the war, and Stalin. He promised a huge MP in
the corridor that he'd break his neck if he dared come in to
him.

One of the army's telephone operators tore off every stitch
of clothing and offered herself to the head-hunter in the corridor.

"Come in here and I'll give you everything you want if
you'll only let me go afterward," she whispered confidentially.

A Russian peasant girl who had to count on getting shot because she had sheltered two deserters yelled fanatically: "Long live Stalin! Long live the Soviet Union! Death to Hitler!"

"And to you, you bitch," the MP answered.

On the opposite side of the corridor knelt a captain, praying silently.

I don't know in how many places God is invoked, but His name was cried out everywhere in the last war. In hundreds of prisons the prisoners implored Him for mercy. I've heard a divisional general pray to God for help against the panzer columns of the Russians when his anti-tank regiments gave up.

Adolf Hitler shouted God's name in his speeches and prayed for His protection of the Pan-German Reich, at the same time as his SS units were hanging priests in the liquidation camps. These priests, in their turn, called out God's name, making it reverberate among the desolate, lice-infested barracks till their cries were stifled by the rope.

SS men who were found with robbed gold teeth in their pockets and were sentenced to death by one of the many court-martials blubbered to God for help. They meant of course that He should help them get into the SS uniform again.

But God was deaf. He didn't hear the condemned in the GPU prison. He didn't hear the priests under the gallows in the liquidation camp. He didn't help the general against the T 34's. He didn't relieve the pains of the amputee case in an army hospital.

God was deaf.

There was a good deal of truth in what the little Legionnaire said: "A loaded tommy gun and a brace of hand grenades is better than a couple of Bibles and a chaplain."

One by one they were hauled before the court-martial, which sat in the office of the former GPU boss.

Everybody was showered with the same words: name, age, detachment. A brief whisper among the three judges and a rustle of papers. Exactly sixty seconds. Then the little judge in flashing rimless glasses rapped out the next question.

"Do you have anything to say in your defense?"

But before the accused had managed to get properly started, the judge would interrupt.

"Rubbish, we know all about that."

Again some whispering between the three of them. A stamp was slammed down on some papers. Then the presiding judge banged his rubber-stamp signature to the whole thing.

"In the name of the Führer and the German people: Sentenced to death by firing squad. Next!"

Again and again. Hour after hour. The leaders of the Third Reich thought they could thus win a war.

At the other end of the corridor, where the stairs ascended, was heard a hoarse whisper: "In single file after me!"

The firing squad had arrived.

With lightning speed they tore open a cell door, chosen at random. The prisoners could never guess whose turn it would now be.

A nurse past fifty had to be carried out into the yard. She threw herself down and refused to get up. Then they tied her to a clothes post, hands raised high above her head. Three short commands. Twelve shots crashed.

The next one was brought out to the little yard.

The same routine, with short pauses, the whole day and night. Every other hour the firing squad was replaced with a new crew.

They dragged out the Captain by his legs. He seized hold of every iron bar, every railing. Each time they kicked his hands, till finally they were a pair of bloody stumps of meat.

He bellowed like a wounded bull. They shot him lying down.

Ewald shrieked insanely when they came for him. Somehow he slipped away from them and ran a race through the different floors. Finally he leapt over the railing on the fourth floor and fractured both legs as he landed at the bottom of the shaft.

They lashed him to the clothes post and shot him.

The truck driver who was to go to Cologne, but had lost all his papers when his vehicle burnt, walked out to the twelve shots under the clothes post as if drugged.

Two days later he was reported missing by his regiment, but then it was too late.

Before the five of us came before the court-martial, the head-hunters, to their great chagrin, had to let us go. Lieutenant Ohlsen had appeared with papers from the regiment which proved that we were under his command and were not deserters.

We were marched off toward Drubny, where the regiment stood.

Without taking aim, the strange sergeant fired a volley at the invisible opponent by the forest.

The answer was a shower of bullets. They whipped up the dust round the hole we were lying in.

Again the sergeant pressed home the trigger and emptied his magazine into the brush.

"Ass," the Legionnaire growled. He tore the sub-machine gun out of the nervous infantry sergeant's hands. "You don't shoot like that!"

The Legionnaire crawled out of the hole, pressing to the ground like a partridge. He raised the sub-machine gun and blazed concentrated fire against every single bush.

A couple of figures in the brush stood up and tried to run off, but the Legionnaire's well-directed bullets got them. He changed the magazine and fired again.

chapter xiii

Back at the Front

IN NUMBER 5 Company we were received by First Sergeant Barth, nicknamed "Fatty." Tiny later altered it to "Fatso."

He examined us carefully with his small spiteful eyes under the large irregular cavalry cap with which he adorned himself like an officer. His eyes moved from left to right and back again from right to left.

What he saw apparently worried him. Sulky wrinkles appeared on his round pig's face. He resembled a spoiled child just before he starts bawling and smacks his fist into his bowl of gruel. He thrust out his fleshy lower lip and played with a notebook peering out between the third and fourth button of his coat.

He nodded as if his worst suspicions had been confirmed. He huffed himself up before the East Prussian and asked gruffly: "What's your name?"

"Otto Bülow."

"Ah, really? Maybe you're an admiral in the U-boat fleet of Lichtenstein?"

"Nah," the East Prussian answered good-humoredly, "I'm a corporal."

"For Christ's sake, really?" Fatty whispered. "And I suppose, my honorable Herr Corporal, that I am only a pailful of trench dirt?" Fatty pushed his big head right up to the East Prussian's face and waited for an answer.

"Nah, you are first sergeant."

"You bet I'm first sergeant, you caveman. Your bad luck, you bag of monkey puke. What are you? What's your name?" He bellowed the last words into the face of the short stocky East Prussian. His voice rang against the dismal peasant huts and ripped at the gray depressing fog.

"Herr First Sergeant, Corporal Otto Bülow reports as ordered to Number 5 Company of 27th Regiment after being discharged from Reserve Army Hospital 19, Hamburg."

"Lie down!" Fatty snarled. He fired the words at the East Prussian, who lightning-quick threw himself in the mire and went into regular guard position, with both heels pressed against the ground.

Fatty examined him carefully, stepped on his rear and yelled: "Down into the dirt, all the way, you flat-footed water rat!"

Then he towered up before the little Legionnaire, but even before he could say anything the Legionnaire clicked his heels and crowed in the manner typical of veteran soldiers:

"Corporal Alfred Kalb, Herr First Sergeant, reports back after being hospitalized in Reserve Army Hospital 19, Hamburg."

Barth glanced at him, walked around him twice and took his stand behind him, waiting to see if he'd move as much as a finger.

Nothing happened. The Legionnaire held himself rigid as only a soldier of many years' service can.

Barth removed the Legionnaire's cap and noted briefly: "Hair too long, in violation of regulations. Lie down, African son of a bitch!"

"And what do we have here?" he growled, touching my shoulder with his finger.

"Color Guard Sven Hassel, Herr First Sergeant, reports back from Reserve Army Hospital 19, Hamburg."

He pulled at my belt and concluded: "Too loose. Not dressed according to regulations. Lie down!"

The same thing happened to Stein. A bawling-out and "Lie down!" The last words sounded like a detonation.

Finally he puffed himself up before Tiny, who was just as big and broad as he. But what was fat and mere flesh on Barth was swelling muscles on Tiny. At his slightest movement, an intense play of muscle became visible under his skin. His broad chest arched tautly over his flattened belly. His face was a caricature, low-browed and with two small quick eyes emitting a foxy gleam. His nose was flat and lumpy, ruined by countless fights, his mouth crooked and conforming to no known laws of anatomy.

Fatty glowered at him as if he couldn't believe his eyes.

"Great God, what face is this? Could anything be that revolting? I can't fathom it!"

"It amazes me too," Tiny answered, tilting his head and smiling blithely. "By the way, they call me Tiny, but that's not my real name. My mother, that pig, decided my name should be Wolfgang, after that piano-pounder Mozart, in case I should turn out to have a mind for music. And then she called me Leo after a Russian liar of a writer, if I should take that path. But since all the signs said I'd become a rowdy, Mother thought—the devil take her!—I'd also better be named for one of that sort, and so finally I got the name Helmuth, for Herr Field-Marshal von Hindenburg. But nobody could remember all these names, and so the whole thing was reduced to 'Tiny.' From my old man, that sop, I'm called Creutzfeldt, which is plain sailing, 'C' as in cow.

"For the rest, I've piles and sweaty feet and occasionally bad breath. And you're First Sergeant Barth, and in a moment I'll get down beside the other guys, so don't trouble giving the command. You might get hoarse from all that shouting. It happened to a prison guard in Fuhlsbüttel, where I did three months for an honest burglary at a greengrocer's in 'Grosse Freiheit.' When I got out I gave that oaf such a going over that he thought he'd turned into a squashed tomato."

Tiny slowly made ready to lie down beside the rest of us.

Heaven knows what Fatty was thinking at this moment. His brain showed all the symptoms of paralysis. In his long service he had never yet experienced the like of it. He had broken many stubborn characters, tamed more snotty fellows than he could keep count of. Pompous asses with college educations, showing off their puffed-up souls and rimless glasses, had had their noses rubbed in the dirt so thoroughly that they never quite recovered from it. Fatty's reputation for toughness was known far beyond the limits of his division. No one had dared answer First Sergeant Barth in this manner, not even in his sleep.

He snorted.

"What the hell! Sweaty feet, piles, bad breath! What a flat-headed fool!" He shook his head, not knowing quite what to do. Then he started shouting and cursing, the normal way of finding release for an NCO when his rage threatens to break him up. You could always think of something to do while shouting.

Fatty shouted and cursed for a very long time.

Tiny observed him with interest. He seemed to be laying a bet how long he could keep it up.

Fatty chased Tiny down the filthy village street.

"Down in the dirt, you son of a bitch!" he yelled. "Double time march, march, march! In place jump, jump! Thunder and lightning, I'll make you squeak, you miserable rat! Before I'm through with you, your ear canals will be sweating. Lie down! Forward crawl! In place jump, feet together! Double time march, march! Lie down! Fifty push-ups! Faster, you lazy bum." He yelled savagely. Every little nook in the village rang with his animal howl.

Tiny grinned, fell down and grinned. Tiny ran, but the outline of his grin never left his face. When he stood at attention, the grin was there as before. When he crawled on his belly across a creek and clambered out like a seal on the other side, he was grinning all the time.

Fatty ran out of breath before the grin vanished from Tiny's face.

"When I see your service rank," Fatty hissed, spitting, "cold shivers run down my spine. In my opinion, every person who gets to be a corporal has already lived too long."

He spat again and grimaced.

For a moment things were quiet. Chewing loudly on his cud, Fatty looked at Tiny, who stood severely at attention in front of him, all smeared with mud.

They looked at each other. What each of them thought is hard to say, but their thoughts were definitely not kindly.

Tiny was the one who broke the silence.

"Corporal Ti—" He hastened to correct himself. "Wolfgang Creutzfeldt requests leave, Herr First Sergeant." Smiling at Fatty, he continued. "Three weeks' wedding leave. I'm to be spliced with a husky gal called Emma. She's my fiancée, Herr First Sergeant. She's a hot one."

Fatty simply lost his breath. His whole body stiffened. His lower jaw dropped like a shutter fallen off its hinges.

"What do you request?" he stammered.

"Leave," Tiny smiled. "I'm to be spliced, Herr First Sergeant."

Fatty's face turned completely white. His whole figure was transformed. He swayed. His squinting eyes opened wide and became round and large. He pushed back his cap and stared. This was the limit. He was convinced that the world would end in a few seconds. This was simply impossible. It simply couldn't be true that a man he'd been chasing around so zealously for the last thirty minutes could stand up in front of him and, with complete composure and a stupid grin on his face, request leave. A fellow who for the last four months had been screwing around in an army hospital. An oaf who'd barely escaped being court-martialed. No, he must be dreaming. Something like that simply didn't happen. It was unmilitary. Undisciplined. If such a thing could happen, you might as well throw all army regulations into the fire right now. But—no, it *was* true, by God. There the man stood before him large as life making his request! And the big stupid ox was smiling into the bargain. A vile stupid grin which could drive you mad. Besides, he had the guts to take up an impossibly slovenly posture right in front of his eyes, the eyes of First Sergeant Herbert Barth, nicknamed "Iron Herbert" in the school for non-commissioned officers in Berlin. The toughest first sergeant in the whole 4th Panzer Army.

He stood there gaping. A tremor shot through his whole body. The blood came and went in his puffed-up cheeks.

Then he planted his feet firmly on the ground. He resembled a tank road block which could be removed only with explosives. His mouth opened to a steaming chasm. From the depths of this chasm came a noise which was not a scream, not even a roar. It was a purely animal noise, insensate and prolonged.

The Cimbrians must have howled this way as they streamed across the Danube into the province Noricum to rob, burn and rape.

But the ending was as lame as the beginning had been violent.

In the middle of his fury, Fatty had noticed that Tiny was smiling. He just stood there smiling. Like all veteran first sergeants he knew an old corporal could be chased around indefinitely. But never beyond the point where the corporal started smiling. Once this happened he was dangerous. The smile was the symptom of incipient insanity, a boiling and foaming madness that could only be put out by a well-directed burst from a sub-machine gun. And long before this could be done, Fatty would have been torn to bits and scattered across the village like mincemeat.

He sent Tiny an angry look and said quite low: "Get out,

get out all of you! And let me see you only as names on
the list of the missing!" He pointed at Tiny. "And you'll
never wish to see me again!" He about-faced and almost
ran into the office.

With the provision crew we marched out to the position,
where the 1st and 3rd Battalions fought as infantry.

As always the regiment was short of tanks.

Joseph Porta went into hysterics of laughter when he saw
Tiny.

"Oh, you gracious young maiden," he broke out jubilantly
—"have you come back to the country again, you big cow?"

Tiny grumbled something about a "punch in the face"
and a "cardboard soldier," but Porta didn't care. He crowed
gloatingly.

"To see you here is the best thing that has happened
to me for a long time. The only thing that can beat this
is for you to get one through your head this time instead of in
your ass, like last time. On that day I'll dress up in my
Sunday uniform and get potted."

Tiny began swinging his arms ominously, but Porta pru-
dently managed to keep some distance between them.

"Did your ass shrink after the operation, Tiny?" he called.
"I hear you've only half an ass now. Is it true?"

"When I get my hands on you," Tiny growled, "you
won't have any!" Ducking, he hurled an empty shell case
after the roaring Porta, who barely escaped getting hit by
the heavy hunk of steel which would have smashed his skull.

The Old Man came walking up to us, swaying his body
like a sailor.

"Back to the muck again," he said, greeting us in his curt
but warm manner, while pulling vehemently on his old
lidded pipe. "Müller is dead. Ivan picked him up during an
attack. We found him three days afterwards—so now you
know that."

The East Prussian raised his eyebrows. "Stretched between
two birch trees?"

"Naturally," the Old Man nodded. "Hugo Stege is on leave.
He's in Berlin, though actually he was going to Dortmund.
It's something about a girl, he wrote in his last letter."

"What sort of a whore is he sweet on?" Tiny asked. He
cleaned his nose on his fingers and wiped them off on the
seat of his trousers.

Nobody took the trouble to answer. To discuss women
with Tiny was useless.

Doubled up we walked through the communication
trench to the bunker of Number One Platoon.

There was the whistle of a bullet. An NCO gave out a brief scream and collapsed. The point of impact was visible just under the helmet, straight between the eyes.

"Siberian sniper," Porta said.

The Legionnaire poked the dead man with his foot. "*Voilà*, he didn't feel as much as a rap."

Together we shoved the corpse up to the edge of the trench and rolled it down the slope. Some dust flew up.

"Amen," Porta said. We went on to the bunker.

As we were sitting in the bunker playing blackjack late in the evening, Lieutenant Ohlsen came in to us. He had taken over the company after Lieutenant Harder, who'd been killed a few days ago. He sat down on a gas mask container and looked at each of us in turn.

Porta handed him a canteen with cognac. He stuck his thumb into the neck of the canteen, flipped it around and drank, just like the rest of us. He cleared his throat and wiped his mouth with the flat of his hand.

"Beier," he turned to the Old Man. "You and your Number One Squad are taking an excursion tonight. If you like to, you may appoint someone else to head the squad. The regiment has ordered prisoners to be picked up."

"Holy Mother of Kazan!" Tiny snapped angrily, throwing his cards on the table. "Let the front quiet down for a brief moment, and the brass asses behind it start itching right away."

Lieutenant Ohlsen laughed loudly. "Whoever said that you're going along, Tiny?"

"Herr Lieutenant, I have to. My job is to be nurse for the tired heroes. Just look at Julius Heide. He's stupid as an ox and spoils everything if Tiny isn't around to give him a slap on the jaw."

The Old Man started putting on his belt. The little Legionnaire got up.

"Old Man, stay here. I'll head the squad. You have a wife and children, and it's people like you that'll be needed after the war's over." He waved his arm at the rest of us. "Tiny, Porta and the rest are good only for the garbage can. It doesn't matter so very much if we're blown sky-high."

The Old Man stubbornly shook his head.

"You're wrong, Desert Rambler. I'm coming along, and it won't be One Squad as Lieutenant Ohlsen requests, but Number Two and I'll be the one to head it. Color Guard Paust will take over the platoon in the meantime."

"Holy Moses," the East Prussian groaned, tearing off his

leather things. "What a club of heroes! Here one can never retire!"

"Shut your filthy Königsberg mouth, or I'll smack you in the kisser," Porta threatened.

At eleven o'clock we stood in the trench ready to go. The regimental commander, Lieutenant Colonel Hinka, had come out to the position personally to keep an eye on us.

Tiny was scolding.

"Dr. Mahler said I should look out because I'm a little backward, but evidently no one pays any attention to that here. Who has to take the lead when there's trouble? Tiny! My good Holy Mother of Kazan, what a crappy war this is!"

"Cut it out, Tiny!" Colonel Hinka laughed. "Some day your gabbing mouth will get you a rope around your neck!"

The watches were synchronized.

"Eleven-o-nine on the dot," Hinka said, adjusting his watch.

From the sector to the right of us came the sound of artillery fire. A light harassing fire.

"That's in the sector of the 104th Rifle Regiment," the Legionnaire said, following the long comet's tail of a rocket shell with his eyes.

Tiny sat up on the edge of the trench stuffing himself with biscuits and black pudding.

Fatty, who had arrived together with the provisions crew, caught sight of him. He stood for a moment contemplating his guzzling. Then he exploded.

"May God help you, you clownish ape, if a report comes in about the tiniest bit of stolen biscuit. Then you'll lose your cabbage head for looting." He took a deep breath. "It'll be the most wonderful day in my life when I can bring you up before a court-martial which only deals out death sentences."

"Certainly, Herr First Sergeant," Tiny grinned, his mouth stuffed with biscuits. He clicked his heels without getting up.

Fatty opened and closed his mouth. Then he asked inquisitorially: "Where did you get the biscuits?"

Again Tiny clicked his heels, without getting up from his comfortable position at the edge of the trench.

"From a whore in Dubrasna, Herr First Sergeant. She sent it to me by a Vlassov Cossack on a dappled old mare."

"Sassy fellow," Fatty snorted. He would have liked to say more but got tongue-tied and hurriedly left. He felt unpleasantly affected by the glance of Colonel Hinka, fixed on him as if saying: Wouldn't it be a good idea if you and

your shock troops moved forward? The thought itself was
enough to make Fatty quake all over. What business did
this monkey of an officer have bringing him, the company
sergeant, out to the position, as if a command noncom had
anything to do here? A hell of a crazy idea! These young
puppies of officers thought they were somebody. Nah, it was
the old active NCOs that formed the backbone of the Army.
Wasn't the Führer himself an ordinary NCO, no more no
less? And he got the better of all the golden pheasants. Fatty
grinned aloud at the idea that generals had to click their
bony legs together for an NCO.

Colonel Hinka looked at him in surprise and asked what
the joke was.

Fatty faltered. "Something funny just occurred to me,
Herr Commander."

"Is that so?" answered Hinka. "Not, by any chance, a
shock unit in full battle dress?" Lieutenant Ohlsen smiled.

"Maybe the First Sergeant would like to come along?"

Tiny gave a howl. "Then he'll shit in his pants!"

Hinka gave Tiny a sharp look. "You'll be kind enough to
keep your mouth shut and spare us your stupid expressions.
The First Sergeant is your superior. Don't forget that!"

Tiny again clicked his heels and crowed:

"Certainly, Herr Commander, I'll surely never forget that.
I wish I could."

Hinka had difficulty keeping a straight face, but managed
to mumble: "Watch out!"

"Ready, Beier?" Lieutenant Ohlsen whispered, tapping the
Old Man's shoulder.

Tiny took his stand beside the Old Man, holding the light
MG in front of him like a shovel. Colonel Hinka shook his
head resignedly. But he didn't say anything. To discuss regulations with Tiny was simply hopeless.

"Keep the sapping equipment in your hands so it won't
rattle," said the Old Man, "and be sure to keep your eyes
out for each other so no one will get lost."

We rolled across the edge and crawled on our stomachs
across the dismal no-man's-land toward the Russian positions.

We sneaked noiselessly forward along the gallery, lunged
like panthers through the wire and crept cautiously into the
darkness lying ahead of us like a velvet wall. The Legionnaire and I crawled right behind the Old Man. Behind us
were Tiny and Porta. Heide trailed the little bag with the
bundled hand grenades to shatter the bunkers with. He was

breathing noisily as if he had asthma. When he was afraid
he always did.

All around us there was an ominous silence. The earth
was breathing. Vapors rose from the swamp. There was a
scent of burnt wood.

We felt terribly alone. Death lurked on every side.

Noiselessly the Old Man adjusted his heavy equipment and
looked at his sub-machine gun, checking whether the long
magazine had got stuck. Heide passed his hands over the
grenades in the legs of his boots.

The East Prussian shoved the intrenching spade in front
of his face.

Tiny was about to light a cigarette.

"Imbecile," the Legionnaire whispered, "do you want to
make soaring angels of us all?"

"Pig," Tiny answered under his breath.

"Shut up, man," the Old Man nervously whispered in return.

Bauer put his head on the bag with the hand grenades.

"This will never end well," he whispered pessimistically.

Lying squeezed together, we looked over a mound toward
the Russian positions, which were uncomfortably near. We
could touch the enemy's minefield just by stretching out our
hands.

Tiny set up the machine gun and stared at the Old Man.
"How do you plan to get through the minefield?"

The Legionnaire bit his lip. "We'll be hitting the clouds before we can say boo." He didn't say any more. Some sound
came to us. A slight clinking. Every muscle in our bodies
tensed.

"Death and damnation!" Porta whispered. He nudged
Tiny. "Watch out on the left!"

Once more a clinking noise in the dark and low cursing:
"Yob tvoyemat'!"

"Ivan in person," Tiny whispered cheerily.

The Old Man gave him a savage kick.

He didn't speak, though we felt he wanted to say something.

We pressed tight to the ground and held our breath. Tiny
swung the machine gun into position, ready to sweep the
terrain clean of enemies.

Porta's eyes glittered in the dark; he held the battle knife
in his hand. Stein unscrewed the cap of a hand grenade. The
porcelain ring made a small clink.

Sounds of laughter came from the darkness.

"*Mille diables!*" the Legionnaire whispered, "he'll soon forget about grinning."

Four dark figures popped up a few yards from us. All we had to do to get prisoners was to put out our hands. The problem solved without any fuss. It looked so simple.

"Go for them!" the Old Man whispered.

On noiseless cat's feet we sneaked up on the four figures, who didn't have the slightest suspicion of the danger in store for them.

We could hear them whisper and laugh in low voices.

All at once a crashing noise and a short outcry cut into the stillness of the night. Heide had fallen into a hole.

In the same instant things started moving. The four Russians jumped to their feet and plunged head over heels toward the Russian positions, screaming: "*Germanski, Germanski!*"

Tiny sprang up, gave a roar and hit the nearest Russian a slanting blow on the shoulder with his short intrenching spade.

From the Russian positions star shells shot hissing into the air, flooding the whole glacis with a crude glaring light.

Heide, who was out of the hole by now, lunged behind the machine gun and raked the positions with concentrated fire.

A man pounced upon me. I barely glimpsed a contorted Mongolian face brushing past me. An almost childish voice snarled: "*Pyos!*" Dog!

I sent three shots from my .38 into his broad face with the lightly slanted eyes. He keeled over and lay still.

From the Russian side came muffled reports from the heavy infantry guns and trench mortars.

Brandt, our top provider, was hit by a Russian spade and fell over, with blood streaming from a big open wound between his neck and shoulder.

This caused us to lose our heads. We hit out savagely with no thought for our object: to bring back prisoners.

"*Pomoshch! Pomoshch!*" cried a wounded soldier lying some distance away. Medics! Medics!

"Do you have any prisoners?" the Old Man asked in agitation while we were lying together in a hole catching our breath. "We can't go back without prisoners. That was the whole point, you know." He cast an inquiring glance toward the screaming Russian. "What about that one?"

Tiny indifferently shrugged his shoulders. "He's weak. I've made mincemeat of him. My spade is all bent from hitting him."

"Damn ass!" the Old Man shouted at him. "Do you have to do everything wrong, you lunkhead? When you've finally managed to get hold of a Russian you have to kill him right away. I curse the day we got burdened with you."

"Shove it up your ass," Tiny yelled loudly, disregarding the fact that the Russians could hear him. "I always get hell. If I drag in a Russian marshal some day, you'll jump on me straightaway: 'Tiny, you stupid ass, why didn't you bring Stalin and Molotov?' And when we start our revolution some time and I hang SS Himmler, you'll call me a dirty son of a bitch because I didn't hang Hitler!" He furiously pounded the earth with both fists, then he stretched to his full height and roared loudly: "But don't you worry, everything's all right, you cry babies. Now I'm going over to Ivan to pick up your colonel. Then maybe you'll be content!"

"Tiny!" the Old Man called, horrified. "Get down!"

A couple of Russian sub-machine guns started pounding away. The tracer bullets brushed right by Tiny. He ran ahead in complete indifference, swinging the sub-machine gun above his head.

He disappeared in the dark, but we could hear him roar savagely.

"God, he's mad, stark raving mad!" the Old Man groaned. "We've got to catch up with him before he jumps into Ivan's trench."

"This is the most dim-witted bunch in the whole 'Disarmed Forces', and here is where I had to end up," Heide said hopelessly.

"Don't preach so much," Porta said and ran after Tiny.

We found him in a shell hole bundling hand grenades for bunker cocktails. We made such a racket shouting and scolding that it could be heard far away. Tiny, who was half demented, yelled for Ivan. The shooting stopped on both sides. Watchful silence. Evidently they thought we had gone mad.

An hour later we jumped down into our positions, where we were received by Lieutenant Colonel Hinka. He was in a rage and gave the Old Man hell because we hadn't brought back any prisoners, as ordered.

"This whole company is nothing but a bunch of cows. The worst one in the entire army," he stormed. "But we'll have another talk!" He about-faced and took off without giving his hand to Lieutenant Ohlsen.

Tiny stood leaning against the wall of the trench.

Next night the company was ordered to send two platoons behind enemy lines to find out what the Russians were really doing.

When Lieutenant Ohlsen made the Commander aware that it would probably cost most of the men their lives, he went completely wild.

"Who are you to tell me, Herr Lieutenant?" he yelled. "The war is a fact, and the duty of a soldier is not to save his life, but to fight. The Division has ordered me to reconnoiter behind the lines, and this order must be followed out at whatever cost. The only thing that matters is that one single man out of the sixty-five returns and can report what goes on back there. Thousands of lives depend on this."

Lieutenant Ohlsen tried to say something, but Colonel Hinka interrupted him brutally:

"You think too much, Herr Lieutenant. Walk around dreaming of honor and such empty phrases. An order has to be obeyed, unless we want to wait for death holding hands in some passageway at Torgau. Forget what you have on the ball as long as you have to wear a steel helmet. We're the last filthy remnant of the 27th. Try to realize that! Within six hours I'll await your report, Herr Lieutenant. Over!"

Lieutenant Ohlsen stood there with the receiver in his hand. He looked lost, as if expecting Hinka's snarling voice to begin all over again.

For a long time we had heard a whirring of engines from the Russian side, but the German observation fliers hadn't been able to see anything. As was customary with the Russians, everything was expertly camouflaged. Every single tank track had been erased by working parties, and now they made use of an old standby: infantry recon.

In the marrow of our bones all of us veteran soldiers felt that something was up. The Old Man said: "I don't like this quiet. Something is happening, and something big, too. Ivan has brought together great quantities of matériel back there."

The East Prussian snorted scornfully. "They'll make a regular hare-hunt for us when they come."

"Why exactly do we have to go out on this recon?" Heide grumbled. "As soon as there's dirty work, it's 1 or 2 Platoon or all of 5 Company that has to do it."

"Because you're a stupid pig," Porta answered, "and serve in a regiment of a special sort, every single member of which is meant to have his brains blown out. I always knew you were a maned sheep and rather slow, but I'd no idea you're as stupid as you now seem to be."

"You'd better shut up, you bull," Heide shouted and threatened him with his knife. "Some day I'll get at you! You may take my word for it!"

Porta was about to jump at Heide, but the Old Man held him back.

"Why don't you cut out your perpetual squabbles and fighting! Use your strength when we get to Ivan!"

"And become the heroes of Greater Germany," Porta scoffed. "Just wait and see! We'll have our portraits displayed in Potsdam, with inscriptions in gold lettering: 'The heroes from the 27th.' I hope we won't choke on our own bravery!"

"I am brave," Tiny said. He made a threatening movement with his head toward Porta. "I've more guts than anybody else in this whole war," he cried loudly. He snapped a rifle butt with a single blow. "I'll take care of my enemies in the same way. You're one of them, Julius Jew-hater," he said, turning to big brawny Julius Heide.

At the same moment Lieutenant Ohlsen entered the bunker.

"Here are some letters," he said, throwing them on the wooden frame table. "There's one for you too, Tiny."

Tiny was speechless with amazement. His lower jaw dropped.

"Letter for me?" he stammered, glancing almost timidly at the dirty gray envelope inscribed, in pencil, with childish clumsy letters: Panzer Corporal Wolfgang Creutzfeldt, Panzer Replacement Unit 11, Paderborn. Obviously, the sender hadn't been in contact with Tiny for a long time. It was more than four years since Tiny had been at the Paderborn garrison. The garrison unit had written our field post number underneath: 23745.

"Holy Mother of Kazan!" Tiny whispered, "it's the first letter I've received in my whole life. I haven't the damnedest idea how to open it."

"Oh, come now," Lieutenant Ohlsen said, "that shouldn't be a problem."

Clumsily Tiny tore the envelope with his finger and pulled out a piece of gray wrapping paper, covered with grubby writing.

We nearly had a shock when we saw him turn pale as he laboriously spelled the letter through.

Julius Heide raised his eyebrow and asked circumspectly: "Bad news, Mac?"

Tiny didn't answer, only stared at the letter as if hypnotized.

Heide nudged him with his elbow. "What's happened,

Mac? What's made you so blue about the beak? Tell us.
Why, you look like a poisoned abortion."

Tiny flared up. "What damn business is it of yours what
has happened? Do I ever ask you about your crap?"

"Come now," Heide reassured him. "Why get excited, you
stupid boor? I meant well, you know."

Tiny let out a scream. He grabbed Heide by the throat
and flung him against the wall. Then he pulled his knife
and rushed at him.

"Now you're going to die, you wretch!"

Lightning-quick the Legionnaire tripped him. He tumbled
right in front of Heide, who was paralyzed with fear.

Tiny whirled around and glared madly at the Legionnaire.
"I'll get your head for that, you Arab gigolo!"

The Legionnaire wasn't insulted. He quietly lit a *papirosu*.

"He'll never be a gentleman," Heide muttered. "His language isn't decent."

"Nor do I want to be," Tiny yelled. He got up and
walked over to the furthest corner of the room, picked up
the letter he'd flung away and smoothed it out on his knees.
Then he began slowly struggling through it again.

The Old Man sat down beside him. He rolled two cigarettes from bits of an old newspaper, handed one to Tiny
and took the other himself.

"Can I help you, my friend?"

"Yes," Tiny growled, "by leaving me alone till Ivan or
the SS puts a bullet through my head." He stood up,
pushed the Old Man aside, crumpled up the letter and threw
it on the floor. Then he made for the exit. With a kick he
sent a bag of hand grenades lying by the door to the other
end of the bunker. He gave a big NCO in his path such a
punch in the belly that he lost his foothold and keeled
over with a groan. He kicked the unconscious man, then
turned to us, watching for his chance. "One word more,
you crappy heroes, and I'll strangle you slowly one after
another!"

He picked up a machine gun and hurled it at us. Then
he vanished into the trench.

The Old Man shook his head, picked up the letter and
unfolded it. "It must be a tough letter making him act up
like that."

"He's a stupid bastard," Heide muttered, stroking his
tender neck.

"So are you," Porta said grimly.

"We can report him, you know, and get him removed,"

said one of the fresh recruits, Corporal Trepka, whose father
was an infantry colonel.

"Why don't you do it?" Heide said, shifting his feet.

"Well, why not?" Trepka said and walked over to the table. "The nasty fellow is a criminal and ought to have been
stuck up against a wall long ago."

The Legionnaire muttered a French oath and glanced at
the Old Man.

"Are you going to report Tiny?" Heide asked watchfully,
looking at Trepka.

"If you like," Trepka answered. He pulled out a piece of
paper and started writing.

Heide was looking over his shoulder as he wrote.

"That's a great report," Heide leered. "Hand it over to
the commander of the regiment! I can promise you his eyes
will pop out of their sockets!"

"No," Trepka said, "the Commander won't get it, the Political Commissar will. He'll get it when we are relieved." He
put the prepared report in his pocket. The report would
mean execution for Tiny.

The Old Man waved the Legionnaire and me over. He
handed us Tiny's letter, which we read together:

My dear son Wolfgang,

I have rheumatism in my legs, but I'll write to you
anyway to let you know you're not my son any more,
even if I did bear you. I curse that day! Your father,
that scoundrel, was a regular drunk, but you're a thousand times worse. You're a criminal, and your poor mother has to pay for it. I got a pair of woolen stockings
from Mrs. Becker yesterday. I'm sure you remember Mrs. Becker, she helped me place you in that institution with the good brothers and sisters. She wished
only the best for you, as she does for everybody. But
you were ungrateful and ran away from there just because of a little flogging, which I'm sure you honestly
deserved. You've always made mischief. You're a regular good-for-nothing. Many fine ladies and gentlemen
wanted to help you when I did their cleaning. I was so
ashamed when you stole a mark out of greengrocer Mül-
lerhaus's frock pocket. The Schupo's ought to have finished you off when they beat you up for drinking Police
Sergeant Grüner's milk. You excused yourself saying you
were thirsty, you rascal, as if water wasn't good enough
for a guttersnipe like you. I, your poor mother, have
done so much for you. The day you went to the reform-

atory you got a pair of brand new wooden shoes and
two pairs of socks, and the rheumatism in my shoulder
didn't keep me from thrashing you every day you needed it. All those wet blots you see on the letter are the
tears of your poor mother. On the work assignment card
it says you're a habitual criminal, and Herr Managing
Clerk Apel, who's such a good person and fine gentleman, says that if only you were dead I could get work,
again, but you're an anti-social element and a clog
around your mother's rheumatic feet, but when you're
dead they will review the case, says Herr Managing
Clerk Apel. I've got a new red coat, Wolfgang, with
nice gray fur on the collar. It's so becoming. Herr
Breining, who presented it to me, tells me the same.
Now be a good boy, little Wolfgang, and give your poor
mother just one little joy. Hurry up and get killed. It
can't be so difficult out there in Russia. Everyone says
it's very easy. But of course you won't do it, you scoundrel, just because you want to distress your mother.
Wolfgang, we don't have any coke left at all. It's your
fault, I'm told at the distribution office. The other day
Herr Schneider at the post office, you know, the man
at window 3, where you pay money you owe, said to
me when I was over there to pay four marks for something that's none of your business, you punk: Is your disgusting son still alive, little Mrs. Creutzfeldt? Like all
the other fine gentlemen he says it's terrible I should
have to be burdened with you, you sot. Your poor
mother is cold, Wolfgang, it's very cold here, and my
rheumatism is bad. I've even gotten three catskins to
apply. Every night the Tommies come dropping bombs,
and though you get to hear a lot of news in the cellar,
it's still bad. Yesterday I managed to exchange a
butter coupon for a coffee coupon. This was with Mrs.
Kirse on the second floor. But now, really, be a good
son, Wolfgang, and hurry up and get killed, so I can
go up to Distribution and say: My son Wolfgang Helmuth Leo Creutzfeldt has died for the Führer and the
Fatherland. I cry bitterly when I come to think how
well off we could have been if you'd been a good boy
and joined the Party like Mrs. Schulze's Carl on the
third floor. You know, those people who had a gray
cat with a white tail which you threw into the Elbe.
Carl is now a fine gentleman. Comes often home on
leave. He is SS *Unterscharführer* and has many decorations. Mrs. Schulze says he has seen the Führer, and

SS Himmler bawled him out once. He'll become something grand, mixing as he does with such distinguished gentlemen. Mrs. Kirse thinks so too. His mother has great joy of him. Last time he was on leave she got a ring and a necklace of real gold and with a red stone in it and ten butter coupons and a piece of pork. He had received the jewels from an anti-social element to spare the monster's life, one of those who exploit us poor Germans. But trust me, the SS know how to take care of those nasty people. Carl has been telling us about it. We were lucky we got the Führer to clean up this mess. Wolfgang, now I hear Mrs. Schulze calling me. I'm going up for coffee. Be a good boy now, you drunk, and die like a hero so your poor mother can get her coke. I don't wish to send you my love, you bastard. Your birth was so hard, but you've always been inconsiderate.

> Your faithful mother,
> Mrs. Louise Creutzfeldt
> née Weidner
> Bremer Chaussée 65.

Ask your comrades to send me a picture of your grave when you're dead, so I can show it to Herr Managing Clerk Apel.

"By Allah, what a nasty old bitch of a mother," the Legionnaire exclaimed.

The Old Man nodded with clenched teeth.

"Let's get Tiny before something happens!"

Heide asked what was in the letter.

"Why don't you ask Tiny?" the Old Man said, putting the greasy letter in his pocket.

We found him by a battered machine gun bunker. When he saw us he let out a grumble.

"I've read your letter, Tiny," the Old Man said. "Your mother's a swine!"

Tiny was puffing away at his *papirosu*. For answer he made a deep growling sound, like that of a bear ready to attack.

"My mother is a stinking bitch, a sewer. She once reported me to Kripo for cleaning out a rotten cigarette machine. I even gave her three packs. She wanted to have half of it, that bitch, but I refused to give it to her, and so she reported me. When Stapo once came visiting and found some magazines around which one of her fine gentlemen had left behind, she simply said, cool like anything, that they were mine, but, hell, everybody I knew could swear I never fooled around with crap like that. And every time the same story. I'll eat my steel helmet if she won't be on her way to the Gestapo again pretty soon to put one over on them about me. As you can see from the letter she has become stuck on the idea that I must die." His eyes burnt ominously under his heavy bushy eyebrows. "You see, Old Man, I was born like a rat, grew up like a rat, was chased like a rat, and now they want to have me killed like a rat!"

The Old Man patted him on the shoulder.

"Take it easy, Tiny. It's true, when you joined our gang long ago you didn't introduce yourself in any specially nice way and you've brought loads of trouble on our necks. But little by little we've come to like you. And though Colonel Hinka and Captain von Barring have given you hell for being a pig, they like you and will stand up for you if the SS try to get you."

The Legionnaire gave Tiny a friendly poke in the belly with his clenched fist. "When we're through with this war some day, you're welcome to come with me if you've no other place to go!"

"So you don't believe that Emma meant a word of what she said? Did she say it all just to get me hepped up?"

"No, no, Tiny, of course she meant it, but all sorts of things can happen," the Legionnaire consoled him.

"Christ, I was so happy when Lieutenant Ohlsen handed me that letter. It was the first letter I'd ever received and I said to myself: Damn it, Tiny, you're a fine gentleman now, receiving a real letter with stamp and everything. I sat thinking about all the people who'd troubled themselves over my letter. And then, look what a crappy letter it turned out to be."

"You shouldn't let that worry you," Julius Heide cut in. "A great many people write letters that should never have been sent. I bet your mother has regretted it already."

"Do you think so, Julius?" Tiny asked, skeptically. "It would be darned wonderful if she had."

At this moment something happened we'd have thought impossible and never would believe if anyone told it to us: Tiny, with his ice-cold eyes, burst into tears. Tiny, whose eyes never smiled even if his whole body shook with laughter. The tears made light stains on his grimy cheeks.

Julius Heide put his arm around his shoulder.

"Hell, Tiny, cut that out. I swear you'll make me cry too. My mother makes the best potato pancakes in the world, and in my house I'll let you eat as many as you want when the war's over. You can sleep in my den. We'll take turns sleeping in the hay. Say to hell with your mother, that bitch. She isn't worth crying over, and if someone is out to hurt you, just let Julius Heide know about it. If we two stand back to back we can fight a whole panzer army."

But Tiny was crying to break one's heart.

We gave him schnapps. We gave him cigarettes. We gave him pictures of girls, the kind he used to collect.

Gifts were piled up before him on the edge of the trench like birthday presents.

The East Prussian handed him his jackknife and said with a lump in his throat: "You can have my knife!"

But Tiny was inconsolable. The griefs and privations of years had broken through. No one had ever said good night to him or stroked his hair when he was a little boy. You don't do that with a rat.

Lieutenant Ohlsen came by and asked what was wrong. He looked at Tiny in amazement.

Without a word the Old Man handed him the letter. He read it and shook his head.

"There's just no limit to human meanness;" he said in a low voice. He gave Tiny a tap. "Hold your head high, my boy! You have us and we're your friends. I'll give this letter to the Commander."

The head officers of the Division were throwing a party. The wine had loosened their tongues.

No one cared to hide his contempt for the conduct of the Government. In their eyes, it consisted of people who weren't fit for their exclusive company.

"What good would the Party be without us?" said the commander of the artillery regiment. He looked around the circle of officers, all with high combat distinctions on the breasts of their uniforms.

Like most high officers, they showed in opposition when they felt sub rosa. It was part of good form to express reservations about the Party, but the critical pronouncements were not rooted in principle. They sprang from self-interest.

For, actually, they didn't have very strong objections to the Party. They only resented the fact that it didn't recognize the sovereignty of the Armed Forces.

They had nothing much against Hitler and his war. Only, they didn't like to see the former corporal assume the pretentious role of an expert strategist.

The aristocratic staff officers wanted to win the war, even if Hitler and his Party would be the real victors.

chapter xiv

Behind Enemy Lines

JUST BEFORE midnight we were in the field waiting for zero hour.

"Extra portions of schnapps and the whole afternoon off," Joseph Porta muttered. "That means we're really in for it. A triple portion of schnapps means slaughter!"

The Division had altered its order of 12 noon, so that now not only two platoons but all of 5 Company were to push ahead for deep penetration recon. The company would be divided into two independently operating units.

"Not a single man will get back," Lieutenant Ohlsen had said, shaking his head.

The Legionnaire was feverishly polishing his machine gun, an MG 42, a new quick-firing weapon.

"All the same, one feels quite at home with this sprayer," he said, whisking away a speck of dust from the lock. "There's a lot to be said against our trip to the woods, but nothing at all against this sprayer. With this rod it isn't half bad even if the whole field swarms with Russkis."

"Really, come down to earth, will you," the East Prussian muttered. "Let's continue our talk in six to seven hours, if we're still alive!"

We were equipped with camouflage from our helmets to our boots. We looked like spacemen. A never-ending, unchanging line of men armed to the teeth.

"Thirty seconds," Lieutenant Ohlsen croaked. He stood between the Legionnaire and Tiny, sub-machine gun across his shoulder and stop watch in his hand. "Forward," he commanded. Like weasels we clambered over the edge of the trench.

A grenadier first lieutenant said ominously: "I'm glad I'm not going. It will turn out badly."

"Squirt," Porta grinned, hustling after the Legionnaire and Heide.

One after another the squads vanished over the edge and plunged into the darkness.

To throw the Russians off the scent short fierce artillery fire started up in the adjacent sector.

"Watch your snouts!" Tiny warned. "There are mines around. I can smell those contraptions ten yards away." He wormed his way ahead of the squad and piloted us across the tightly packed minefield. "Forward, heroes! Follow Tiny!"

"For Christ's sake, shut your trap, Tiny," the Old Man said. "You're blabbering so loud it can be heard for miles!"

"Don't scold me," Tiny warned, "or I'll go crazy and get up and start calling Ivan!"

We got through the Russian lines and reached a village about four or five miles behind the front.

It was Porta who discovered the expertly camouflaged tanks.

"Holy Mother of Kazan!" Tiny exclaimed. "A whole army of T-34's!"

"If these start rolling we won't even have time to tighten our ass-holes," the East Prussian followed up.

"Shut up," the Old Man said, looking nervously about him.

"Don't get excited, now," Porta grinned, "in a moment we may flutter around with the angels blowing trumpets!"

"Jesus Christ, I get goose pimples just looking at all those T-34's," Stein exclaimed. "Must be at least a hundred of them."

"May I offer you a piece of good advice?" Tiny asked. "Let's take the through train to the German lines. You can smell murder for miles around here—neck-shots!"

"You're right," the Legionnaire said. "Let's get away from here mighty fast. We've seen all we wanted."

"Very well," the Old Man muttered. "Let's clear out!"

"I've got my racing shoes on," Tiny grinned. "Just follow me and it won't take long to get home again, I promise you!"

"You're just about the biggest chicken I've ever run across," Corporal Trepka scoffed. "To run before those inferior Russians is a disgrace!".

Tiny scrutinized Trepka's arrogant Junker face, with its spiteful staring eyes. He gave a grunt.

"You're welcome to stay behind and talk with those inferiors. As for me, I've no desire to be a hero."

"Keep shut, Tiny, and let's get going," came resolutely from the Legionnaire.

With Tiny and Porta in front we rushed head over heels through the forest. They guided us across the narrow and often submerged paths with unerring instinct.

We had barely reached open country when four green star shells went up and turned the night into a hall of phantoms. Our faces took on a corpselike look.

Quick as lightning we threw ourselves down for cover. Everything suddenly came alive around us, as if an invisible hand had pushed a button.

Shrill voices of command and the screeching of pea-whistles came from the darkness. The air quivered with the roar and rumble of hundreds of engines. There was a clanking of heavy tank chains. The ground beneath us shook as self-propelled artillery and T-34's rolled forward in battle formation.

"Holy Mother Bridget!" Tiny exclaimed, halfway getting up. "I'll be hanged if we aren't right in the middle of the concentration area. This is the fault of that damn black cat I ran across this morning, but just let the grinning thing wait till we meet again!"

"Imbecile," Trepka hissed, "it's hard to believe you're normal."

Tiny turned his head and put out his fist at him, but Trepka drew back instantly.

"Is that so?" Tiny growled. "It seems the two of us

should have a little talk, you little cardboard soldier!"

"What are we to do?" Grenadier Schmidt whimpered, peering to see where the droning sound in the forest came from.

"Just go on lying quite still and count the stars," the Legionnaire answered, "and then follow the rest of us when we take off."

"When you want to get out is your own affair," Tiny said, "but I'm getting out right now, because in a little while Ivan's infantry will turn up and then there will be neck-shots. I can't stay with you, because I promised Emma I'd come back home."

"How do you know that infantry are coming?" Trepka asked doubtfully.

"What a greenhorn!" Heide snorted. "You've a lot to learn yet. The infantry usually come after the tanks, and if they find us here you'll forget about being a hero."

"Then may God help us," Bauer continued.

"There they are," Porta said, pointing toward the edge of the forest.

A long line of figures came out of the forest in single file: Russian infantry.

A moment later the tanks started rolling towards the German lines.

" 'Bye, heroes, Tiny's moving out." And he was off.

The Old Man and Porta followed. Then the Legionnaire and I beat it. Trepka tried to hold Heide back, but he cut loose with the butt of his sub-machine gun.

Star shells were sent aloft.

Behind us the Russian infantry were roaring, *"Ura Stalin!"* and firing wildly in every direction.

Wave upon wave of brown-clad infantrymen were pouring out of the Russian trenches.

The whole front came alive. It turned into some terrible inferno. Shells of all calibers tore up the gutted ground. German and Russian artillery vied with each other in making hell perfect.

In one jump the Legionnaire and I landed in a deep shell hole, still warm from the explosion. Vague parts of a man lay at the bottom, but we didn't care. Anything for cover against the shells.

Someone fell on my back. I screamed in terror.

"Quiet, you fool!" came Tiny's voice. He was smeared all over with blood. He had had a hand-to-hand fight with a Russian.

The sounds of clanking chains were coming closer.

"A T-34—they must have seen us," Tiny whispered. "Lie

where you are till he's almost on top of us, then we'll run."

The hateful sound of rattling chains came closer and closer. I could feel a sickening fear crawling up my spine, but I knew it meant certain death to run a second too early.

The Legionnaire's lips quivered like a rabbit's. In his fear he dug his fingers deep in the ground. Tiny looked as if the whole thing didn't concern him. Suddenly he roared: "Go!" We saw the nose of the T-34 by the edge of the hole.

How we got out I don't know. All I know is that our legs moved of themselves.

The tank wriggled across the hole, crushing everything in it.

Then it rumbled on.

We landed in another hole, where we lay with open mouths gasping for breath. Our motley camouflage clothes were too tight, as if set on strangling us.

Tiny bunched together six hand grenades for an extra strong sticky-bomb, muttering: "I'll settle their hash for them. Damn Stalin-fry trying to keep Tiny from getting back to Emma!"

Again chains rattling.

"I can't stand it," I screamed.

"Then why don't you send a telegram to Zhukov so he can pause while you recover?" the Legionnaire sneered. He raised his head above the edge of the hole to look for the tank we could hear approaching.

It stopped. The engine idled. The turret searched the terrain with its long gun. Then the heavy diesel engine whined again.

Once more the uncanny clatter of chains.

There was a clank and a roar. A shell flew from its gun against a German machine-gun post, which blew up in a shaft of flame.

Tiny swung back his arm with a triumphant leer. The big bunch of grenades hissed.

"Let them go, damn you," the Legionnaire yelled, with a hypnotized stare at Tiny's hand.

He held them maddeningly long before he threw them, then dropped back in the hole.

We pushed our faces in the mire. An ear-splitting explosion. We were surrounded by a sea of flames.

"Now we can take off, boys," Tiny said, looking exultantly for a moment at the burning tank. A man hung halfway out of a turret hatch, shrieking insanely.

The Legionnaire fired his sub-machine gun at him. "A new kind of anesthesia," he groaned.

Lieutenant Ohlsen rushed out of the forest like the rest of us. Right behind him fifteen fresh recruits ran in a close huddle.

A T-34 spotted them. A searchlight flared and caught them in its blinding light.

"Run," cried Lieutenant Ohlsen. But no one heard him.

From a depression in the ground where he lunged for cover he saw the reddish-blue and green tracer bullets sweep the fifteen recruits off their feet.

Sergeant Schneider ran headlong toward the silenced German lines. A fifteen cm. high-explosive shell grounded before his feet. A dazzling flare of fire. He was torn into three pieces.

NCO Grunert and tank gunner Hauber came into the sights of a T-34 driving around doing target practice with its machine guns.

Hauber was hit by a tracer bullet. It went right through his breast. He stopped, fell on his face and uttered a loud ringing scream. His arms and legs thrashed the earth. The T-34 ran over him. His bones scrunched, and blood and shreds of flesh squirted to the sides of the heavy chains. It looked like a car driving through a puddle.

NCO Grunert stood petrified in front of the steel monster. He stretched out his arms as if trying to stop it with his hands.

The T-34 rocked gracefully in its chains as if about to dance a quadrille. In the joint of the left chain hung one of Hauber's hands. It seemed to be waving. Blood dripped from the two front rollers.

Grunert's eyes nearly popped out of their sockets. Then the heavy engine roared. The gears shrieked. The vehicle curtsied.

Grunert screamed and started running. He fell. In the next moment everything in him seemed to get crushed. Fifty-five tons of steel trundled over his legs and turned them into pulp. He dragged himself along the torn-up ground, the mush-like stumps trailing behind him.

A Russian infantryman caught sight of him, cursed and fired half a score of bullets at his back. He collapsed and gurgled. Then he lay still. The infantryman had only smashed his shoulder.

Lieutenant Burgstadt, second in command, panicked and ran into a mine which sent him flying. His abdomen was torn up. His right leg dangled from a couple of muscle fibers just below the knee. When he was found by two Russian infantrymen, he was squatting. He pressed both hands tight against his abdomen, trying to hold back his intestines. The blood oozed out between his fingers. His mouth was wide open, but no sound could be heard.

"*Pyos!*" one of the Russians grumbled and sent a bullet through his nose.

"*Chort germanski,*" the other said, plunging his long triangular bayonet into the chest of the nineteen-year-old Lieutenant. He did it very slowly and deliberately. His sister had been hanged by the SS in Kharkov. He followed the motto of Ilya Ehrenburg: "Kill, you Bolshevik soldiers of Russia! Hate, you riflemen of the Red Army! Slake your thirst for revenge in German blood!"

He grinned to his comrade and shouted: "*Davay!*"

The men in the third platoon, under the command of Sergeant Major Dorn, ran around like stray sheep in no-man's-land. Three T-34's blazed away at them.

They sought cover in a hole, where they huddled together one on top of the other. Russian infantry stormed toward them from the edge of the wood.

Sergeant Dorn roared his brief snarling command. They opened fire on the Russians with their three MG 42's. The T-34's fired some high-explosive shells at them.

They stood up and stretched out their arms, despite Sergeant Dorn's threat to report them for cowardice.

The Russian infantrymen, who were under cover, stood up likewise. They raised their sub-machine guns and used the shocked third platoon for target practice. They didn't stop till the last man had hit the ground.

"Now we know what we have to expect," the Old Man said. "There's only one thing to do: Get back to our own lines as quickly as possible and fire at anything that stands in the way!"

Joseph Porta sat on the edge of the trench, a large can of beef in his hand. He lectured Tiny about the connection between beef and heightened potency. He made an eloquent gesture with his hand to get Tiny to understand what was meant by potency, but was interrupted by long rumbling detonations from hundreds of guns.

The blast from the firing was so tremendous that Porta and his can were sent flying and hit Tiny's head. Tiny had been sitting cross-legged at the bottom of the trench.

In a few minutes the entire trench system had been pulverized beyond recognition.

The dive bombers poured from the sky in swarms. Napalm bombs exploded.

From the forest the Russian artillery belched forth destruction against the German lines.

There was no earth. No sky. No sun. No grass. The world consisted of explosions, yells, roars, groans, and screams.

Those who were already dead were again and again hurled high in the air.

Thousands of shell splinters hissed around both the living and the dead.

The Division existed no more.

chapter xv

The Partisans

THE REMNANTS of 5 Company stood at the edge of a forest seventeen miles to the southwest of the original German front line area. Some of the men, twelve in all now, were sitting; others lay around. The men were Lieutenant Ohlsen, Fatty, Porta, Tiny, the Legionnaire, the Old Man, Bauer, the East Prussian, Stein, Heide, Trepka, and myself.

Tiny was chewing on a sappy twig, trying this way to quench his flaming thirst.

Lieutenant Ohlsen had aged ten years in one night. His deep-set eyes were bloodshot and fixed in a glassy stare.

"Twelve men," he groaned. "All that's left of 225! What in the world are we going to do?" He looked despairingly from one to the other.

"Herr Lieutenant!" Fatty rapped out. "Allow me to make a suggestion."

Lieutenant Ohlsen waved his hand in a tired gesture. "Let's hear, First Sergeant."

"I propose we walk over to the Russians all together!"

Tiny guffawed. He called to the Legionnaire, who was sitting on a windfall: "The command NCO has got war fatigue. He thinks he can go to Ivan for a rest cure!"

Fatty flared up. "Be kind enough to shut your mouth, Corporal!"

Tiny openly grinned at him. "You fat pig, by the proposal you made a moment ago you lost every right to command either me or anyone else in this gang."

Fatty swallowed. He turned to Lieutenant Ohlsen.

"Herr Lieutenant, I request that this man be immediately court-martialed for open mutiny!"

"Come down to earth," Julius Heide said, cutting into the conversation. "You can't be quite sane, Fatty. If it suits us, Tiny and I can set up a court-martial right now and hang you from the nearest tree."

"Herr Lieutenant, this is mutiny!" Fatty bawled.

"No, First Sergeant," came sharply from Lieutenant Ohlsen. "As a matter of fact, by your proposal to run over to the enemy you've made yourself guilty on three counts, for which a court of the whole crew may send you to the gallows."

Fatty gaped in astonishment.

Tiny grinned and tickled him behind the ear. "You fat clod, how I'll make you blow when I hang you."

"Leave him alone, Tiny," the Old Man said. "He's always been a swine. Now besides he's a cowardly swine. We'll settle with him when we get back—if we do get back."

He glanced across at the roller conveyor, where the Russians were pouring west, in the direction Lvov-Brest-Litovsk and Tolochino. To us it sounded like an ominous storm. Thundering tanks, rumbling engines, rattling chains, neighing horses, and then the artillery following behind, with the boom of its long-range guns quickly drawing nearer.

Porta and Tiny had found a commissariat store, but very little had been left behind: fourteen cans of beef, nine packages of hardtack, a few soggy crackers, and a cat. Except for Tiny and Porta, everybody was disgusted with the cat, but Tiny pushed back his bowler and sneered.

"Some day you'll be wiser, you pampered soldiers." He waved his hand at the forest. "That copse over there is about sixty miles deep and chock-full of partisans. In a couple of days you'll be ravenously hungry. Your mouths will be one big gaping hole, and you'll just be dying to sink your teeth into pussy."

"You stinking pig," Trepka exclaimed, disgust written on every feature of his refined face. "That a fellow like you should be allowed to wear a uniform and carry arms at all is a riddle to me."

Tiny whirled around. "Just say one word more, my boy, and I'll snap your spine. *Ponimayu*, you super shit?"

Trepka turned pale. He gave Tiny a hateful look and mumbled something that couldn't be made out. He felt for his pistol, but noticing Heide's eyes upon him, gave it up.

"Herr Lieutenant," Tiny said and chucked the bag of provisions over to Lieutenant Ohlsen. He held the cat in his hand like a killed rabbit. "Would you divide the provisions?"

The Lieutenant nodded. He divided the provisions into twelve portions of exactly the same size, so exactly that at the end everyone received a fourth of a cracker.

When the provisions had been distributed, Tiny looked at each of us in turn. He swung the cat above his head.

"So none of you would like to have any part of pussy?"

No one answered.

"Very well, you monks," he went on, "you'd better make sure not to come to me afterwards and ask for a leg of it." He pulled his tobacco pouch out of his pocket. "Here I have tobacco. Every morning I'll roll twelve weeds and each of you may come and get his when he wants to. But it's no present. It's a loan, and I want to have it back. The interest will be a quarter for each whole one!" He threatened with a large fist. "And for your information, this fist is my lawyer and the other the bailiff, and you bet distresses are levied promptly. *Ponimayu?*"

"Just how much ammunition do we have?" Lieutenant Ohlsen asked, glancing up.

"Damn little, Herr Lieutenant," Porta answered, shying a rock into the little lake. It skipped five to six times over the tranquil surface. "But I guess there is enough for a bullet through the skull of each of us."

"Shut up, Porta, with all your tiresome twaddle," Lieutenant Ohlsen flared up. He shoved three ammunition boxes over to the Old Man. "These ones are full. How is the MG? Is it okay?"

"Yes," the Old Man answered curtly and kicked the toe of his boot with the other as if miserably bored.

"I say!" Porta bawled. "Three boxes of gunpowder and a real machine gun! If we don't win this war, we are simply not worthy to be called Teutons, sons of the Nibelungs."

Lieutenant Ohlsen pretended not to hear Porta's mockery. He turned to the Old Man: "What other arms do we have?" –

The Old Man was tapping an anthill with a twig. He answered indifferently:

"Three sub-machine guns—one Russian. Seventeen hand grenades. A flame-thrower, and a stovepipe without ammunition."

"Holy Mary of Sankt Pauli!" Porta rejoiced. He doubled up with laughter. "I'll be damned if it isn't enough to hold one's own against a whole army. Let's just hope it won't get through to our colleagues what a dangerous bunch we are, because then they might run again!"

"Shut your damn mouth!" flashed Lieutenant Ohlsen. "Your endless twaddle doesn't help us a bit. Why don't you instead give us some hint how we can steer through the partisan territory and get back to the German lines. There must be a new front line somewhere."

"Pardon me for interfering," Tiny cut in, "but I believe the new front line is being set up in the vicinity of Berlin."

"This is disloyal talk!" Trepka cried. "I request court-martial in accordance with the Führer's Order Number 8!"

"Trepka, you can't be quite sane. Do you imagine we've time to lose over that kind of nonsense here behind the Russian lines?"

Trepka clicked his heels and looked at Lieutenant Ohlsen with a fanatic gleam in his eye. He crowed like a Bantam cock.

"Herr Lieutenant, every German soldier regardless of rank may request court-martial proceedings against defeatists and traitors!" He handed Lieutenant Ohlsen his written denunciation of Tiny.

Lieutenant Ohlsen read it through in silence and then tore it up. He looked sharply at Trepka, who stood before him straight as a ramrod, completely sure of himself.

"In your place I would forget about that denunciation. The idea of court-martial seems to have gotten stuck in your throat."

Tiny, who sat on a tree stump between Porta and the

Legionnaire, let out a shout which rang through the forest. "Let's see how eager our budding colonel will be to court-martial poor Tiny after Ivan has picked us up. Julius Jewhater has told me all about that dirty report."

"Cut out the clamor, will you!" Lieutenant Ohlsen admonished him, "or we'll be on our way to Kolyma before we know it."

"*Saperlotte!*" the Legionnaire grumbled. "I definitely prefer the Sahara to Siberia."

"I say, to hell both with your Sahara and Siberia if only Joseph Porta can get to Bornholmerstrasse, Moabitt, Berlin."

"And how does Joseph Porta propose to get there?" Lieutenant Ohlsen jeered.

"We lift a truck from Ivan. It's better than to walk," Porta answered nonchalantly.

Lieutenant Ohlsen looked at the Old Man and shook his head. The Old Man shrugged his shoulders.

"A crazy idea," he muttered.

Porta got up, slung his machine gun over his shoulder and trudged off into the forest.

Like a faithful dog Tiny followed in his tracks, lugging along the ammunition boxes.

Lieutenant Ohlsen shook his head once again. He commanded: "In single file after me!"

For hours we pushed our way through the jungle-like evergreen forest. We cried. We cursed. We fought. But the drive for self-preservation and the fear of what we had to expect from the Russians if we fell into their hands compelled us to keep moving.

With the unerring instinct of wolves of the wild, Porta and Tiny led us through brush and swamp until, after four days of intolerable exertions, we saw the glare from some fires.

In our fright we hid among the pine trees. Except for Porta and Tiny we were all agreed that we must get away from those fires, but in the end Lieutenant Ohlsen surrendered unconditionally to Porta and Tiny, though deep down he looked upon both as insane.

"If there are fires, there are Ivans, too," Porta said with conviction, "and where there are Ivans there are trucks, and we are going to use a truck. Tiny, come, let's look into it."

They vanished in the darkness. The Old Man and Lieutenant Ohlsen cursed savagely.

Returning two hours later they squatted down beside us as we lay in the tall grass.

Tiny pushed back his bowler. He was gurgling with laughter.

"We ought to have met a long time ago, Joseph Porta. Think of all the things we could have fixed on Reeperbahn. You'd have conned the dudes and Tiny would have socked 'em."

"A gem of a truck," Porta mumbled.

"What do you mean?" Lieutenant Ohlsen asked impatiently.

"A cross-country armored vehicle for tank gunners, crammed with gasoline cans, enough to take us to Bornholmerstrasse!"

"And the crew?" Lieutenant Ohlsen asked, staring at the dark crowns of the trees.

"Nothing to speak of," Tiny answered, jabbing at some mosquitoes. "Just eight yellow monkeys sitting around a coal-basin getting soaked. *Ponimayu?*"

"They have at least three quarts of vodka," Porta said, "which they have pinched from one of their QMC officers, with guarantee."

–Tiny laughed softly. "And now those two Tartar baboons are sitting there lapping it up as if the war would soon be over. I can bet they sit there thinking: The Germans, that Nazi riff-raff, have almost been chased back to Poland."

Porta laughed loudly. "And suddenly there we are pinching their armored truck. They'll have a fit!"

We lay for a little while in silence. You could feel everyone pondering that truck.

Porta rolled a *papirosu* for himself.

After a moment Lieutenant Ohlsen stood up. "Very well, let's pick it up."

And now one of those countless dramas never reported in communiqués took place behind enemy lines. The only consequence of such incidents is that a few names are struck from the muster roll.

Corporal Vasily Rostov and tank gunner Ivan Skolyenski of the 34th Panzer Brigade had just walked over to their wonderful new troop transport truck to pick up a couple of pieces of smoked mutton, when they felt a pair of steel fingers around their throats.

Slowly everything went black before their eyes. The new truck seemed to float in the air. Vasily just managed to put his hand to his throat and touch the strangling fingers. Then he died.

Ivan saw his two children before him. He got only a brief glimpse of them. He wanted to call them, but not a sound passed his lips. His legs twitched a bit. The Legionnaire slightly tightened his grip. Then he died too.

Porta and Tiny quickly pulled the dead men's blouses over their black panzer coats and put on the Russian helmets. They had a brief whispered exchange with the rest of the squad. Then all of us sneaked up to the fires, where a few Russians, the rest of the truck's crew, could be made out.

"*Yob tvoyemat*'," Porta cursed loudly.

The Russians by the fire laughed. One of them called: "Hurry up now. We're waiting."

"Right away, my boy, right away," the Legionnaire whispered. You'll soon be home in the garden of Allah!"

We approached from the smoking side of the coal-basin, noiselessly, like snakes. Julius Heide readied his steel sling. The Legionnaire massaged his wrist and tightened his grip on his Moorish dagger. The Old Man tested his short intrenching spade, turning it in his fist. Each and every one tried out the feel of his special weapon.

Spades and knives flashed in the glare from the small fire. A sickening gurgle came from a couple of the surprised tank gunners as knives and spades cut into quivering flesh.

Julius Heide lunged at a sergeant. He pressed his face into the glowing embers of the fire, which went out with a fizz. He released his victim only when he didn't move any more.

Lieutenant Ohlsen vomited.

The whole incident happened so incredibly fast—without noise, without heroism—that we looked in astonishment at the corpses of the Russian tank gunners. One of them had a piece of bread in his hand. Another held an overturned messtin. The *kapusta* had poured over his breast.

"Not one eye will be dry when the message of the heroes' deaths gets to the village," Stein grinned. He poked the corpse of the sergeant with the toe of his boot.

The Old Man sat rocking, head on hands. He was deathly pale. He had thrown the bloodstained spade some distance away from him. Lieutenant Ohlsen went on vomiting bile.

Those two could never get used to it.

Tiny and Porta had forgotten the dead. They had jumped into the brand-new armored truck. Porta behind the wheel. Tiny behind the machine gun.

When they discovered how many weapons it contained, Julius and Stein stood up in the back of the truck and uttered one joyous exclamation after another. It was crammed with ammunition: two machine guns and one of those peerless Russian trench mortars.

Porta screamed with joy. He revved up the engine and let it roar till the air quivered.

"This is quite a coach, isn't it?" he gushed. "You won't find its match in the whole German army!"

Lieutenant Ohlsen and the Old Man jumped in when the engine started roaring.

"Have you gone completely out of your mind?" Lieutenant Ohlsen rapped. "That roar can be heard as far as the roller conveyor. Make it run more quietly."

"Can't be done, Herr Lieutenant," Porta yelled back. "Ivan doesn't know how to build noiseless engines. They have to creak and bang." He took a turn with the heavy truck. The chains clattered over the burnt-down fire and the corpses. "Ivan Stinkonovich, this is Joseph Porta, Corporal by the Grace of God in Hitler's defeated army!"

He put on the brakes. The chains made a squelching noise and clouds of earth flew about our ears. He put on the headlights, which again made the Lieutenant shout.

"Turn out those lights, man, and I order you to shut your mouth!"

"Herr Lieutenant, if I do as you say we won't get very far. Now we're no longer scared Germans but bold Ivans. We've won the war, thrashed the Nazis, chased them deep into Poland. We'll soon be in Berlin which has real china toilets. So why drive in the dark and in silence, *Gospodin Leytenant*? Lots of light, oceans of light! Mother Russia is rejoicing! The victory is ours! The proletariat is mighty! Long live Daddy Stalin! *Yob tvoyemat'*!"

Lieutenant Ohlsen pointed a finger at his forehead and looked at the Old Man. He thought Porta must be insane.

Like one possessed he guided the heavy truck through the night. He and Tiny sat on the driver's seat, dressed in Russian uniform coats and steel helmets.

Often we would pass by camps where the narrow road didn't permit him to turn aside. He just speeded up the truck and raised his fist for the Red Front greeting, while bearded, wild-looking, half-uniformed men waved and yelled to us, swinging their weapons above their heads.

"*Uraaa* Stalin! Long live the Red Army!" partisans flushed with victory roared after what they took to be a Russian armored car.

"To Warsaw and Brest-Litovsk!" Porta yelled back. "Down with the *Germanski*! We'll wash and crap in cans made of china in Berlin!"

"Put away a can for us too, brother Gospodin," the partisans bellowed for good-bye.

Hour after hour the sound of clattering chains was heard as the truck rumbled through the big forest. When we halted during the day, the truck was camouflaged. It couldn't be seen from a yard's distance. Half of us stood guard behind machine guns and trench mortars, while the second half slept.

Somewhere deep within the forest a partisan unit under the command of a lieutenant from the Red Army were busy with some sort of court-martial. A young Russian woman, hailing from the Volga district, had fallen into their hands. To get board and lodging the girl had served as a kind of office help for a German regimental staff. Then the offensive started rolling. Chaos. Panic. She was forgotten more or less deliberately. There were plenty of girls wherever they went. The red braiding of the artillery officer has always appealed to girls. The last thing she saw in the village was a cloud of dust after the departing regimental staff.

Quickly she packed her few things in a couple of bags, slung them across her shoulder and set out on the roller conveyor. Around her, German soldiers were being bawled out and cursed by brutal MPs as they poured back from the front. She fell. She got up. She staggered. She wept. For a few miles she was allowed to hold on to a cavalryman's stirrups. He was her countryman, a Cossack.

Finally the Cossack increased his speed. She couldn't keep up with him any more. She stumbled and fell. The horse pranced. The Cossack swiped at her with his long *nagayka*, gave out a short *"Nichego!"* and spat after her. He spurred his horse and galloped down the roller conveyor with the sunlight reflected in the red crown of his cap.

For a short stretch she rode with an infantry kitchen truck. Then she was chased off by a lieutenant.

Before she knew, the soldiers of her own country had popped up on the roller conveyor.

She ran into the forest to hide, though she had more enemies, and more dangerous ones, in the forest than among the army soldiers on the road.

For hours she sat in a thick brake, paralyzed with fear.

Early one morning she ran into the arms of two shaggy-bearded partisans. They dragged her before Lieutenant of the Guards Turyetza, chief of the partisan unit. He was a tall slim man, and had been the best in his class at the military academy in Omsk. At the age of fourteen he had denounced his mother for counter-revolutionary ideas. She was killed by a piece of falling rock in Sib-Chicago near Novosibirsk.

When Pyotr Turyetza was notified of his mother's death by the head of his Komsomol unit, he just shrugged his shoulders and remarked: "She got what she deserved."

He was intelligent, fanatical and quick to make a judgment.

When he saw Maria enter the camp between two of his men, he immediately noticed the Wehrmacht socks, the gray pullover with the green border, and the characteristic green scarf.

He smiled icily. "Traitor!" he hissed. He spat at her face and struck her with his fur cap. "What's your name? What are you doing here? Where do you come from?"

His slap gave her courage. From deep down, the characteristic obstinacy of her race surged up. Her pretty eyes became narrow slits as she lapped up the blood streaming down her face. She screamed at the Lieutenant of the Guards.

"I come from my mother's womb, you oaf! And I'm running away from the Germanski. You who hide in the woods and kill from ambush don't know maybe what's happening on the highways and in the villages today!"

"So this is how you want to play it, you slut." He called his second in command, Staff Sergeant Igor Poltonek, a little Kalmuck. A Cossack who didn't give a rap what was his or what was coming to him, but always gave himself most. He clicked his heels before the Lieutenant and growled tersely:

"At your service, *Gospodin Leytenant!*"

"Take care of that bitch," the Lieutenant snarled at the bowlegged Cossack NCO, who grinned with satisfaction and secret understanding as he dragged the girl away.

They beat her. They broke two of her fingers. They petted her.

"Marisha," Lieutenant Turyetza whispered. The pet name for Maria. "So you were going to spy on us for your German friends?"

"*Nyet,*" the girl moaned.

"You were going to inform against us?" the Lieutenant whispered, nearly twisting her neck out of joint. He grabbed hold of her breasts and squeezed till she screamed. "You're a traitor, you've whored with Germanski." He gave her a kick.

They tore off all her clothes. They swung her over a branch, where she hung like a bow while they cut little narrow gashes in her flesh and rubbed the wounds with salt.

They took her down again.

She said she had sold Russia. She had stabbed the Red Army in the back. She had derided Papa Stalin. She was a Vlassov traitor.

They forced her to drink vodka. They poured it over her face directly from the bottle. The Lieutenant shrugged his shoulders.

"Do what you want with her." Then he left.

Igor Poltonek, the Kalmuck, flung himself on top of her. He whispered: "Marisha!"

When he was satisfied, he drew a swastika on her forehead with a red-hot nail.

They cut off all her hair and burned it on the fire. Then they spat at her and walked off.

When they set out at dawn they just left her lying there. When Turyetza asked Igor if she was dead, he lied and said "yes." He hoped she would die slowly in the damp forest, but she didn't die. She was from the Volga, and people from the Volga region die hard.

When she woke up, there was only one thought in her throbbing, burning head: She had to kill the Kalmuck before she died.

Sobbing, she staggered on her way. Instinctively she walked west.

Three days and nights later she was sitting on a windfall, wishing herself dead. The worst pains had gone. The burn on her forehead didn't smart any more, but she was oppressed by an overwhelming, murderous fatigue.

She chewed sappy twigs to still her thirst, but chewing hurt. Her teeth had been knocked loose and the mouth was heavily swollen.

Suddenly she heard a snarl, and in the same moment a pair of fingers closed around her throat and pulled her back. Almost paralyzed with fright she stared into Tiny's grimy bandit face beneath the Russian steel helmet.

"A broad!" he roared. "A broad with a mark on her skull!"

"Ass!" the Old Man hissed as he came crawling from the brush like a lizard, followed by the Legionnaire. "Why don't you let go of the poor girl, you're choking her!"

Tiny got up and helped Maria on her legs, but didn't miss the chance of passing his large fist over her well-formed body, only half covered by the torn rags she had for clothes.

"Holy Mother of Kazan," Tiny exclaimed. "What a sweetie!" He winked at the Old Man and the Legionnaire. "Let's cast dice who'll be first to hop on her."

"Swine," the Old Man scolded. "She'll be brought to Lieutenant Ohlsen."

"You can take her first," Tiny offered magnanimously. "I bet she'll only be too glad if we do it to her."

"Shut up," the Old Man answered. "If you touch her I'll shoot." He tipped his sub-machine gun.

Tiny pawed the girl like a chicken before its head is chopped off.

"Holy Jesus, my whole front armor is getting hot," he groaned, all excited. "Really, Old Man, be a good pal and let poor Tiny have his hard-earned pleasure. Everybody is so mean to me. Remember mother's letter—that bitch," he added.

"You won't touch her," the Old Man decided. "She has to be questioned by Lieutenant Ohlsen."

"Fine," Tiny cheered up, "then let's have a preliminary investigation. Like the cops when they pick up someone, to soften him up for the big grill."

"No tricks now, Tiny. Just forward march!"

When they were well into the spruce forest Tiny suddenly yelled:

"*Yob tvoyemat'!*"

Maria shrieked hysterically. The Old Man whirled around, horrified.

"The whore has no panties on. I've just checked." Turning to the girl he laughed: "Will you play *Moy lyubimets,* play love with Tiny?"

"Cut out that filth!" the Old Man fumed, swiping at Tiny's hand with his sub-machine gun. "Her gang, the partisans, may be right by, and you can think of something like that!"

Covered by the Old Man's sub-machine gun they marched into camp.

Porta whistled long and suggestively when he noticed Maria in her tattered clothes and Tiny's lustful face. But before he could say his mind, Tiny trumpeted:

"What a nice little piece of furniture, collapsible and all. And she has no panties on! Her ass grins gaily under her rags like on a sow in heat on its way to the boar. A real hot piece. Just my size."

Lieutenant Ohlsen sprang up. He faced the Old Man. "What have you done to her?"

The Old Man looked at him with unwavering blue eyes. He didn't answer.

Lieutenant Ohlsen felt embarrassed. "Forgive me, Beier. Naturally nothing happened, since you were there." He held

out a fumbling hand to the Old Man, who accepted and
squeezed it with a wry smile.

The girl was questioned.

First they threatened her. But the swastika branded on
her forehead spoke a plain enough language. There was no
ground for doubting her story.

She related jerkily. It took her an hour and a half to finish.

"Where are the partisans now?" Lieutenant Ohlsen asked.

Maria pointed east, into the forest, *"V lyesu."*

"Are there many?" the Old Man asked.

"Da," Maria nodded. "You get away quick. *Davay, davay! Nix nemma!* No sleep!"

"No," Lieutenant Ohlsen said. "Let's get out!"

The girl got a seat between Porta and Tiny. A Russian infantry cap was pushed over her forehead. With her slanted
eyes she looked exactly like a young Caucasian soldier.

Julius Heide handed her a sub-machine gun.

As she felt the cold steel in her hands, she gave an evil
grin.

"I take revenge. Shoot dead the Kalmuck Igor. Only I that
do," she said in broken German.

Porta shrugged his shoulders.

"He's the last one you should want to meet, my girl, especially now when you're with us. You would die very slow.
It would take you at least two weeks."

Hour after hour we pushed ahead on the narrow forest
road. At every halt Maria told us what had happened to her.
She told us things that made us see red.

Lieutenant Ohlsen interrupted her story again and again
and urged us on. He had become quite a different man since
the offensive had rolled over us. He urged us on without rest.

"His neck is itching for a medal," Porta grumbled.

But it wasn't true. Lieutenant Ohlsen had no desire to be a
hero.

"His hustling drives me insane," Julius Heide growled. "The
only explanation is that he's eager to get some tin around
his neck."

In the midst of our grumbling conversation Lieutenant Ohlsen came over and threw himself down beside us. As if he'd
heard what we'd been talking about, he said:

"You're probably thinking I aim to be a hero, that I'm
running after tin. I'm not, only I want to get away from this
vile forest. Only two things drive me on: homesickness and
the desire to survive." He pulled out his wallet from his
breast pocket and handed us a snapshot. "That's Inge and

Gunni. My wife and my boy. He is seven. I haven't seen him for three years." He spat. "So you see it is pure selfishness which makes me hustle you. No one ever gets away from this damn country by himself."

We sat silent for a moment. He seemed to expect us to say something.

Heide hummed quite softly:

Long is the way back to our homeland,
So long, so long, so long...

"I can use you, as you can use me," Lieutenant Ohlsen went on. "We can choose. To croak as slaves in this country's endless *taigas* or help each other get home. No highfalutin words about fighting for the Führer and for Greater Germany. All we want is to go home. To die in this rotten forest is far too senseless."

Porta glanced up.

"I guess all of us want to live! We do and so do our opposite numbers on the other side, and yet damn few of us will."

"That's because we are swine, born of swine and meant to be, slaughtered," the Legionnaire said. "We have only a slightly stronger instinct for self-preservation than our fellow-creatures with snouts. We are like wolves that snap at the knife that butchers them."

"I think you're right," Julius Heide broke in. "We're a herd of nasty cattle. Too cowardly to give up."

"No," Lieutenant Ohlsen shouted, "this is precisely the danger. We must feel and think as the SS feel and think about Hitler and the NKVD guard units about Joseph Stalin. Except that the object of our feelings and thoughts should be an iron will to survive, no matter what. We should be ready to gnaw our way through forests and mountains to reach home!" He wiped the sweat from his forehead and kicked his steel helmet, sending it rolling some distance away.

The Old Man drew a deep breath.

"I don't want to discourage you, but I don't think any of us will return home. For me, a workshop, a wife and three children are waiting, but I know they'll never see me any more."

Lieutenant Ohlsen caught the Old Man by his chest and pulled him to him. He whispered almost imploringly: "You mustn't think this way, Old Man. Deep inside you, you must believe that we will get home. The war's almost over. It *must* be over. The Russians are chasing us like rabbits. Our new soldiers are worth nothing. We're short on arms. Ammunition. Gasoline. Provisions. We loot to fill our bellies. Our police and military police are hunting us like rats, and at home they're smashing one house on top of the other, while our coolies in Italy are being chased just as we are. It's only a question of a few weeks or months, then the whole pigsty will collapse."

"Yes, and then the super-butchers will go to work," the Legionnaire sneered. "The victors will take bloody revenge on us soldiers. Don't make the mistake of thinking we've survived just because the war's over. They'll lock us up behind a barbed-wire fence and starve us till we start devouring each other."

"No, that'll never happen!" Lieutenant Ohlsen cried. "They won't do that."

"Who'd stop them?" Julius Heide asked.

"They can use us," came despairingly from Lieutenant Ohlsen.

"No," the Legionnaire answered. "No one has any use for us worn-out starving hired killers. We're superfluous material. The sooner we pinch our ass-holes together for good, the better. Because we've forgotten how to work."

"It isn't true," Lieutenant Ohlsen yelled. "It can't be true. I could begin at the office tomorrow. I'm dying to, just as the Old Man is dying to get back to his cabinetmaker's shop."

The little Legionnaire shrugged his shoulders and blew some dust from the lock of his sub-machine gun.

"Stay in the Army like me. There you get board, clothes, lodging, a bit of money so you can get drunk in your free time, and, best of all: an instant death to put an end to it all."

"The Army, ugh! Not for me," Porta said tersely. "I certainly won't need the aid of that stinking club to keep my ass afloat." He clicked his tongue, raised his finger and looked around as if about to share a great secret with us. He lowered his voice. "D'you know what I want to do? I'll catch a pack of sluts, just like the head-hunters catch deserters. Then I'll give them a kick and send them flying into the bunks of a first-class whorehouse—and I'll be the manager. Do you realize what kind of money such bitches take in?" He wiped his mouth with the back of his dirty hand and pushed back his silk topper. "That'll be the time, boys! I can sense things acting up in my pants already."

"Swine," Lieutenant Ohlsen sneered. He spat.

"Why, Herr Lieutenant?" Porta asked dumbly, fanning away some mosquitoes with his topper. "The girls don't mind, and why not make business out of pleasure, and profitable business at that? There are few women who would mind taking a crack at that profession. They just don't have the courage and opportunity."

"Jesus Christ," Tiny exclaimed. "Would you let me be your bouncer, Porta? You won't have to give me very much for it, as long as I'm allowed to feel the goods when I like."

"That would be quite often, wouldn't it?" came from Heide.

"That's as it should be," Tiny nodded, licking his lips. "If I knew for sure there were enough broads in Siberia, I'd stick my thumbs up my ass and ride there on my elbows without changing trains in Omsk!"

In dead earnest Porta started giving us all jobs as employees in his future business—except Lieutenant Ohlsen and the Old Man.

Two day later we came upon the MPs.

Heide was the first to see them. He had walked into the woods together with Tiny and Maria. They were looking for partisans. Instinct told us there were some.

Tiny cut a fiendish grimace and readied his steel sling, but Heide signaled him to lay off.

When the rest of us got there, with Lieutenant Ohlsen in front, the head-hunters—there were three of them—were at first surprised to see us turn up in the woods. Afterwards they became insolent. They had altered their uniforms so one couldn't really see they were MPs. One would take them for ordinary infantrymen.

One of the three, a first lieutenant of fifty or sixty, large and heavy, requested our marching orders from Lieutenant Ohlsen, who literally gasped at this piece of insolence.

There was a moment's silence. Then the MP officer again opened his mouth.

"Lost your voice, Lieutenant? Or are you slow? I wanted to see your papers, so I can determine with what right you are roaming around in these woods."

"Christ, you must've been bitten by a mad dog," Heide exploded.

"Shut up, you dirty fink," the MP officer roared with an ominous thrust of his lower jaw. The muzzle of his submachine gun pointed straight at Lieutenant Ohlsen's breast.

At the same moment a piercing voice from the brush behind the MPs cut into the silence of the forest.

"Lay down those sprayers!"

As if they had burnt their hands on their weapons, the head-hunters dropped their sub-machine guns to the ground with a clatter.

"Up with your paws, and make it snappy," the voice from the brush went on.

Three pairs of fists shot up. Then Porta and the Legionnaire came out. Porta carried our heavy machine gun in a strap across his shoulder.

The Legionnaire gave the First Lieutenant a kick.

"On your knees, you son of a bitch. Pretty soon your balls will be loaded."

Puffing, the heavy officer fell on his knees.

The two NCOs got their faces slapped by Tiny.

"You also kneel down!"

"Leave them alone!" Lieutenant Ohlsen ordered.

"You shall pay for this," the First Lieutenant threatened, not even trying to conceal his rage. "You'll find out that laying hands on an MP during discharge of duty is punishable with death in accordance with Section 987."

"As far as I know, desertion is punishable with court-martial and hanging," came dryly from Lieutenant Ohlsen.

The MPs didn't suspect what Maria had told us, even less that she was with us.

She knew the MPs had been with them. Had heard them discuss running over to the Russians as ordinary infantrymen. Their idea was to let the offensive overtake them, then wait till it was quiet behind the front and pass themselves off as Communists. A brilliant job had been done on their forged papers. They had also talked of crossing the mountains to the Balkans. Maria knew they had their pockets full of blank marching papers with a faked general's signature. The First Lieutenant was in possession of a special order which would open most doors and remove most stumbling blocks for him and his pals.

"So you've stepped off the dung-cart?" Porta leered, jabbing at the First Lieutenant with his battle knife.

A gurgling sound came from the lips of the fat officer: "You shall pay for this!"

"Dear me!" Porta grinned. "We'll know before dawn, but by that time your ass will for certain be cold, my boy. Tiny is dying for permission to strangle you."

"Shut your mouth, Porta," Lieutenant Ohlsen cursed. "Search them," he went on curtly.

"I protest!" the First Lieutenant yelled. "Doing this to an officer is defamation."

"You bet it isn't," Tiny grumbled. "It's preparation for hanging."

Porta laughed malevolently. "I dare say it must seem strange to you that this time you are the victims. You may be sure we'll do a good job of it, nothing shall be omitted. You'll be permitted to stand up when Tiny strangles you. He'll use his steel sling and hold you at least four inches from the ground till your very last gasp has hit the clouds."

"I told you to shut your mouth, Porta!" came sharply from Lieutenant Ohlsen.

The Old Man handed him some papers we had found in the pockets of the MPs, among them three blank special orders with a general's signature.

"I guess this tells the whole story," Lieutenant Ohlsen said, waving the compromising papers. He sounded tired.

"May I strangle them now, Herr Lieutenant?" Tiny grinned. Out of his pocket he pulled a long piece of steel wire with two pieces of wood at either end—the steel sling for noiseless strangulation.

Lieutenant Ohlsen fumed. "You're not going to do a thing. The three of them are going back with us to our own lines. When I'm in command we'll have no so-called drumhead court-martials. Remember that," he added threateningly.

Heide and Fatty were ordered to lead the three prisoners over to the truck, where they were tied up, hands behind their backs.

They caught sight of Maria and went pale. She slowly came walking up to them, stopped in front of the heavy MP officer, spat in his face and hissed:

"*Chort!*"

Maria had known his love in a forsaken hut by the roller conveyor. He had almost strangled her when she refused to give in to him. He had caught her brutally under her dress. He had puffed and panted, slaver dribbling from the corners of his mouth while he tore at her body. He had sunk his teeth into her breast. Yet, he was not a pervert. He was a heavy stupid peasant in an officer's uniform who was boiling over with lustful desire. An animal in human form. Not a sick animal. Not a sexually depraved individual. He was simply stupid and inexperienced.

When he felt satisfied he had let his staff sergeant take her.

Maria let him.

The thick lips of the staff sergeant dribbled with hackneyed words of love. He thought this was part of rape.

Meanwhile she lay as if stone dead.

At the end he had forced open her mouth with two fingers and with complete composure spat down her throat.

She had vomited. It was worse than the partisan lieutenant. The lieutenant was wild and wicked, but the staff sergeant was repulsive and sickening. A human gutter.

A rock hit the large broad staff sergeant in the back of his head.

Maria laughed like a hyena.

Tiny handed Maria another rock. "Throw it straight at his face!"

Maria collapsed, weeping, and dropped the rock.

Tiny shook his head, unable to grasp that Maria had no desire to kill the staff sergeant. He shrugged his shoulders and gave the man a kick which made him fall forward. Tiny stood for a moment contemplating the big lump on the ground. Then he took careful aim and calmly and deliberately kicked the prostrate man in the groin.

A long drawn-out animal howl rose toward the tree tops of the black forest. The large body curved upward like an overarched bow.

Lieutenant Ohlsen came running. He was in a rage. Tiny stood at attention and let the shower of abuse flow over him.

The MP lieutenant, who sat on the ground beside the truck with his hands tied up, yapped indignantly.

"This is torture. Perverted sadism. But I'll take care to get that man executed. He has manhandled my staff sergeant, an active non-commissioned officer. You'll pay for it."

No one bothered to answer the ass. When we got back to the regiment he and his two subordinates would get short shrift: desertion, forgery and cowardice in battle.

It was the Old Man who discovered that the prisoners were gone. It happened just after dawn. We were shocked when we realized what had happened.

Fatty had been on duty. He lay unconscious beside the tree the prisoners had been tied to.

Lieutenant Ohlsen blew up. He questioned us, but all Fatty could say was that he had suddenly fallen down. He started sobbing when Lieutenant Ohlsen threatened him with court-martial for having gone to sleep on duty. With tears streaming down his face, he swore he'd not been asleep. His whole pig's body shook under Lieutenant Ohlsen's fit of rage.

"They must've cleared out," Tiny grinned, looking at Porta and the Legionnaire who sat chewing a turnip each, with Maria between them.

The Old Man looked up and scrutinized the four of them.

He nodded without saying a word, slung his sub-machine gun across his shoulder and walked into the forest.

"You're our comrade, aren't you?" Porta called after him.

The Old Man turned around without a word. Then he walked on.

We had finished packing the truck when the Old Man returned.

"Did you see anything?" Lieutenant Ohlsen asked inquisitively.

"Yes," the Old Man answered curtly, staring at Porta and Tiny who stood by the truck playing craps. They were laughing noisily after a good throw.

"What's the matter?" Lieutenant Ohlsen asked, following the Old Man's glance.

"That's what I'm not so sure of," the Old Man answered.

The Legionnaire came strolling up to them. He was cleaning his nails with his long Moorish battle knife.

"What's up?" he asked. A cigarette dangled between his narrow lips.

"Were you up last night?" the Old Man asked.

"Naturally," the Legionnaire answered. "I'm up every night to play pranks."

"You didn't notice anything?"

"Nah, not really, I was too drowsy," the Legionnaire laughed.

"Was Maria near you?"

"Yes, she was lying between Porta and me." A faint threat was audible in his voice. "But what the hell do you mean playing Gestapo like this?"

"I've found the prisoners," the Old Man answered.

"What did you say?" Lieutenant Ohlsen gaped.

"But that's great," the Legionnaire grinned, tossing his knife in the air and catching it again. "I guess we'd better hang them then."

"It can't be done," came softly from the Old Man. "They have already been hanged."

Lieutenant Ohlsen turned dark red. "Show me the bodies and God help those who've done it!"

All of us except Fatty went into the forest.

We found the three bodies a good distance within. Ants crawled over their dark blue faces. A blowfly sat rubbing its wings on one of the First Lieutenant's glazed eyes. The bodies were a horrible sight.

Porta bent over the First Lieutenant's mauled abdomen.

"The partisans must've done it," he said.

The Old Man gave him a knowing look.

"I had the same idea, but when I noticed what the two corpses had in their mouths I thought of Maria's story, and an uncanny suspicion came to me." He turned his eyes on the Legionnaire, and stressing every word separately he went on: "Wasn't this what the women did in the Rif Mountains?"

The Legionnaire put up a broad grin. "Yes, the Russian partisans seem to have learned something."

Lieutenant Ohlsen took a deep breath and placed his arm around the Old Man's shoulder. "Let's think it was the partisans. The three of them succeeded in escaping and then ran straight into the arms of the partisans."

The Old Man nodded and whispered: "Men can be such swine!"

Tiny yelled, loud enough to be heard for miles: "Those partisans are some dirty fellows!"

The Old Man ran up to him and caught him by the collar. "If you open your mouth once more I'll shoot you on the spot!"

Tiny gaped but said nothing.

The Legionnaire stood throwing his knife into the air, while squinting at the Old Man and Tiny. Then he whispered through the corner of his mouth: "Those three didn't deserve any better. There's a war going on!"

The Old Man turned around and looked at him. "Do you really think so?"

The Legionnaire nodded. "I do, and I also think you should go to a nerve clinic when we get back to our lines."

The Old Man gave a tired laugh and glanced at Lieutenant Ohlsen, who stood beside him.

"Not such a bad idea at that! Normal people will get locked up while murderous sadists are honored!"

The Legionnaire's knife sank into the wood right above the Old Man's and Lieutenant Ohlsen's heads.

"I thought I saw a squirrel behind you," he said smiling.

"I'm glad your hand didn't shake," came dryly from the Old Man, "or your conscience might have made things awkward for you."

We sauntered back to the truck and went on packing in silence. When we halted later in the day Tiny threw away his steel sling. He hurled it into a deep creek. Porta thought this was the best thing to do.

The Old Man noticed. He spat, but said nothing.

The Legionnaire grinned. He consoled Tiny saying he would get a new one soon.

Fatty sat on a tree stump. He had a headache and cursed savagely. He was somewhat dazed. He couldn't understand how three prisoners tied up like pigs could get loose and knock him; an active first sergeant, over the head.

"I just don't get it," he muttered. "I sat there staring at those three stinkers, and all of a sudden my skull exploded!"

"It must've been a partisan," Tiny proposed, feeling a bump the size of an egg.

"That partisan had tried it before," Porta grinned, passing his hand over Fatty's head.

The next morning we made it to the river. We took cover, waiting till night to cross.

Only two of us didn't know how to swim. Fatty and Trepka.

"You can stay with me," Tiny offered Trepka, "and I'll float you across."

"Who'll help me?" Fatty asked miserably.

Everybody grinned when Porta suggested he could stay on the side where he was.

Just before nightfall we heard a shot. The sharp report of a carbine .98.

A little deeper within the forest we found Maria. Her head was shattered. She had put the muzzle of the gun into her mouth and pulled the trigger with her toe.

"What a gyp!" Tiny called. He felt terribly cheated. "Since she'd decided to kick the bucket anyway she might just as well have let us take a crack at her first."

"You rotten pig!" the Old Man fumed.

Tiny pouted and kicked at a big branch his feet had gotten entangled with. It put him in a perfect rage.

When we walked back to camp Tiny lifted up Maria's dress, shook his head and said to Porta in surprise:

"Cripes, she too has shit in her pants. All do when they die. I wonder why? Do you think they're afraid?"

Porta pushed his topper over his forehead and scratched the nape of his neck.

"Nah, Tiny, it isn't from fear, but you see they bungle the whole thing when they get into a tizzy like that. It is just like when you want to sneak out a secret fart after stuffing yourself with split peas and pork from a diseased sow. Then there are surprises!"

Lieutenant Ohlsen heard the tail end of their conversation and told them off, calling them brutes and bastards. They looked at him in reproach and felt deeply hurt.

At midnight we swam across the river. In the middle of the rapid current Trepka panicked, but Tiny brought him safely to shore.

The report had been forgotten. Trepka had grown up.

Heide and Porta swam with Fatty, who snorted like a seal from terror and exertion.

We pushed the Russian armored car into a swamp next to the river.

In it lay Maria.

The whole gang went with him to the train. The little open four-seater Volkswagen almost broke down under the ten of us.

On the hood in front lay Heide and Tiny. We lost Tiny twice and had to stop to pick him up again.

In honor of the event we all addressed Lieutenant Ohlsen familiarly.

The train took off.

We stood there waving till the last wisp of smoke had vanished.

Lieutenant Ohlsen sat musing by the window. He didn't see the scorched trees, the ruins, the burnt-out car wrecks and the smashed locomotives which had grown tired and now rested on the sloping railway embankment.

He saw only Inge and Gunni. His stomach was in knots from expectant joy.

Inge, Gunni, Inge, Gunni, the wheels were singing.

He saw Inge's warm smile and laughing eyes. He heard little Gunni's voice while he looked at a dissolving cloud in wonder.

"Now the cloud is going away, Father. Is it going home to the Lord?"

chapter xvi

The Reunion

LIEUTENANT OHLSEN had gone on leave. The first one in three years. He was wild with joy as he said good-bye to us.

When the train stopped in Breslau a friend stepped into the compartment. A rousing reunion after all those years. The friend whispered some things in his ear, and they were tempting.

"When we get to Berlin, come with me out to Darlem. I'm in charge of a sort of theatrical troupe. A service

theatrical troupe," he added, laughing boisterously. "We have
the greatest times. Lots of girls." He clicked his tongue,
rolled his eyes to the ceiling and made a motion of embrace with his arms. "Oceans of booze. Torrents of champagne. Shovelfuls of caviar. Anything you could want. The
boss is an SS *Obergruppenführer.*" Again he laughed noisily.

Lieutenant Ohlsen laughed softly.

"I only want one thing, Heinrich: to get home to Inge and
my little boy as quickly as possible!" He clapped his hands
from sheer joy of anticipation. "I feel like getting off the
train and sprinting ahead."

Heinrich laughed. "I understand you, but pay us a visit
anyway some day. We have a black-haired witch who can
do it thirty-three different ways. Afterwards you feel like a
castrated stallion. And you should see some of the boys we
have, even if they are SS men. They are game for anything.
If someone grumbles, hey, presto!—he's gone. No one asks
any questions. It's just as easy as pulling the plunger in the
can."

Lieutenant Ohlsen shook his head. "I had no idea you
were in the Party or the SS."

"Nor am I, damn it, but so what, Bernt? I prefer to co-
operate with those on the bridge to rotting in a trench. And
even if I resisted, do you think the system would be over-
thrown?"

"Wasn't your brother hanged in Buchenwald?" Lieutenant
Ohlsen asked in surprise.

"Yes, and my father, too," came blithely from Heinrich,
"but that's not my fault, after all. They were foolish, wanted
to be heroes, but were forgotten. They floated to heaven
through a chimney because they didn't get off the old shaky
wagon in time. Liselotte and I were wiser. We sniffed
Adolf's star and made sure to become good citizens at the
right moment."

"Then be sure you remember to step down before Adolf's
wagon tips over at the turning," Lieutenant Ohlsen warned.

"Don't worry," Heinrich laughed. "Today the SS. Tomorrow
the NKVD or the FBI. As long as I sit on top I don't give
a hoot what they are called. Never in my life have I been
a fool enough to swim against the current. When it's customary to shout 'Heil,' fine, I shout 'Heil,' and if tomorrow
I have to swing a pig over my head and shout 'Green
front,' I'll do that too. If you'll take my advice, Bernt, and
come with me, you'll never see the front again!"

Lieutenant Ohlsen shook his head.

"I'm afraid I'm not clever enough to pull back my nose at the right moment."

It was evening when they reached Berlin. They separated on Schlesischer Bahnhof. But first Heinrich had given his address to Lieutenant Ohlsen. Then he ran laughing down the platform and disappeared.

Lieutenant Ohlsen took the trolley to Friedrichsstrasse. He felt a bit uneasy and lost as he stepped off at the familiar station. He was overwhelmed by sudden terror. A terror that took his breath away.

An old militiaman saluted stiffly, but Lieutenant Ohlsen couldn't bother raising his arm for the salute. He nodded chummily as usual.

A cavalry captain came up to him. He saluted in a friendly way. The captain's mouth smiled, but his eyes were a piercing blue, like the dragoon facings on his cap and collar.

"Herr Comrade," he lisped, "allow me to bring to your attention that discipline requires an officer to salute his subordinates in a military manner, under no circumstances like a friend. It verges on sabotage, Herr Comrade." The captain of dragoons saluted and nodded. "Have a nice leave! Greetings to the heroes in the trenches!" Then, spurs clinking, he danced along the platform, saluting cheerfully to all sides.

That was his way of waging war.

Lieutenant Ohlsen wiped the sweatband in his little field cap and followed the captain with his eyes. A bit further down the platform he had stopped a sergeant. Lieutenant Ohlsen shook his head, hitched up his two bags and trudged down the stairs to Friedrichsstrasse.

He was tired, terribly tired. Something told him that he didn't quite fit in here any more. He had become a combat swine.

Fear surged up in him. Fear that the little Legionnaire was right after all. He glanced down his dusty, faded black uniform, his worn-out boots with the heels worn down on one side, and his rank-and-file belt with the holster—a black .38 holster, not the dashing brown Mauser holster worn by officers in the hinterland. He was a peculiar mixture of private and officer. Only the silver shoulder straps were an officer's.

He drew a deep breath, passed his hand over his eyes and whispered: "Berlin, my Berlin!"

He saw Tiny's brutal face before him. He saw him kick the MP. He saw the long knife of the Legionnaire swish into the tree behind himself and the Old Man, a sharp warning not to continue the questioning about the execution of the MPs. He shivered, as if he felt cold at the thought of the three mauled bodies. He saw Maria lying dead by the river in a pool of blood. He brushed off his thoughts and looked about him. In the dark, everything looked hopeless. Gutted ruins everywhere. When he walked, there was a scrunching of broken glass. On the walls were announcements in chalk: "Mother at Aunt Anna's in Bergenwalde." "Müllers on third floor is alive. Inquire at Uncle Theo's."

He hurried off so as not to waste a single minute of the three short weeks he was privileged to be a human being. One week for each year at the front. In his mind he saw an announcement from Inge: "Gunni dead. Inquire at Father's." He began sobbing in sheer fright. He started running.

No one turned around to look at him. Seeing a man run weeping through Berlin was nothing unusual. Here even the rocks and the walls wept.

There was no announcement. He stiffened. The house was gone. Erased. Simply razed to the ground.

He slumped down on one of his bags and covered his face with his hands. He groaned, sobbed, cursed. He wished the gang had been there. His gang. Big, bellowing Tiny. The fatherly Old Man, jabbering Porta. Captious Julius Heide. The hard brutal Legionnaire. All of them. The death-gang.

A hand was placed on his shoulder. The grimy, chapped fist of a worker. He raised his head and looked into a weather-beaten, wrinkled face with a day-old stubble peering out.

"Herr Graup!" he exclaimed surprised, taking the old man's hand.

"You've come back, Bernt," the man grumbled, "and you've become a lieutenant. Your wife and boy are safe. It took three days to dig them out. We rescued nineteen. A heavy blanket of bombs fell Saturday two weeks ago and cleared the street. Didn't your wife write you about it?"

Lieutenant Ohlsen shook his head.

"Inge doesn't write very often. She has so much to do."

"I guess she does," the old man said, spitting out a plug. His words seemed to have some hidden meaning.

"Where are they?" Lieutenant Ohlsen stammered.

"At her father's, or more correctly in her father's house. Your father-in-law is supposed to have been inducted. Call up before you go there. It's better that way," the man called, but Lieutenant Ohlsen didn't hear. He rushed off.

"Inge, Inge," came a whisper from inside him as he was running. "You are alive, thank heaven! You're alive!"

The old man again spat out a stump of tobacco.

"What a pity," he muttered, "but that first sergeant day before yesterday had it tougher. Wife and five children killed, and now he's locked up in Plötzensee for making disparaging remarks about the Reich." A cat rubbed up against his leg. He scratched it behind the ear. "You're lucky. You're chased only by dogs!"

Lieutenant Ohlsen rushed back to Friedrichsstrasse and took the train to Hallensee. He was on the point of getting into a scrape because he didn't notice a general on Kurfürstendamm. He straightened up stiffly and let the abuse pour off him while he whispered to himself:

"They're alive, Inge and Gunni are alive. You can't understand that, you ass. They're alive."

"Certainly, Herr General, no discipline at the front." They are at Father-in-law's. "Certainly, Herr General, compulsory salute is the basis of victory and the successful course of military operations." Father in heaven, thanks for letting them get away. "Certainly, Herr General, the incompetence of an officer shows itself through his failure to salute in accordance with army regulations." You red-striped shit, I wish a Tommy-bomb would send you to the top of Brandenburger Tor. "Certainly, Herr General, won't happen again. Thanks, Herr General, that Herr General will overlook it." You old sclerotic nitwit, I wish you'd lose your war soon so Ivan can chase you around. "No, Herr General, I don't want to have my leave cancelled. Certainly, Herr General, I'm not worthy of wearing an officer's uniform."

The General put three fingers in deerskin gloves to the peak of his cap. Then he wobbled down the street on his knock-kneed old man's legs. He bleated like a goat over the incident.

Lieutenant Ohlsen brought together his slanted heels with a bang and rushed off. In passing he just managed to tip a regulation salute to a major with the red stripes of the General Staff on his light gray trousers.

Berlin, lovely, stinking Berlin, rotten to the core! If only the Revolution would soon come so that all the gangs from out there could sweep you clean. What a lovely sight: Porta and Tiny behind a machine gun on Brandenburger Tor. Seeing all those hick-town heroes run for their lives! Thank God, they're alive.

He turned down Joachim-Friedrichsstrasse. He lost one

of his bags, stopped, swung it over his shoulder and continued at breakneck pace.

A girl called after him. He didn't hear. She laughed and hissed: "Stupid pig!"

She had been dead certain of a pound of butter and a bottle of vodka when she saw that lieutenant.

But he probably had battle fatigue. Stupid pig.

Then he stood in front of the house. A large stately building with polished granite steps before the ornamented portal. A marble staircase with gold-ornamented mirrors on every landing and trumpet-blowing angels all the way up. He had kind of grinned at those angels the first time he came to the house. The whole thing was wide, vast, ostentatious.

On the second floor was a tall oak door with a bright brass plate, inscribed in Gothic letters: "Von Lander," and under the name in somewhat smaller letters the lovely title "Regierungsrat."

Lieutenant Ohlsen stared at the name. He saw his arrogant parents-in-law and his gossip-mongering sister-in-law in his mind.

He drew a couple of deep breaths before he pressed the button. Far off he could hear the bell ring. He rang again. Not a sound. He knocked, first softly, then more strongly.

Silence.

No one home? he thought. Odd. He drummed with his fingers on the carved oaken door. Then he slumped down on the stairs. Stared forlorn at the door. Far away he heard a clock strike twelve. It was midnight.

Inge just had to be home. Gunni was always afraid to be alone. He listened. What was that? Something moved. It was only a slight noise, like the rustle of silk. He was dead sure he heard it. There was someone behind the door.

He stared at the double doors, which seemed to grin at him in mockery. Someone was walking stealthily about. Someone who didn't want to be heard. He jumped up and hammered away at the door.

Not a sound.

He tried to peek through the letter slit, but something hung in front of it so he could only catch a glimpse of a red runner.

Open up, damn it, he thought. He started pounding on the door with both fists, but everything remained quiet.

He thought he could hear a whisper of a man's voice. He knew there was someone inside. His Inge? Impossible. She had always written she would wait. The last thing she said the day they parted on Anhalter Bahnhof was that she would wait.

With heavy steps he walked down the stairs. He slammed the door behind him so loudly it could be heard upstairs. Then quite softly he stole up to the landing, from where he could keep an eye on the door of his parents-in-law.

He was breathing heavily and with difficulty. He clenched his fists about the handles of his two bags. He glanced up at the angels. They also seemed to grin at him. He spat after them.

Again, shivering, he thought of the little Legionnaire: We're swine, superfluous swine. Allah is wise. He knows why. Come with me to *La Légion Etrangère* and die by a true believer's knife. Allah will rejoice!

He grimaced.

An elegant couple, a lady and a gentleman, came up the stairs. They stopped. They kissed. They laughed. The lady hit out at her partner's exploring hand.

"No, Otto, wait till we're upstairs," she whispered. Silence and heavy breathing.

She uttered a little scream.

"No, not here. Are you crazy, what if someone came!"

They began walking up the stairs. Noticing him, they became nervous and scrutinized him with timid glances. Even Germans could confuse the black panzer uniform with the SS. The big hussar death's-heads on his lapel recalled death excursions in black cars at night.

They hurried past. Glanced over the banister from the fourth floor. Whispered briefly together.

Ohlsen caught the words: Raid. Gestapo. A door clicked.

Now their night is spoiled, he thought, lighting his forty-third cigarette. He glanced at his watch. Almost three!

Finally he heard the door being opened. A big powerful man in well-fitting clothes. He heard them kissing.

"Good-bye, sweetheart," he whispered.

"See you again," she said.

"Yes, on Thursday," he whispered. "I'll send the youngster a package."

Then he ran down the stairs. He didn't notice Lieutenant Ohlsen hiding in the niche. He seemed to feel very self-confident.

Red spots danced before the eyes of Lieutenant Ohlsen. There was a buzzing in his ears. Desperately he pounded on the wall with clenched fists. His body was shaken by uncontrolled sobbing. A weeping that made his stomach muscles contract in convulsions.

"What can I do?" he whispered. "Inge, why?" Suddenly a terrible thought took hold of him: Gunni, what about Gunni? Was it he the man had meant with "youngster"? Gunni was his! He would go to the Gestapo. To the SS. He would shun no recourse to keep his boy. He knew that his comrades would despise him if they found out he had gone to the Gestapo. The gang, his gang, would turn their backs on him. The Legionnaire might murder him. But he didn't care. Better take the contempt and mockery of his comrades than losing his boy.

He walked up the stairs slowly, step by step. Stood for a moment in front of the ostentatious door. Then he rang and knocked.

On the fourth floor he heard a door being opened. Whispering voices.

"It is at von Lander's," he heard a woman whisper.

Behind the closed door a deep woman's voice asked: "Who is it?"

Some time passed before he could pull himself sufficiently together to answer. He had to draw several deep breaths to quiet his upset nerves. When he answered he couldn't recognize his own voice:

"It's Bernt, Inge."

The woman behind the door seemed to need some time to collect herself.

Then she stood in the open door. Slim, dark. Her brown eyes laughed. Her mouth smiled:

"Bernt," she whispered. "Oh, you!" She threw herself into his arms. He hugged her. For a moment he believed that everything connected with the strange man was only a dream.

They kissed. They kissed savagely.

He slammed the door with his foot. They walked into the room. The large room with the costly rugs he had been afraid to walk on at first. She had been amused at that.

She jabbered away. He picked up only half of it: Bombs. Everything gone. Rescued. Father inducted. On the QMG's staff in Leipzig. Mother taking a cure in Karlsbad. Anni with Aunt Ingeborg. She talked, talked, talked.

A bottle of wine popped up. Tall rummers appeared on the table.

She had on a tight-fitting Japanese kimono. Verdigris green and black. She crossed her legs.

He noticed she was naked under the heavy silk.

She smiled. Her eyes glittered.

You bitch! he thought. You disgusting, dirty bitch!

He nonchalantly swung one of his booted legs. His boots were dusty. Russian dust. Again he saw the Legionnaire's sneering face when they had pipe-dreamed about the time after the war.

Suddenly she realized he hadn't said a single word since he stepped inside.

Again she poured out two full glasses. He flushed down his in one gulp.

She raised one of her well-shaped eyebrows, curled her mouth in a faint smile, and again filled up his glass.

"Would you like to take a bath?"

He shook his head.

"Are you hungry? I have some cold turkey. Father sent one."

Hungry? He probably was, but he shook his head.

"Are you tired? Do you want to go to bed?"

He was dead tired, but he shook his head.

She looked closely at him and asked sharply: "What's the matter with you?"

He forced a smile. "It's only that we are at war, my friend. Our home is gone. We have lost everything!" He held the word "everything" on his tongue for a moment, to taste it, then repeated it.

She laughed, relieved.

"Is that all? That, you know, you shouldn't take to heart. Father will get what we need, and more. He has the best connections in the Party and the SS."

"Where is Gunni?" he asked.

She glanced up at the large crystal chandelier in the ceiling and slowly lit a cigarette before she answered.

"He is at the National Socialist home in Bergen by Lüneburg."

He slammed down his glass and gave her a squinting look. In a low, menacing voice he asked: "Why, if I may ask?"

She was blowing smoke rings. Staring fixedly at the crystals, she answered: "Because I thought it was the best thing we could do. Father and Mother thought so, too."

"So that's what you thought? You and your family don't seem to realize that as Gunni's father my advice should also be asked! Do you realize what it means to send him to a Nazi home? You have sold your own son to the Party in cold blood!"

She bowed her head. "I knew that."

"What did you know?" he jeered. He was boiling with rage. His temples were throbbing. He opened and clenched his fists while he whispered to himself: "Easy, easy, for God's sake don't do anything rash!"

"I knew you wouldn't understand anything at all," she almost snarled. Her eyes flashed. "You're as stiff-necked and conceited as ever. One can clearly see where you're from."

He gave a tired laugh. "Yes, one can see where I come from, Inge. I'm a little office louse picked up from the gutter to lick the dust before the distinguished Lander, *von* Lander!" The last words came out as a sneer.

Restlessly he began pacing the floor. He kicked the leg of a sofa. "You still haven't told me why you sent Gunni to the Nazi home."

"That boy is impossible, " she yelled, losing her self-control. "He's like you. He's disgusting. Sulky. Stubborn. When you asked him to do something he threatened he'd tell you all. He's a liar." She checked herself.

He stopped pacing. "Tell me all? What in the world can he tell me that I shouldn't know? That your family runs me down, that I know. Your ravishing sister, as you know, loves to put her nose into everything that doesn't concern her. The stupid bitch," he added.

"Be kind enough to control your language here in my house," she warned, drawing herself up.

He leaned back laughing, went into convulsions of laughter.

She gaped in astonishment. "Have you gone mad?"

All at once he stopped his hysterical laughter. He looked at her. His eyes were dark. He blew out waves of smoke.

"Is 'bitch' improper? What then do you think of 'pig,' 'slut,' or 'whore'?"

She got up and bent forward a little. Her voice was quite steady. "That will do, Bernt. Go. Get out!" On the finger with which she showed him the door gleamed a diamond ring. "This is my father's house. Not yours. You've no business here. I've been given shelter here. Not you."

He threw down his glass. It broke.

She looked reproachfully at him. "Why didn't you open when I rang and knocked last night?" he asked, pushing his angry distorted face at her.

She looked quietly at him. Suddenly she discovered she despised him the way he sat there in his filthy uniform.

"Well, I suppose because it didn't suit me to open for you. That should have gotten through to you long ago."

He gasped for breath. His stomach contracted. Their roles had been exchanged. No longer was she the mouse. He was.

Not let me in, he thought, his face distorted with mental

pain. His Inge, whom he loved, quite calmly said she wouldn't let him in. She didn't apologize for anything. Didn't explain anything. Everything can be forgiven, even infidelity, but here no forgiveness was asked. Was it over? By God or Allah, it mustn't happen! He could endure the war, even if it were to last for ages yet. He could endure everything, but if Inge left him ... that he couldn't bear. And his boy? He swallowed a lump in his throat and looked into her dark velvety eyes.

She returned his glance firmly. She didn't falter a bit. She passed a slender well-kept hand over her glossy black hair.

"But why wouldn't you let me in, Inge?" His rage was gone. Only sorrow, deep, unbearable sorrow remained. "I have three weeks' leave."

She raised an eyebrow, pursed her lips. She walked over to the phonograph and put on a record.

"Because I had company, my friend."

"Company?" he asked.

"Yes, as I'm sure you know very well. I assume you were hiding somewhere near by and saw Willy leave." She smiled.

He nodded.

"Yes, you're right. I was standing on the landing below." He slumped down into the chair. "Do you want a divorce?"

She swayed her hips, walked a moment back and forth humming Zarah Leander's song: *"Davon geht die Welt nicht unter."*

"Divorce?" she answered, pouring out a glass of cognac for herself. "That didn't occur to me till you mentioned it. Might be a good idea." She sipped her cognac. Lit another cigarette. She was smoking from a long gold cigarette holder, ornamented with five small diamonds. "I'm tired of waiting, at any rate. Right now I'm in love with Willy, but I suppose you, with your soldier's morals, won't believe that a woman can't live only on letters. Our relationship has been a misunderstanding from the beginning."

"You said you loved me, Inge, and then we had Gunni."

She smoked feverishly. Emptied her cognac glass. A vein stood out sharply on her forehead.

"One says so many things. How many couples, do you think, really love each other? It becomes a habit. If you had been magnanimous instead of picking at trifles, we could have lived nicely together and this whole stupid scene could have been avoided." She looked at him. Her eyes became mean. Her mouth jeered. "I could have gone to bed with whomever I wanted and you with anyone you liked. We could have been friends. Friends with a wedding ring."

"But that just can't be done, Inge!"

"No?" she laughed hoarsely. "As if you had the foggiest idea of what can be done!"

Again he felt a lump in his throat. What had happened? His Inge couldn't talk like that. He adjusted his belt, noticed the pistol and rested his hand pensively on it.

She noticed it and curled up her mouth in a wry smile.

"For God's sake don't turn this into a classical drama, where the unfaithful wife gets shot. It would make both of us look awfully ridiculous."

He dropped his hand and shrugged his shoulders.

"Would you like me to go, Inge?"

She nodded.

"It's the best thing to do. In any case, you are too old-fashioned to go on the way I'd like to. If you want a divorce, Bernt, you can always write to me about it."

Her kimono had come apart. He saw her long legs, slender pretty legs. Those legs he had so often caressed. He couldn't grasp it was all over. It was too absurd. Too unreal. Almost ridiculous. She stood there smiling prettily. Though alive, she was still dead. At any rate to him.

Again he felt for his pistol. He opened the holster and passed his fingers quickly over the cold steel. Then he thought of the boy. He could see the Legionnaire's mocking glance. He dropped his hand.

"Won't you have a drink before you go?" she asked.

He nodded. Imagine her asking me, her husband whom she has just thrown out, if I would like a drink before I go.

He wanted to ask her about something, but they had already become strangers to each other.

They drank together. She said something about his dusty boots and soiled uniform. Mentioned something about a hotel where he could sleep. Then he suddenly burst out with:

"Are you in love with Willy?"

"I told you so, didn't I? I love him."

"Have you slept together?"

She flung back her head and laughed. Her laughter was provocative. He felt a desire to strike her. Once more his hand strayed down to his pistol. Once more the boy's face popped up before him. Tomorrow he would go to the Nazi camp where Gunni was.

When he left she raised her hand to wave good-bye. He noticed she wore a bracelet he had given her long ago. The one with the blue stone he had bought in Rumania. She had kissed him savagely and lifted her legs from the floor. Afterward they had had a wild and reckless night of love. That was five years ago.

When she closed the door he was on the verge of tears.

He slept in a guardsmen's barracks in Potsdam.

Next day he went to Bergen to see his boy.

The camp, a camp of huts, was situated far out on the moor, remote from inquisitive glances. One had, after all, enough sense of shame not to want everyone to know how the boys' minds were being systematically destroyed and perverted.

An SS *Obersturmführer* who had lost an arm in 1941 took him out to the camp in his car. Every time this officer, who wore the emblem of murder on his black-edged cap, called him *"Herr Kollege,"* Lieutenant Ohlsen startled. He told Lieutenant Ohlsen that he was responsible for the boys' military education.

Lieutenant Ohlsen pumped him about life in the camp.

"They're slackers when they get here," the SS officer shouted to make himself heard above the roar of the Kübel car. "But before we've had them for very long they're real demons." He waved his half-empty sleeve in rapture. "They would even slit the throats of their own mothers."

They halted about a mile from camp. The SS officer pointed at a unit of brown-clad boys worming themselves ahead across the field.

"There's our sabotage detail, *Herr Kollege.* This puts the finishing touch to our education." He laughed as he said "education." "Once in a while we also give them a Jew to play with. Watching the boys knock off a Jew like that is better fun than either dog races or cockfights. Afterwards they'll learn to do it to real people."

Real people! Lieutenant Ohlsen looked with revulsion at the face of the officer, handsome in picture postcard fashion.

The camp commandant, Hitler Youth *Bannerführer* Grau, had a surprise in store for him.

With a smile he was informed that he no longer had a son. His son belonged to the Führer. There could be no question of his seeing or talking to Gunni. He could send him a package, which the boy would receive as if sent by the Movement.

"After all the Movement is all of us," Grau said, smiling.

There was a smile here for everything. Even for pronouncing a death sentence.

Lieutenant Ohlsen protested against the State having adopted his son. He hadn't signed the papers.

"It's of no consequence," the *Bannerführer* smiled, "Your wife and your father-in-law are warrant enough, and you can hardly have any objections to your son being educated as a true disciple of the Movement. The home is not the right place for our youth. With us, on the other hand, they become tempered, tempered like Krupp steel."

They drove him in to Bergen, not to do him a courtesy, but to prevent him from communicating with his little boy through illegal channels.

*In front of the villa sat a man without legs, without arms.
He sat on the undercarriage of a perambulator.*

*He was in plainclothes and on his jacket gleamed the
Iron Cross, First Class.*

SS Obergruppenführer *Berger stepped out of his Horch,
wrinkled his forehead and looked disapprovingly at the in-
valid.*

*"Get that thing away from here," he mumbled to his
adjutant.*

*The man tried to resist. He screamed loudly as they lifted
him up and drove off with him.*

*They threw him into an oven together with some Jews
and gypsies.*

*The frame of the baby carriage rolled slowly across the
street, where a boy began playing with it.*

The unpleasant sight no longer annoyed the arriving guests.

chapter xvii

An Evening Party at the SS

ONE EVENING Lieutenant Ohlsen drove with his friend Heinrich and an SS *Obersturmführer* out to a large villa in Wann-
see.

Before the gate, which was ornamented with SS runes and
a majestic eagle peculiar to this corps, stood two guards in
the full-dress uniform of the SS.

There was a crush in the large hall, where zealous SS men
in white jackets took the guests' things.

From the hall one walked into a large room splendidly illuminated by numerous crystal chandeliers, whose lights were
reflected by large wall mirrors decorating the room from floor
to ceiling.

In the middle of the room stood a horseshoe table, covered with damask cloths and Sèvres china. Twelve-branched
candelabra of beaten gold were placed one after another on

the table. Each place setting had several crystal glasses, wreathed with artfully woven flower festoons. The silverware was sterling, heavy and old.

At the lower end of the room stood half a score of SS officers. They stared hungrily at the entering ladies in their extremely low-necked gowns.

Heinrich pulled Lieutenant Ohlsen over to this group and introduced him to a tall powerful man wearing the brown uniform of the Party. He had the coldest eyes Lieutenant Ohlsen had ever seen, a human being without a trace of human feelings. A living robot in the Party apparatus.

He held out his hand to Lieutenant Ohlsen and gave him a handshake reminiscent of old dough. He mumbled something about it being an honor for him to greet a combat officer and advised Lieutenant Ohlsen to do justice to the food. Then he walked up to a lady in a lilac sheath dress. Lieutenant Ohlsen was forgotten.

The company sat down to dinner.

A long line of SS men in white jackets marched in with the food. The whole affair went off in parade-ground style. They immediately began serving and filling the glasses.

It was a menu to which rationing was unknown. Even the most jaded palate could find everything it wished for.

"This is what I call a menu," grinned SS *Obersturmführer* Rudolph Busch sitting across from Lieutenant Ohlsen. He was already a little drunk. "That's something," he said, smacking his lips and taking a bite from a pheasant leg which he held with both hands. He had convinced himself he looked like an old Teutonic hero when he ate in that way.

Heinrich had told Lieutenant Ohlsen that Busch had hanged his own sister in Gross Rosen two years ago. And judging by his looks he seemed very capable of doing a thing like that.

"An internationally composed dinner," he growled contentedly, indicating the splendid table with the gnawed pheasant leg. Then he chucked it over his shoulder. It was picked up by one of the SS men in attendance.

No one took offence at this, because here SS Teutons feasted in the style of old Valhalla.

"Here are artichokes from Yugoslavia," he yelled in a rapture of conquest, "Belgian truffles, French mushrooms, Russian caviar, Danish butter and ham, Norwegian salmon, Finnish grouse, Dutch shrimps, Bulgarian pheasants, Hungarian mutton, Rumanian fruit, Italian chicken, Austrian saddle of venison, and Polish potatoes—grown in sandy soil! Actually, the only item missing is a delicious English beefsteak." Again he flipped a bone over his shoulder. "But what isn't here now may still come—" he licked his greasy lips—"just wait, Lieutenant, till we jump across the creek! I'm looking forward like hell to setting up concentration camps in Scotland and making the English lords vault over the buck."

My God, thought Lieutenant Ohlsen, here apparently no one knows that we are losing the war. Here they are still winning victories and storming forward.

"What do you think will become of Germany, *Herr Kollege?*" Busch grumbled, tearing into a haunch of venison with his teeth. He resembled a gorgeously uniformed cannibal.

Lieutenant Ohlsen shrugged his shoulders, saying he was sorry he didn't know. At any rate he would make sure not to say what he was thinking: pigs, born of pigs, to die like pigs on a military dunghill. He saw the mocking face of the Legionnaire before him and shivered.

"Germany will become the mightiest empire in history," maintained the SS officer—he had gradually become quite drunk—"and we've appetite in plenty," he added reflectively. "A scorching appetite. Just take a look at our guests here this evening!" Grinning, he snarled, "Today eating is more important for these gentlemen than culture and combat. Look how they jump at the trough. I'm speaking about the men."

"Certainly," nodded Lieutenant Ohlsen. He couldn't keep himself from asking: "And what about the ladies?"

"Just wait, Herr Lieutenant, and you'll see!" He laughed omnisciently and slurped from his glass. "Here everything goes by SS regulations. Here it's not as deadly dull as in your club, Lieutenant. When we've filled our bellies we proceed to Act Two." He took a bite from a peach. The juice flowed over the breast of his light gray uniform jacket. He tried to wipe it off with his hand. "Act Two: alcoholic introduction." He belched, then nodded apology to his dinner partner. "Next follows furioso grandioso." He pursed his lips and smacked his tongue like a glutted sow. "And finally, Herr Lieutenant, pastorale amoroso. We are always sticklers for etiquette in the SS! The fact is, Herr Lieutenant, that in the SS we are what the English call gentlemen."

He stopped speaking and sucked lightly on his finger, on which some horseradish sauce had got stuck. He glanced sideways at Lieutenant Ohlsen and said, while he kept sucking his finger: "Horseradish sauce always makes me think of whores, but class-A whores," he added, contracting his brows.

He scrutinized Lieutenant Ohlsen and decided to say something he'd long wanted to say to an army officer. "You angel-hair fellows in the Army don't have the slightest notion of good form. You are common peasants, the whole lot of you." He grinned and waited eagerly for Lieutenant Ohlsen to object.

But the Lieutenant wasn't listening. He sat there thinking of all he would do to get even with Inge and his father-in-law.

"My father-in-law is a stupid pig," he confided to Busch.

"Give me his name and I'll pass it on to my friend in Prinz Albrecht-Strasse," Busch offered. "All stupid pigs are to be liquidated. *Lebensraum,* that's what matters," he imparted confidentially.

Further down the table an SS *Obersturmbannführer* shouted: "Shut up, Busch, you drunken sot, or you'll get grilled!"

"Certainly, *Obersturm,*" Busch cackled and flushed down his cognac. He glowered about him and muttered, "They are to be liquidated. Throw them to the bears." He looked across at Lieutenant Ohlsen. "One should be kind to animals," he explained.

Lieutenant Ohlsen looked at him but didn't see him. He saw Inge, his wife, before him in a Japanese kimono which brought out her slender legs. He drank and only half heard what Busch was saying.

"The ladies here are eminent ladies, rich ladies. They have an itch in their shafts, the tide is running strong." He grinned with delight at his own wit. Suddenly he became philosophical. *"Herr Kollege,* life is strange. You're an officer of hussars, lieutenant in a combat regiment, and what am I? A lousy prison guard in a camp." He wrinkled his forehead in concern and swept a heap of gnawed bones off his plate. Then he glanced briefly at the empty plate and flung that down, too.

"I'm a very unhappy person. A profoundly unhappy person." He looked about him frantically as if he were drowning and was looking for a lifebuoy. He bent across to Lieutenant Ohlsen to entrust him with a great secret: "My life has been a disappointment. *Herr Kollege,* would anyone believe my greatest desire was to become a pastor?"

"Definitely not," came with conviction from Lieutenant Ohlsen.

"And yet there's nothing I'd rather do than stand in a pulpit in a black frock and drill with the congregation. Christ, how I'd make them jump, *Herr Kollege!* And what did the whole thing come to?" He spat his contempt on the floor, nearly hitting his lady. "Ugh, to have become an officer in the Guards. But I have a good idea, *Herr Kollege*. When the war's over I'm going to take an accelerated course in theology. In that way I hope to end up as archbishop of Cologne. Then the whole thing will have shape to it.

"When the distinguished ladies present have had a sufficient amount of bubbly," he continued, "we extend the front to the second floor." He grinned omnisciently and winked vehemently at Lieutenant Ohlsen. "There we stage a French pastoral!" He stopped talking and thought hard. He passed an exploring glance round the room. Then he pointed at a slender brunette in a low-necked dress of silver lamé. "The one over there with the tinsel work, *Herr Kollege*, is a thigh-swinger stinking with dough."

Looking in the direction indicated, Lieutenant Ohlsen noticed a popular movie actress from UFA.

"Will all the ladies be taking part in that pastoral play?" he inquired dubiously, scrutinizing the well-known movie actress who was flirting quite openly with a general of the police.

"Not all," Busch conceded, "but the prim ones will be asked to resign, and they are then left out in the cold. The tinsel girl over there—" he clicked his tongue—"is one of the right sort. In her films she lisps like a Gretchen from the YWCA, but here . . . ooh, la, la. *Meine Ruh' ist hin.* . . . Here she turns into a Clymestra, or what the hell the name of that Greek mare was."

"Do you mean Clytemnestra?" Lieutenant Ohlsen smiled, hoping he pronounced the name correctly.

He was eager to annoy the drunk SS officer.

"Don't put on airs, you clown from Circus von Kleist!" Busch flared up.

Lieutenant Ohlsen laughed and shrugged his shoulders. He had accomplished what he wanted.

Busch sulked and muttered something about liquidating the whole Army, which was comprised of traitors and other outcasts. Suddenly his face lit up.

"Do you know what the letters on the license plates of the Army mean? WH?"

"*Wehrmacht Herr*," Lieutenant Ohlsen answered promptly.

"You missed!" Busch cried in rapture and pointed accusingly at Lieutenant Ohlsen. "They mean *Weg nach Hinten*, the way back." He slapped his thighs in rapture and brutally poked his lady dinner companion with his elbow.

Lieutenant Ohlsen leaned back in his chair.

"Do you know what the Army calls the SS?"

"Nah," Busch answered, his curiosity roused.

"*Arsch, Arsch,*" Lieutenant Ohlsen said. "Ass, ass."

The ensuing silence around Lieutenant Ohlsen was oppressive. He laughed, raised his glass and called out: "To the Army!"

But when the glasses were raised somewhat slowly, he added with malicious pleasure: "To Adolf Hitler's Army!"

However reluctant they were to do so, they now had to drink to the Army and then break the glasses afterward, because Adolf Hitler could be toasted only once from the same glass.

Looking at the large pile of broken crystal on the floor, Lieutenant Ohlsen vowed to drink to Adolf several more times before he left.

After dinner the guests scattered about the large villa.

"What's the mood at the front at the moment?" a police officer wanted to know.

"I'm on leave and have no knowledge of the momentary situation and mood."

"Leave?" cried Busch. "What's that? To us in the SS it is an entirely unknown concept. What it comes to at most is an official trip to pick up traitors and such vermin. Nah, you at the front are well off. Much better than we. Just hearing the name of the *Wehrmacht* nauseates me."

His glassy eyes had started to get watery. "Look at those stinking generals strutting about with corset boots on their spindle-legs! Lice, I tell you." He was getting warmed up. "If I was the Führer..." he slit his eyes and knit his brows, "I would have them impaled. By God, I would." He turned to some SS officers standing by. "Isn't that right, boys? The Army is a flock of cantankerous billy-goats who only know how to bleat."

They nodded agreement. One of them muttered something about a "cowardly bunch."

"And those red-braided gentlemen have the guts to show off in front of us, the SS guard of the Führer! They look down on us, think we're nothing." He spat at the Persian carpet. "Those squirts completely forget that it is through us they've become what they are today. What would they have been without us?"

Lieutenant Ohlsen indifferently shrugged his shoulders. He glanced at a lady sitting on a sofa with her dress pulled high above her knees. An SS officer was measuring her thighs with a piece of string.

"What were those dogs before?" Busch asked obstinately, nudging Lieutenant Ohlsen. "They were shits, small stinking shits without red stripes and they had to appear for inspection to get their stamps just as in the Weimar time." He again spat on the carpet, then rubbed it in conscientiously with his foot. "You *Wehrmacht* studs get orders and medallions by the sackful for the bit of fighting you do!"

Someone tried to quiet down Busch, who by now was extremely stirred up. But he didn't listen and went on:

"What about us?... You don't answer me. I ask you, Herr Lieutenant Hero-face: What about us?"

"Really, Rudi, cut it out," someone said. "It isn't the panzer lieutenant's fault that you don't have any combat ribbons."

"Let me finish what I've got to say, you oaf!" Busch protested, catching Lieutenant Ohlsen by the lapel. "Our war is much harder than yours. Just look at my hands, how they tremble!" He shook his hands violently in front of Lieutenant Ohlsen's face. "Executions by the hundreds, *Herr Kollege*, mass executions. You should just try commanding firing squads hour after hour, day after day. True, those we plug are just inferiors, but still they scream because they're afraid to die."

He licked his full lips. "Sometimes we bury them before they're really dead. Not because we are inhuman. Remember, I wanted to be a pastor, *Herr Kollege*." He puffed, emptied his glass, had it refilled, emptied it again and had it filled once more. "We're busy, *Herr Kollege*, busy like hell. All Jews must be liquidated before the war's over, the Polish and Russian intelligentsia come next—so you can imagine, Herr Lieutenant, what a regular dunghill we have to get through. We gas them, shoot them, hang them and guillotine them. On the whole we do a lot to clear the air."

Lieutenant Ohlsen felt nauseated and turned away from Busch.

The mood became more abandoned. On the stairs they drank champagne out of ladies' shoes.

In a little room they were spinning the bottle and stripping off their clothes. In a small niche two high-ranking officers were pulling the panties off a squealing lady. A girl in a blue dress danced on a table. She kicked her shoes to the ceiling. She hit the crystal chandelier, making a bulb blow out with a bang.

An SS *Hauptsturmführer* pulled his pistol and shot down two more bulbs.

"It was necessary," he explained. "The bulb struck me. I followed the Führer's order: two for one." He inserted two fresh cartridges in his Mauser and put it back in his pocket. He noted with satisfaction that most of the ladies present had noticed his pistol. There was something very manly about carrying a gun.

Lieutenant Ohlsen stood looking at one of the costly paintings. An SS *Standartenführer* placed himself beside him. He pointed at the painting. "Beautiful, isn't it?"

Lieutenant Ohlsen nodded.

"This is an absurd house, don't you think, Lieutenant?" Without waiting for an answer, he went on. "All of this used to belong to some Jews." He made a sweeping gesture with his arm. "These Talmud pigs have held their disgusting orgies here." His face twisted with nausea at the thought of the immoral goings-on in the house he called "absurd." "It was about time we got this Augean stable cleaned out." He laughed and tapped Lieutenant Ohlsen's shoulder with his white gloves. "I took part in it myself." He tilted back his head. "It was glorious, *Herr Kollege.*"

"What became of the owner?" Lieutenant Ohlsen asked.

The SS officer almost lost his voice at this naive question. He simply couldn't understand that a normal person in uniform could ask something so foolish.

"In a camp, naturally. What else? But first we had this Talmud brood thoroughly *gestäupt.*"

Lieutenant Ohlsen looked dumbly at him. "*Gestäupt?*"

"Yes, of course, *gestäupt,*" nodded the SS officer. "Manhandled. From what I hear you do the same thing with the partisans." He danced laughing up to a lady and ran his hands up her thighs, tearing her dress in the process. Jubilant at this, he tied the two pieces together in a bow in such a way that the lady's legs were exposed behind. It looked comic. She was very knock-kneed.

"Aren't we soon going to bed?" yelled an SS *Sturmbannführer* from the *Kz*-guard of the extermination division.

"That's the second in command in Oranienburg," a police lieutenant explained. He offered Lieutenant Ohlsen a glass of wine. "A genuine Veuve Cliquot, can be had only with us in the entire Reich." He kept the bottle in his pocket and liberally refilled the glasses. "Have you found a heifer for yourself, Herr Lieutenant?"

"A what?" Lieutenant Ohlsen asked, surprised.

The police officer laughed. "Well, you see, a heifer is one of the fresh ones. A cow is the run-of-the-mill lady. Mares are acrobats who perform in public."

"I guess that would make the men bulls and stallions?" Lieutenant Ohlsen couldn't help saying.

The police officer laughed uproariously and ran off to join a couple of ladies.

Lieutenant Ohlsen again ended up over in the corner, where Busch stood explaining to a tall gentleman in dark civilian dress what the SS were doing while the others enjoyed life at the front.

"We're nothing but refuse collectors," he explained to the dumbly attentive gentleman, on whose lapel gleamed a microscopic Party emblem in gold.

Slowly the civilian gentleman lit a cigar. He was obviously a connoisseur. He was one of those mysterious Germans who had lived in South America in the time between the wars. Once he had been consultant to the secret police of Bolivia. Later he sold Krupp arms to Paraguay, Bolivia's opponent in the protracted war between the two states. At present he was one of the big wheels in Berlin, with an office on the top floor in Prinz Albrecht-Strasse.

"We liquidate everyone," Busch shouted in a thick voice, swaying ominously. He spilled cognac on his uniform. "First we'll knock off the Jews, every damn one of them." The gentleman with the black cigar nodded in silence. "Then comes the turn for the gypsies." The gentleman with the black cigar nodded once more. Busch slurped from a bottle of cognac which one of his comrades had filled half with vodka, half with Danish akvavit. He belched. "Then we plug the Polacks. You see, we boys are creating *Lebensraum, Lebensraum* for the victorious German people. They'll gape in amazement when our Special Action Groups get rolling. Whole nations will vanish from the surface of the earth. There's room only for us Germans. Forward, comrades, long live the SS!" He slammed his heels together, raised his arm and bellowed: *"Sieg, Heil!"*

All those present joined in, roaring rapturously. Someone started singing the Jew song. Others joined in at the line: *Jewish blood shall flow.*

An SS *Hauptsturmführer* from Eicke's extermination division jumped on a chair and screamed frantically: "The last Jew will be hanged on Brandenburger Tor!"

"We're the greatest nation in the world," Busch bawled. "We'll liquidate all the others."

He was interrupted by a girl who tore screaming through the room. Her hair was disheveled and she had no dress on. She was hotly pursued by an officer in shirtsleeves, with wide peasant braces flapping behind him.

An officer with the black badges of an SS general on his lapel commanded: "Ready, to the beds!"

A yell of enthusiasm almost blew off the ceiling of the villa.

This was the signal for a wild woman hunt. A refractory lady was taken by force in a window niche. Another stood on her hands, exposing her elegant black lace panties, which revealed more than they concealed. An officer poured red wine from the Rhône valley over her. He did it very slowly and with feeling. That much one owed the good wine, thought SS *Obersturmführer* Stenthal. He formerly had a wine cellar in Bonn. Now he was director of interrogations in the police unit at Buchenwald.

He pulled the panties off the acrobatic girl and carried his jest further, with no one apparently taking offence at it. Meanwhile three of his comrades sang:

Röslein, Röslein, Röslein rot,
Röslein auf der Heide.

They outdid one another in insane erotic whims. They bellowed like royal stags at rutting time.

Lieutenant Ohlsen had gotten drunk. He straddled a chair as if astride a horse. Before him on the floor lay a naked woman. The only thing she had on was stockings. Long stockings, held up by wide black garters with red roses. An SS officer lay half across a chair. He was dressed only in jacket and long underwear. Underwear with a patch, poorly sewed on at that.

Lieutenant Ohlsen grinned at the patch on the long underwear.

"Super Teutons in long patched underwear." He spat out what he had in his mouth and succeeded in hitting the patch on the SS officer's underpants. "Slime," he said in a tone of complete conviction. "Tomorrow I'm going over to Prinz Albrecht-Strasse to find that acquaintance of Heinrich on the fifth floor. I'll tell that dog some things about the whore I'm married to." He grinned again.

A platinum blonde came over to him and sat down on his lap. She stroked his hair.

"You may call me Ilse if you like," she said.

"Ilse," Lieutenant Ohlsen said. He spat once more at the patch on the SS underwear.

Ilse doubled up with laughter.

They sat silent for a moment examining the patch.

Another lady came up to them. She had on a golden dress, cut to her hips in the back.

"You look peeved," she said to Lieutenant Ohlsen. "Why don't you have fun? Don't you like girls?"

"Are you a whore?" Lieutenant Ohlsen asked.

"You're fresh," the girl snorted.

"That's true enough," Lieutenant Ohlsen grinned, "and you're a pig." He kicked at the girl and almost lost his balance with the chair. He grabbed for his glass standing on the floor. It was a one and a half liter beer glass, filled with vodka and cognac. A police lieutenant had said it chased one's sorrows away. That's why he drank it.

An SS *Hauptsturmführer* came reeling over to them. He hauled a chair after him. He had only one eye. The other was covered by a black monocle, which he was constantly losing. But his pockets were crammed with spare monocles. Where the eye had been was a big red moist hole. He just loved making others look at that hole. Seeing it made them lose their appetites.

He slumped down beside Lieutenant Ohlsen and looked around with his one eye, a pitch-black, ferrety eye. He looked at Lieutenant Ohlsen.

"Would you care to come out to the camp tomorrow and have a fencing-bout with the traitors?" He puffed and pointed at Ilse, the platinum blonde. "Shall we be friends and play nookie, nookie?"

"Not with you," Ilse said. "You're a creep."

The SS officer grinned. He lost his monocle. It rolled along the floor.

His red eye glowed. Ilse shivered.

Lieutenant Ohlsen sucked at a cigarette holder and looked indifferently at the moist red flesh that wouldn't cure.

"You're probably quite a little tiger," the SS officer said, grinning at Ilse. "A panther to be tamed with a whip." He grinned fiendishly.

"Why the eye bit?" Lieutenant Ohlsen asked. He drank a little more from his large tankard.

"He's nuts," said the platinum blonde. "He's stark raving mad. They say he has crucified Biblical scholars in his camp."

Lieutenant Ohlsen looked at the SS officer who sat there grinning absurdly. His one eye looked perfectly insane.

The SS *Hauptsturmführer* nodded.

"What you say is true. Four nails, whether it is a black-robe or a Talmud swine." He looked meditative. "Those Talmud guys are the toughest, but the blackrobes squeal louder so it's more fun. Won't you come out with me, Lieutenant, and observe me nailing one of them to the beams? You'll have one too. A new transport has just arrived. In my quarters I've two heads the size of an orange. One of them sat on a Talmud wench. The other is Polish. There's a French girl in the camp. She's in my section. I want her head too. It sort of cheers you up to have a few of these heads on your writing desk. When some day the war's over I'll be sure to make a lot of money from those heads. It's much easier to pick up shrunken heads in Berlin than to go to the heart of South America, and besides there's no hazard."

Lieutenant Ohlsen took three long drafts from his mug.

"What do you have there?" the one-eyed officer asked.

Lieutenant Ohlsen looked at him without answering. He had made up his mind not to have any further talk with the collector of heads.

"Lieutenant, did you ever taste woman's blood in cognac? It has a lovely taste." He grabbed platinum-blonde Ilse and like a striking snake cut a gash in her wrist and squeezed some blood into his glass. He grinned savagely and emptied his glass.

Ilse shrieked with pain and fright. There was a great hubbub around her.

The tall gentleman in the dark suit came over to them, followed by some SS men in white jackets. He listened in silence to what had occurred.

Shrugging his shoulders, he turned around and muttered as he went away: "For God's sake, nothing more. A little jest." He whispered to a huge SS man who helped serving: "Have the bitch arrested and brought to the camp, charged with insult to the SS. But not yet. Later." He lit another black cigar and looked pleased at a couple who were more than slightly engrossed with each other. Then, as he left the room, he hummed: "How beautiful is life, divinely beautiful."

The head-hunter who drank women's blood stood up. He poked the naked girl lying on the floor.

A little later he showed up again. Now he had a light gray cape hanging across his shoulder. His white shirt front and dress uniform were stained. He had put the black monocle in his pocket. The flesh shone fiery red in the inflamed socket. He was drooling from a corner of his mouth. He nudged Lieutenant Ohlsen with the gold handle of his riding whip.

"Are you coming with me to the camp, you army lieutenant, to nail a couple of Talmud swine to the beam?"

Lieutenant Ohlsen looked at him. He would have liked to say a great many things to him. The kind of things that others also would have liked to say. Everything one would say in a novel. But this was not a novel. And Lieutenant Ohlsen didn't say anything. He just took a long pull from his mug, which again had been filled with the mixture. Lieutenant Ohlsen wanted to forget.

The SS *Hauptsturmführer* shrugged his shoulders and turned around, a bit uncertain on his feet. He staggered, lurching ominously like a ship hit by an awkward wave, but managed to right himself. He looked over his shoulder, grinned, and with the back of his white glove wiped the red flesh that wouldn't heal.

"I'm going now, but in case you should change your mind, Lieutenant, ask for *Oberscharführer* Schenk. He'll drive you out to the camp. And if you come we'll separate the Talmud swine from the blackrobes and then we'll be able to see who scream the loudest." He walked out of the room with clanking spurs. He had gold spurs on his ankle boots. He was from the SS cavalry division.

The dark girl asked Lieutenant Ohlsen to unbutton her brassière. It was too tight, she said.

"Are you on leave?" blonde Ilse asked.

"Yes, I'm on leave," Lieutenant Ohlsen answered.

"Don't you have any family?" the dark girl asked. Her eyes were half closed like those of a cat purring by a fireplace.

Lieutenant Ohlsen didn't answer.

"You're welcome to sleep with me," said Ilse, the platinum blonde.

"I'll think about it," Lieutenant Ohlsen said, again taking a swig from his mug. He was very drunk now, but no one could notice it. He put away the mug and looked at the platinum blonde. "If I were you I'd leave this place."

"Why should I?" she asked and tossed her head, making the light flash in her hair, which hung loosely down her back.

Lieutenant Ohlsen smiled.

"Because I'm telling you. Steal out the door without anybody noticing."

"Good Lord, what stupid rot," she snapped. She walked up to an SS *Untersturmführer* with the SD insignia on his collar. Soon his hands were going up her skirt.

They went upstairs together.

Lieutenant Ohlsen didn't see her any more. She was arrested shortly after she had been in bed with the SD man. And it was he who arrested her. They led her out the back way, where you could get out into a side street through a little wicket in the wall.

Next day she was found in Grunewald. A brief notice in the afternoon papers announced that she had been run over by an unidentified car. She was spoken of as one of Berlin's anti-social women. People shrugged their shoulders and said:

"A whore."

Abendblatt carried a picture of the corpse. It was lying on the road with clothes mussed up. The head was covered with a blanket.

"Her head seems to have taken a regular beating," said a drayman in a tavern. He stood leaning against the bar drinking beer while he looked at a sign which read: BERLINERS SMOKE JUNO.

Someone slapped Lieutenant Ohlsen on the back. It was an SS *Sturmbannführer* with the Knight's Order of the Iron Cross dangling from his neck. He was very young. Around one arm he wore a narrow black band, with an inscription in elaborate Gothic letters: *Leibstandarte SS Adolf Hitler.* The bodyguard to the Führer. His breast was covered with decorations.

"Would you like a ginger ale, my friend?" the young SS major asked.

It was the first time someone there had said "friend" to Lieutenant Ohlsen. He looked at him in amazement.

"Ginger ale?" he said. "You get sick from that." He raised his big mug and drank. He drank slowly, but even so he started coughing.

The SS major laughed. He sniffed at Lieutenant Ohlsen's glass.

"Jeez, it's strong."

"Yes, it's strong," Lieutenant Ohlsen said. "It's all strong," he added.

The SS major from Hitler's bodyguard nodded, then looked around the room.

"This is a filthy pigsty."

Lieutenant Ohlsen said nothing. He merely nodded agreement and thought: It's far worse than a pigsty.

"When this war's over we'll all be presented with a long, long bill for everything these guys are doing," the SS major said.

"They crucify people," Lieutenant Ohlsen said.

"I know they do," the SS major said. "Altogether they are a damn tough bunch of boys right now." He bent down over Lieutenant Ohlsen and whispered: "Do you know what I want to do, friend? I want to shoot myself. I want more..."
Again he looked cautiously around him. An ironical smile played about his mouth. "I'm going to do it right here in this joint."

"Wouldn't it be foolish?" Lieutenant Ohlsen asked.

"It might, friend, but they'll all be gaping."

"Are you drunk?"

"Not a bit," the SS major maintained. He couldn't be more

than twenty-five, very slim. Over six foot three. His hair was yellow like ripe wheat. He was very handsome.

He drew himself up to his full height.

"Just watch now, friend.". He walked across the floor in the direction of an SS general with decorations from World War I, the Party emblem in gold, and honor chevrons on his right sleeve.

The young officer flicked at the general's lapel, glittering with silver oak leaves. He smiled and said very loudly:

"SS̄ *Gruppenführer,* now you're going to see something funny. The best joke of all time."

The General, past sixty, looked annoyed at the tall dashing officer. He was standing with the gentleman in the dark suit and three ladies. Ladies from UFA. The ladies laughed expectantly.

"Well, let's hear the joke."

The young officer laughed. His laughter was very contagious and warm.

Lieutenant Ohlsen took another slight pull from his tankard, then made himself more comfortable on his chair. He felt as if he had been specially invited to a theater just before the performance was to begin.

The SS major pointed at the SS general.

"SS *Gruppenführer,* you're a pig, a vicious Nazi pig!"

The General started back. All the blood faded from his bloated face. His mouth opened and closed.

The SS major smiled. "The whole lot of you guys from camps and offices behind the front are a pack of filthy bastards and sex killers. But to your pleasant surprise I am able to announce to you that we have lost the war. Our brothers from the other side are on their way to Berlin, and they are in a hurry."

Someone caught him by the arm. He rapped his hand and snarled: "Your fingers off me, you cur!"

The SS *UnterstURMführer* who had caught him by the arm released his hold. The Bodyguards armband and the flashing Knight's Cross made him cautious.

The SS major drew his pistol and cocked it.

There was dead silence. The General and the gentleman in the dark suit stared hypnotically at the heavy black army pistol in the hand of the laughing young officer.

"I feel like a dog because of the uniform I wear," he said. It came out slowly and with weight on every word. "I am ashamed of my German mother. I am ashamed of the country which is called my own. I sincerely hope that our opponents in this war are sensible enough to shoot every damn one of you like the mad dogs you are. To hang you by your own braces on the walls in your barracks and prisons." He put the pistol to his belly, clicked his heels and fired. He dropped the pistol, swayed back and forth but didn't fall. He drew his blade of honor, the long pointed and sharp-edged weapon he carried on a chain by his side. With the smile still on his lips he slowly drove the blade into his belly and cut from left to right. The blood poured out over his hands. Again he swayed like a tall tree in a storm. He fell on his knees. "That you didn't expect, you filthy swine," he wanted to say, but he didn't say anything.

With violent exertions he again got up. Then he collapsed.

The whole thing took place in three stages. He looked at Lieutenant Ohlsen straddling his chair. He raised his hand for a salute. A hand soaked in blood.

"Wasn't it fine, friend?" His eyes became dim, but he still smiled. The Knight's Cross clinked against his buttons. He tried to stand up. He coughed blood. He was lifted up and placed on a table. They cut his uniform and trousers. He looked into the face of the person who bent over him, someone with bluish skin from his tough beard.

"Damn you all. I have returned my club membership card. Sorry as hell I didn't have the chance to see you hanging on your walls." He nodded. It hurt. God, how it hurt. "Perhaps, my friend, it was foolish after all," he whispered. Kneel down and pray to Lord Jesus, his mother had said. Grandfather was a pastor. He remembered him. His starched white collar was always yellow at the edge from sweat. Grandfather always spoke as if he cried, but he always cheated at marriage when they played in the back room of the tavern where no one could see them.

The sharp light from a crystal chandelier stolen in Prague hurt his eyes. He could hear someone pacing the floor, back and forth.

"He mustn't die," someone said.

He wanted to laugh, but only had the strength to pull back his lips and bare his teeth. You're wrong there, I've resigned. Actually he didn't mind dying now, but it was fun to stall and play a joke on them. But how it hurt. Why the hell did he have to stick that knife in his belly? It was foolish, friend. It was all the fault of those Japanese. It looked smart when a yellow monkey like that committed hara-kiri, but he had never believed it could hurt so much. And not in this way. How could it possibly hurt all the way up to your throat and down your back? If only there was no God. For he wasn't one of the good boys. He knew that very well.

Maybe the pains he suffered now would profit him if God was waiting for him. Maybe Grandfather with his yellow collar would put in a good word for him.

Very pale, the General bent over the table where they had laid him. He looked like a very old man.

With incredible exertion for a dying man the young SS major sat up angrily. Blood surged up in his throat. He coughed, could no longer breathe. The blood tasted sickly sweet.

Abusive voices were heard everywhere. The General's light trousers became bespattered with blood. Furious, he croaked something about a "filthy mess."

A girl sobbed.

He fell back heavily on the table. Now it didn't hurt any more. In fact, he was quite comfortable. He stretched out and died.

Without realizing it he suddenly stood in front of the large gray building, Prinz Albrecht-Strasse 8. He stared at the oval sign with the black SS eagle and the words: GEHEIME STAATSPOLIZEI. Secret State Police.

Mechanically he walked up the stairs and opened the heavy door. The handle was placed so high it made you feel like a little kid.

The SS sentries didn't condescend to give him a glance, in spite of his officer's uniform.

On the fifth floor he halted outside a gray door with a little brass plate inscribed: STAPO B. 2.

He gave himself a shake as if he were cold.

A little further down the corridor a door was opened. Black glittering SS helmets appeared.

A woman was half dragged over to an elevator, which disappeared down to the basement with a buzz.

A tall slim man with flaxen hair and aquiline nose—a figure modelled to Himmler's own heart—asked what he could do for Lieutenant Ohlsen.

"Forgive me, I have come to the wrong place," he mumbled.

He almost ran down the stairs and cleared out of this Devil's stronghold. He breathed a sigh of relief. He would be able to meet the glance of the Old Man and the Legionnaire without feeling ashamed of himself.

chapter xviii

A Casual Affair

IT RAINED as Lieutenant Ohlsen left the villa. He was without a coat. He held his cap in his hand so the rain could flow through his hair.

He stood still, turning his face to the sky. He enjoyed the

294

rain, it cooled his burning-hot skin. That *Leibstandarte*
officer had put up a wonderful performance. God, how wonderful! It spoiled their celebration.

Lieutenant Ohlsen laughed softly at the thought that the
celebration had been ruined.

He again started walking down the street. What if he had
possessed that much absurd courage! He dwelt on the thought.
A wonderful thought: Go home, ring the bell. Ring real long.
Stroll nonchalantly in to his arrogant parents-in-law. Glance
at Father-in-law sitting big and heavy in his wide chair. Tell
him exactly what he thought of him. Tell them they were just
sausage Germans. Sausage Germans with diamonds gleaming
on their pudgy fingers. It would be wonderful to observe their
dull fish eyes as he slipped his bayonet into his belly. The
thought made him brace himself and walk faster.

A black Mercedes with a police license plate swerved by
him. He had a glimpse of some officers and ladies. A woman's laughter came from the car.

He missed his gang. Years seemed to have passed by
since he left them. Perhaps they weren't even alive any more.
Fear crawled up his spine. He saw the little Legionnaire.
The brutal face with the knife scar seemed to hover by the
lilac bush over there. A face without body. Lieutenant Ohlsen
said aloud:

"Hi there, Alfred."

The little Legionnaire smiled his dead smile. Only his
mouth smiled. Never the eyes. He had forgotten how to smile
with his eyes and heart a long time ago.

"You won, Alfred," Lieutenant Ohlsen nodded. "Christ,
how you won. We're pigs, born of pigs, and shall die on a
dunghill like pigs. *Vive la Légion Etrangère!*" Without being
aware of it he shouted the last words loudly. He looked
around nervously.

A Schupo came strolling along. He suspiciously stared at
the wet Lieutenant. The eagle in his helmet flashed. The rain
flowed from the helmet down his raincoat, which glistened
with wetness.

Lieutenant Ohlsen quickened his pace, while the Schupo
stood still, peering after him.

The cop was in high spirits despite the rain. No air raid.
He walked on.

Lieutenant Ohlsen turned the corner. He recalled the
time they were lying in their positions by the Elbruz valley.
It was very hot. The sun was scorching. There were no trees.
No shade. It was long ago. There were alarmingly many head
wounds in those positions by the Elbruz valley. He saw a

long line of faces before him. All of those who received head wounds. NCO Schöler, Pfc Burg, tank gunner Schulze, fire team leader Mall and Sergeant Blom, who wanted to go to Spain and grow oranges when the war was over. He was constantly talking about that orange grove. Though he never got to Spain, he had learned a few words of Spanish. He had an ancient dictionary with a great many pages missing. *"Dos cervezas,"* he would say when he ordered beer, regardless whether he wanted ten or two. He also knew how to say *"mañana"* and *"hermana."* He used to say this to all the girls. To old people he said *"abuelos."* The day he died—the Siberian sniper hadn't hit him quite right, just above the root of the nose, and it took him three minutes to die—he said to those standing by: *"Yo no me figuraba."* The little Legionnaire, who knew Spanish, nodded and answered in Spanish. It cheered Blom greatly. He died with his mind on the orange grove he never got to see. They buried him down by the crooked cactus, where the fallen rock was lying. They buried a tiny dry orange with him in the grave. The Legionnaire squeezed it into his hand. Afterward they trampled the earth very firm. They jumped up and down on it, to make sure the wild dogs wouldn't dig him up and feed on him. They did this only because he was "Barcelona-Blom." Usually, they didn't do it. So many died, and the wild dogs also had to live. But with Blom it was different. All of them knew that orange grove, had heard so much about it. Next day Lieutenant Colonel von Herling was killed. A Siberian sniper hit him right at the edge of his helmet. He died instantly. They didn't pack the earth down on his grave. He was new with them. The next day they found part of him. The dogs had dug him up. The Commander had gone clean mad, had threatened them with court-martial. But it was so hot in the Elbruz valley that before evening the Commander had forgotten all about it. He was Colonel von Lindenau, who later was killed in Kiev. He was burned to death. That they could see when they got to his tank. He was half hanging out of the turret, completely charred. Porta said he looked like a steak forgotten by a cook. Porta said much more. They had laughed noisily at Porta's remarks. Von Lindenau had been with the regiment for a long time, but no one missed him. They left the whole thing there till Ivan came to clear up. Ivan's demolition squad had carried the colonel's corpse on two forks to a hole and thrown some earth on top of it. No one had any idea where von Lindenau, landowner, colonel, count, had been buried.

Lieutenant Ohlsen shook his head in the rain. What a war.

He had gone all the way down to Havel. He sat down on a bench in the rain. He was drenched to the skin, but didn't care. He discovered he was right beside Prinz Albrecht-Strasse, where Heinrich's friend had his office on the fifth floor.

A girl came strolling by. A girl in a red leather jacket and a very wet hat on her head. She smiled at him. He smiled back and wiped the rain from his face.

The girl stopped and sat down beside him on the wet bench. He offered her a cigarette.

They sat smoking for a little while. The cigarettes were damp.

"It's wet here," the girl said. She had heavy legs, he noticed.

He nodded. "Very wet."

"Do you like going for walks in the rain?"

"Nah," Lieutenant Ohlsen answered. "I can't stand it."

The girl puffed hard at her cigarette. "I can't either."

They both laughed.

Then they sat again for a moment, both with their own thoughts. It was the girl who broke the silence.

"You're from the front," she said without looking at him.

"Yes, from the Eastern Front. I'll soon be leaving again."

"Would you like to walk me down the street?" the girl asked and got up. They walked together down the street along the Havel.

"My sweetheart also was home on leave," the girl said and changed step to fall into step with Lieutenant Ohlsen. "He stayed home."

Lieutenant Ohlsen looked at her sideways. She wasn't a pretty girl. Her nose strained upward like a kitten's.

"Did he desert?"

The girl nodded and wiped some raindrops from her face.

"Yes, he didn't want to go out there again. They shot it off him."

"Shot it off him?" Lieutenant Ohlsen asked dumbly.

The girl asked for a cigarette.

"Yes, they shot the whole thing off. What other men have. He had to pass water through a tube. He smelled."

Lieutenant Ohlsen didn't know what to say. Captain Fromm had also been castrated. The Russians had done it. They found him in a peasant hut tied to a table. The whole works were lying on a plate beside him. He was dead when they found him. His entire abdomen was dark blue. They killed seven prisoners with neck-shots for this business with Fromm. Not because the prisoners had had anything to do with it, but it seemed to them they had to do something to someone in retribution. And so they shot those seven prisoners. They knelt on the ground and the Commissar went from one to another, pressing his .38 to the nape of the neck of each of them and pulling the trigger. They fell forward like Mohammedans at prayer. They were seven Georgians from the 68th Grenadier Regiment, a border unit. All of them from Tiflis.

"What happened to your sweetheart?" Now he used the familiar form speaking to her. What had happened to her sweetheart created a bond between them. In a way she had become a combat soldier. It must be bad to have a sweetheart who couldn't do it any more. What was a girl to do? The little Legionnaire had also been castrated. It happened in the *Kz* camp.

"They caught him," the girl said. She took off her hat and whisked off the rain.

"Not so good," Lieutenant Ohlsen mumbled.

"They shot him in Morellenschlucht. They shot him with a general from the Air Force. I picked up his ashes at the central court-martial."

Oh, go to hell, thought Lieutenant Ohlsen. What do I care about your castrated sweetheart?

"I received him in a shoe box," the girl said. "I signed a receipt for him as if it were parcel post."

"What did you do with the box?"

The girl smiled and glanced toward the river. "I scattered him in the Havel." She indicated the river flowing by, gray and muddy. Even wetter than usual. The rain was playing with it. "So I come down here every morning, saying: Hello, Robert. I always throw something out to him. Today he got an apple. And when I've given it to him I say: So long, Robert, the war isn't over yet."

"I understand very well," Lieutenant Ohlsen said, astonished that he really was able to understand it.

They went home to the girl's place. She tossed her red jacket on a chair and said she would make coffee, but discovered she didn't have any. Then she wanted to make something else, but she only had a few bottles of beer and two quarts of vodka which Robert had brought home with him.

They drank vodka. They drank it from tankards.

The girl lay down on the sofa.

Lieutenant Ohlsen kissed her. She opened her mouth. She bit his lip.

He told her about Inge. About Gunni. He told her he would have his revenge.

"That won't help you," the girl whispered, cuddling up to him. "You won't get them back."

He could feel the buckle of her garters through her clothes. She had on a short and very tight skirt.

He put his hand around her knee. She stroked his hair.

"You have beautiful hair. Robert's was just like yours, jet black."

He passed his hand higher up her leg. Her skirt was so tight. He couldn't manage to get his hand very far up.

She pulled her legs slightly apart. As if unconsciously. She sighed, caught him round the neck.

"You mustn't," she whispered.

He didn't answer. His fingers reached a bit higher. He felt the top of the thin stocking. Just above the edge she had a deep scar. He played with his fingers over it.

"What is it?"

She sighed and kissed him. "A bomb splinter. It happened two years ago."

He put his hand more firmly on the scar from the bomb splinter.

She made a little room so he could better feel the two-year-old scar. It had bled a lot that night. A sailor on leave from the minesweeping service had ligated her thigh with his hat-ribbon, with the name "Kriegsmarine" facing front. If it hadn't been so serious she would have laughed. But it hurt terribly. The bomb splinter sat very deep, a jagged edge impinging on the bone. One millimeter further, the surgeon had said, and the leg would have gone. She lifted her leg to look at it.

"I don't have nice legs," she noted.

He looked at her legs. He put his arms around her, kissed her. She opened her mouth. They lost themselves in hot kisses. She panted. He pulled up her narrow skirt. She helped him by raising herself a little bit.

"You mustn't," she whispered. "We don't know a thing about each other."

His fingers, a bit inexperienced, explored playfully.

Suddenly she threw herself vehemently up against him, pressed her half open mouth against his in a long kiss. She was a little afraid of what had to come. Nervously excited. Her tongue played against his. She uttered small screams.

"Not that," she whispered and nevertheless helped him.

Her skirt lay on the floor beside the sofa. She took away his hand and put it around her.

They kissed savagely. They whispered foolish words. He bit her neck, nipped her ear. She was lying on her back with slightly parted lips and closed eyes. Her breast was bare. He kissed her rough nipples and played tag down her shoulders and back with his fingers.

Then they forgot about everything. The point was to find everything in the moment. Tomorrow you will die.

She wept, but why, she didn't know herself. For Robert who was ashes and lay at the bottom of the river? For herself?

An air-raid siren started wailing in shrill treble.

They half got up and for a moment listened closely to the infernal concert sweeping over the city.

Then they fell back into each other's arms again.

"It's the English," she said. "They always come in the daytime."

"Is it?" he said and kissed her.

They could hear airplanes high up.

"How can they really find Berlin in such weather?" she asked, listening for the droning engines.

"I don't know, but they do," he answered.

She nodded. They did.

The bombs started exploding. The windowpanes rattled.

"Should we go to the basement?" Lieutenant Ohlsen asked.

"No, it's disgusting," she said. "Damp and nasty. Let's stay here."

They made love again. Then they fell asleep, closely embraced and exhausted.

When they woke up it was evening.

It was still raining.

They drank, ate, and made more love. They suddenly felt very young.

Next morning her sister came. She worked in the office of the SD. She was always saying: "What crap." She said it so often that Lieutenant Ohlsen got fed up with her.

"I suppose the two of you have been playing house in the dark," she laughed. "What crap it all is. What if you got children. Heavens, what crap." She walked into the kitchen, where she began clattering with pots and pans. "They are preparing a new prosecution," she called into the room. She put her head through the door. "It's secret. What crap. They'll nab the last of the Talmuds. A whole regiment of SS boys have come from Poland and the Sudetenland. One of them, an SD-*U-Scharführer*, snatched me in the toilet. He apparently thinks that Central Security is a brothel. Well, it is one," she added. She dropped an egg. "What crap," she fumed and kicked the shell.

"Alice is a pig," the girl said to Lieutenant Ohlsen, "but she's kind enough. You can say anything to her. She is not a squealer. She has covered up for a Jew beside us here, and she also covered up for a colonel. But she wouldn't help Robert. She can't stand deserters. She says they're cowards."

Lieutenant Ohlsen shrugged his shoulders. When all is said and done those who did't desert were probably the greatest cowards. Because, if they all went back home the war would be over.

"Would you be able to desert?" she asked.

"Who has deserted now?" Alice called from the kitchen. She didn't wait for an answer. "Don't you have a dishcloth?" she called. "Well, here it is. God, what crap."

"I don't think I'd dare," he said.

"It must really be very bad on the Eastern Front. Aren't you ever afraid?" She stroked his cheek.

"Yes, I'm always afraid, but if you stay, you have a chance. If you desert and you're caught you have no chance at all. Then you're tied to a post in Senne or Morellenschlucht."

"Do they shoot many?" She was leaning on her elbow and looking down at him.

He nodded. "Incredibly many."

"Are you setting out again soon?"

"Tomorrow," he answered.

She sighed and kissed him. Her lips were full and swelling like the river Inn in the spring.

Alice brought in the food. She looked them over carefully.

"You can probably do something about it. Heinz will be coming this evening and then we'll do something about it."

They drank cognac and beer with their food. Anything was drinkable if you only could get it, and Alice could get a lot of things. She stole them. But she knew that the others also stole, and they knew she knew. Therefore she stole openly.

"Alice, you've no morals," her sister said. "You can't be sitting here facing my friend in your underwear."

"You can see yourself I can," Alice answered breezily. "Morals, pooh, what crap!"

Heinz came rumbling up the stairs like someone who knows he is entitled to rumble.

"Hi, girl, here's throat-wash and coffee." He laughed boisterously. He was an SS *Unterscharführer*. He was drunk when he arrived. He completely overlooked Lieutenant Ohlsen's service rank, called him "Fritz." Lieutenant Ohlsen didn't care.

They drank and feasted. At last they went to bed.

Alice squealed rapturously. Heinz laughed. He was the perfect peasant lover, a wild bull let loose in a cowshed.

Next morning Lieutenant Ohlsen left. He took off very early. He stole away without waking any of the others. He didn't even have an idea what the girl's name was.

He went to Bahnhof Friedrichsstrasse. The platform swarmed with soldiers on leave who were going back to the front. Some were with relatives, but most were alone. People preferred to avoid leave-takings on railway stations. Little by little it became too reminiscent of a funeral.

He walked up and down on the platform.

Asinine, he thought. To go back before your leave is up.

"Why in heaven's name don't you go out to Charlottenburg?" a railwayman asked a group of soldiers. "It's much easier to get a seat there. That's where the train is set up."

An old non-commissioned officer sitting on his pack laughed mockingly.

"Nah, one should do exactly the opposite. One should go to Schlesischer Bahnhof."

"I can't see that," the railwayman said. "That's the last station in Berlin. The train is always chock-full when it gets there."

"Precisely because of that," laughed a corporal lying full-length on the wet platform with a gas-mask container under his head. "You can't get on the train at Schlesischer Bahnhof. And so you go to the station master, get your leave papers stamped and you've gained one day."

A subway train came roaring in, crammed with soldiers.

The old NCO pointed at it with a laugh.

"Look at all those who are going to try it. I'm ready to bet anything you want that this train will empty out on Schlesischer Bahnhof. But we have to be off anyway. We played it yesterday. If we try again today the head-hunters will nab us, and then it takes some luck to escape being clamped against a wall for cowardice."

Half a score of soldiers came rushing up the stairs, storming toward the subway train.

"They're in a hurry," the NCO laughed. "They spurt to the finish like well-greased lightning."

"Doesn't stop before Schlesischer Bahnhof," called a conductor running alongside the train.

The soldiers grinned.

"Suits us fine. The sooner we'll be home again."

The railwayman who had recommended Charlottenburg looked at the crammed subway train in amazement.

"The Führer will never win the war with a gang like this." He walked away shocked.

A panzer-jäger first lieutenant walked up to Lieutenant Ohlsen and greeted him familiarly.

"Have you tried the trip over Schlesischer?"

"Nah," Lieutenant Ohlsen answered apathetically.

"My dear friend, it means an extra day of leave."

"I can't take the trouble," Lieutenant Ohlsen smiled.

The panzer-jäger officer retreated quickly. Nazi or ass, he thought. Probably both. He walked over to two infantry lieutenants, one of whom shortly disappeared into the subway train.

"It won't take long till we can take the subway to the front," an old staff corporal growled. He spat at a poster with the ostentatious text: *"Räder rollen für den Sieg."*

A warning whistle from an artillery sergeant.

"Watch out, the enemy is listening."

Steel helmets flashed. Three head-hunters strolled along the platform. Suspicious, malevolent eyes glared from under glistening helmets.

The leave train for the front came roaring in. It stopped with wheels shrieking.

The soldiers poured in. Shouts and screams. Cursing and bitching.

"Zurücktreten. Zug fährt ab!"

The train rolled slowly through Berlin. It rolled across the Spree. One had a glimpse of Alexanderplatz with the police presidium, where hundreds of prisoners were sitting in detention prison waiting for their savage sentences.

On Schlesischer Bahnhof there was a mad crush. Only a few got on. The line by the station master's office grew steadily. It was a line with happy faces. Some had been bold enough to make an appointment with their relatives right outside the cordon.

A long whistle. Then the loudspeakers blared warning calls.

The train drove on. It drove toward the East.

Every single compartment was crammed with people on their way to slaughter.

They still had the experiences of two wonderful weeks in their blood. But now other things awaited them. Drum-fire. Panzer attack. Hand-to-hand combat. Blood. Mud. Mutilation. Death. Words, words, words, but what didn't they contain of inconceivable horror!

Lieutenant Ohlsen sat in a corner. He huddled up under his coat. He tried to sleep, but the others played cards, drank and told dirty stories.

Lieutenant Ohlsen wept. He wept silently. He wept for the boy he had lost. He wept because he was completely alone.

And yet! He was not completely alone. He had the gang out there, his gang.

He saw them before him: The Old Man, the fixed point. The little Legionnaire. Joseph Porta. Tiny, big and stupid. And all the others in the gang.

As the train rolled through Germany, the Russians completed their troop concentration behind the lines. They were ready for the greatest offensive the world had ever seen.

Porta, Tiny and a Russian infantryman sat in a deep shell hole shooting craps. They had tossed their sub-machine guns into a corner of the hole. All three of them had been caught behind the lines while on patrol. Tiny had already lost a bottle of vodka to the Russian when the front came alive and to their annoyance interrupted the game.

Two hundred and sixty-three infantry divisions and eighty-five panzer divisions rolled forward to the attack.

THE END

of a Gold Medal Novel

BY SVEN HASSEL

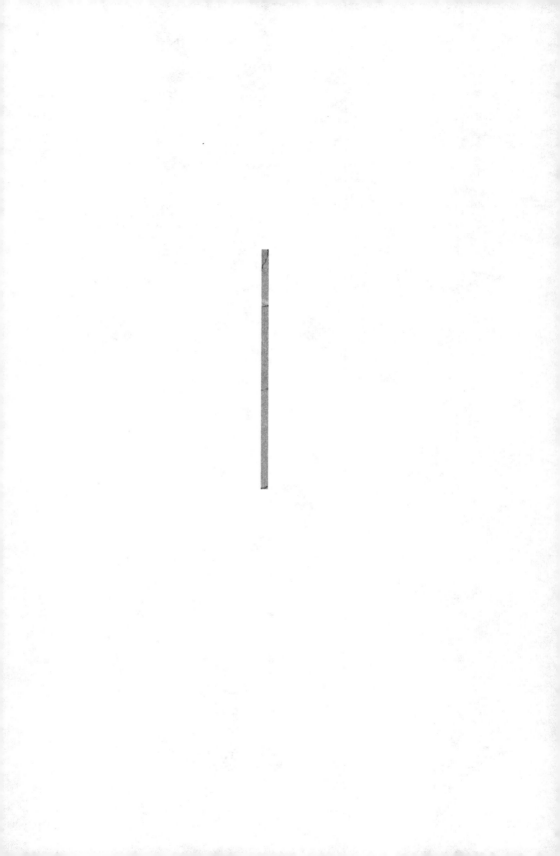

CPSIA information can be obtained
at www.ICGtesting.com
Printed in the USA
BVHW051318080223
658131BV00003B/109